EVERYDAY
LAW

EVERYDAY LAW

STELLA TARAKSON
BEc LLB (Syd), Grad Dip Leg Prac (UTS)

Published by
The Federation Press

with the assistance of
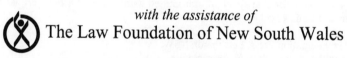 The Law Foundation of New South Wales

1995

Published in Sydney by:
The Federation Press
PO Box 45, Annandale, NSW, 2038.
3/56-72 John St, Leichhardt, NSW, 2040.
Ph (02) 552 2200. Fax (02) 552 1681.

National Library of Australia
Cataloguing-in-Publication entry

Tarakson, Stella.
    Everyday law.

    Bibliography
    Includes index.
    ISBN 1 86287 179 5

    1. Law - Australia - Popular works. I. Title.

    349.94

Typeset by The Federation Press, Leichhardt, NSW.
Printed by Southwood Press Pty Ltd, Marrickville, NSW

Foreword

As Australians we expect and are entitled to expect a great deal from our legal system. To meet our expectations, the law must be accessible, understandable and it must deliver justice whenever the law touches upon our lives, whether as workers, consumers or in our personal relationships.

In response to the ever increasing demands upon the legal system to solve our problems quickly and with minimum cost, the law itself has expanded. Where once people might have turned to a lawyer only for conveyencing, or to make a will, there are now many situations where legal advice or assistance is needed and expected by the community. In addition to the traditional legal services there are many new agencies, each able to offer help in one or more of our problems, whether they concern consumer problems, compensation, dealing with government, family breakdown or neighbourhood disputes. These include Legal Aid Services, Community legal services, Community Justice Centres, Consumer Tribunals, Administrative Appeal Tribunals, Ombudsman offices, Anti-Discrimination Agencies, Human Rights Commissioners, Equal Opportunity Tribunals, Family Mediation Centres and Family Courts, none of which existed years ago.

If we were more aware of the extent of our legal rights and obligations and of the legal and related services available to us, we could avoid many problems, or resolve them more quickly when they arise. Regrettably, when faced with a bewildering array of legislation and legal services, the average person without legal training is uncertain where to start.

Everyday Law is especially welcome because it attempts to deal with these uncertainties by explaining to non-lawyers how the law works. It provides a general introduction to the Australian legal system and to the law-making and court structures of the Commonwealth, States and Territories. It explains the legal services available to the community and sets out clearly the main principles of law in the most important areas for the community. The text is clear and understandable and the entries are easy to find. *Everyday Law* should clear up many uncertainties, provide reassurance and guide the reader to the most appropriate legal service or agency for further advice or assistance.

I am happy to be associated with this publication which brings the law closer to the people, and I congratulate the author and Federation Press for their contribution to the demystification of the law and thereby to the quality of justice in Australia. I suspect that *Everyday Law* will also be popular with lawyers!

Elizabeth Evatt AC
member, Human Rights Committee
under the Covenant on Civil and Political Rights

To Peter Skibinski,
for not divorcing me while I wrote this book.

CONTENTS

PART 1 — ACCESS TO JUSTICE

PART 2 — PERSONAL CONCERNS

PART 3 — PROPERTY CONCERNS

ACKNOWLEDGMENTS

Many people helped in the writing of this book. My thanks must first go to Chris Holt of Federation Press for his continuing encouragement and support. I also want to thank Chris Tarakson for critically yet enthusiastically providing the layman's view.

In addition, many individuals, organisations and government departments helped by providing information and checking accuracy. I would like to thank the following for their efforts and expertise:

- Chris Aird, Building Services Corporation
- Barry Barnes, real estate agent
- Ian Bourke, barrister
- Julie Bourke, solicitor
- John Butler, NRMA Association Solicitor, Legal Service
- Neil Chapman, Rockdale Council
- Meredith Dawson, ASA
- Barbara Hall, Community Justice Centre
- Chris Knox, Legal Aid Commission
- Ourania Konstantinidis, solicitor
- Vivian Kontos, solicitor
- Patrick Latham, Chamber magistrate
- Legal Information Access Centre
- Stephen Lynch, WorkCover Authority
- Jim Macken, former judge of the NSW Industrial Commission
- Carla Mullins, Welfare Rights Centre
- National Children's and Youth Law Centre
- Ingrid Pagura, TAFE tutor
- Anne Radford, Office of the Ombudsman
- Tracey Robinson, medical practitioner
- Peter Skibinski, Reserve Bank
- Maggie Smyth, Anti-Discrimination Board
- Jeremy Stoljar, Consumer Credit Legal Centre
- David Watson, Office of the Ombudsman
- Chris Wheeler, Deputy Ombudsman for NSW
- Lidia Zin, Public Trust Office

I would also like to thank The Law Foundation of New South Wales for their assistance.

HOW TO USE THIS BOOK

No single book can tell you everything there is to know about the law. This book can help, however, by introducing everyday legal concepts and explaining how the legal framework fits together. It summarises basic principles in clear, easy-to-understand language, and points the way for further information and advice.

A word of warning: Laws vary between States, and it is in the nature of the law that it can change rapidly with the introduction of new legislation or a ground-breaking court case. If you have a legal problem you should always check the current legal position in your State, either by seeing a solicitor or one of the free legal advice centres discussed in this book.

This book is not intended to be a substitute for legal advice. But it will help you know what avenues to take and what questions to ask — helping you make the most of the legal services available to you.

THE BOOK'S CONTENTS

This book is divided into three parts. The first part 'Access To Justice' describes the workings of the legal system and looks at its major components — lawyers, the government, courts, and alternatives to court. Sources of legal advice are discussed.

Part 2 'Personal Concerns' covers a wide range of legal issues that affect you personally in your everyday life. Principles relating to family law, children, employment law, accidents and social security are covered.

The final part, 'Property Concerns', covers home and neighbourhood, cars, wills and consumers' rights.

To find information refer to the Contents, or, for something more specific, the Index at the end of the book.

FURTHER READING

A range of useful books can be found at the end of each chapter. If you are looking for references on a specific topic, they can be found at the end of the appropriate chapter. General references on a broad range of topics can be found in the Further Reading section at the end of Chapter 1. Other excellent books of course exist; Further Reading lists do not pretend to be comprehensive.

GLOSSARY

Every attempt has been made to keep the use of legal terminology to a minimum. Where jargon has been used, it has been carefully explained. Even so, it can be useful to have a quick reference for looking up some common legal terms. The Glossary at the end of the book provides simple legal definitions in alphabetical order.

PART I

ACCESS TO JUSTICE

Chapter 1

THE LEGAL WORLD

1.1   THE AUSTRALIAN LEGAL SYSTEM

The law influences many aspects of our everyday lives, but what is it? Where does it come from? And who decides what our legal rights and responsibilities should be?

WHAT IS LAW?

The law is a set of officially recognised rules which govern how individuals and groups act and interrelate. If these rules are broken, action can be taken to enforce them.

ORIGINS OF AUSTRALIAN LAW

Australia was settled by the British, and for a while we used their laws. As time passed this was seen as inappropriate, and the colonies were given the right to pass their own laws. The path towards legislative (law-making) independence was gradual – at first laws had to be approved by the British governor and had to be consistent with British laws.

Each colony had separate laws and parliaments. But some matters, such as defence, could be better handled by one single unifying government. So on 1 January 1901 the colonies joined together to form the Commonwealth of Australia. The colonies became States, and the Commonwealth Parliament was created.

THE FEDERAL SYSTEM

Australia has a federal system of government. This means that the laws affecting most people are made by both a State government and the Federal (also called Commonwealth) Government.

The Federal Government cannot pass laws on any subject that it chooses. Its powers are derived from the Commonwealth Constitution, which limits its law-making abilities. If it tries to pass a law outside the scope of the Constitution, that law may be declared invalid. This problem is sometimes overcome by the States voluntarily referring their legislative powers to the Commonwealth.

Some legislative powers are exclusive to the Commonwealth, such as the ability to pass laws on defence, migration and customs duties. States cannot pass laws on these matters. In other areas there are concurrent or coexisting streams of law, for instance consumer protection. Where laws are passed on the same subject matter and there is a conflict between them, the Federal law prevails over State law.

As a result of the federal system, each State has two sets of governments and two court systems.

The Territories used to be governed by the Federal Government but they are now self-governing.

SOURCES OF LAW

In Australia there are two main sources of law:

- parliament-made law; and
- law made by the judiciary (judges), known as common law.

PARLIAMENT-MADE LAW

What is parliament made up of?

Except for Queensland, parliaments in Australia are made up of two houses, an "upper" house and a "lower" house. This is known as the bicameral system.

The lower house is called the Legislative Assembly (or House of Assembly) in the States, and the House of Representatives in the Federal Parliament. Queensland's single house is known as the Legislative Assembly. A State government's upper house is called the Legislative Council. The Federal upper house is the Senate. Each level of government has a Queen's representative – State governments have Governors and the Commonwealth has the Governor-General.

When a political party is elected to power, the leader becomes the Premier (in a State government) or the Prime Minister (in a Federal government). Some of the elected representatives become ministers. They have responsibilities in different areas and are the heads of government departments. Some of the ministers are chosen to become members of

Cabinet – a kind of committee responsible for the administration of government.

The law-making process

Parliament makes laws in the form of legislation – also known as statutes and Acts. Legislation can either change existing laws or create totally new laws.

The push for legislation can come from various different sources: from the government or opposition, from the Law Reform Commission, from pressure groups, unions or the media.

If the government agrees that the changes are worthwhile, then lawyers employed by the Parliamentary Counsel's Office will be given the task of drafting the legislation. The draft is known as a bill.

When the bill is written it is introduced into parliament where it is read and debated. Most bills start in the lower house of parliament. If they are passed, they then go to the upper house, which is the house of review. There the reading and debating procedure is repeated. Bills are either rejected, changed (in which case the procedure is repeated for the amended bill) or approved.

An approved bill must then receive the assent of either the Governor (if it is a State bill) or the Governor-General (if it is a Federal bill).

Once a bill receives this assent it becomes an Act. But it may not yet be in operation. The date when an Act takes legal effect depends on the terms of the actual Act:

- some specify that they operate on the date of assent;
- others appoint a specified date in the future;
- others come into operation on a day to be proclaimed in the Government Gazette.

Delegated legislation

Parliament does not have either the time or the expertise to pass all the detailed rules and regulations that exist. To deal with this problem it first passes an Act which outlines general requirements. It then delegates some of its law-making powers to people who have the necessary expertise – such as the Governor, local councils and statutory authorities.

These bodies must pass laws within the limits that parliament sets. Examples of delegated legislation include building and health regulations.

JUDGE-MADE LAW (COMMON LAW)

Statutes do not cover every single aspect of the law. And even where statutes do apply, courts still have to interpret them. The body of law developed by judges in this way is called common law.

Courts cannot make their decisions at random. Similar cases must be decided in a similar manner. This is known as the doctrine of precedent. Note that cases that appear to be similar might have different end results. This is because the court might decide that special circumstances apply which differentiate them.

The court hierarchy (see below) determines how precedent is applied. Lower courts must follow decisions made by higher courts within the same jurisdiction. Decisions of courts in different jurisdictions (eg different States) can be persuasive but do not need to be followed. The High Court is the highest court in Australia. It does not need to follow its own previous decisions – but it generally does unless there is a good reason not to.

DIFFERENCES BETWEEN PARLIAMENT AND THE JUDICIARY

It is an important feature of our legal system that the judiciary be independent from parliament. Parliament is elected by the voters and is accountable to them. The judiciary, on the other hand, is independent. Nobody has the right to interfere with a court's decision. Judges are not elected and do not necessarily represent the community.

There is another important difference – judges can only make a decision on the law if somebody actually brings a case before them. And then the decision is usually restricted to what is necessary to determine the case. Parliament, on the other hand, can pass legislation to cover a wide range of matters. It is not restricted to solving past disputes – it can pass laws dealing with future issues.

THE JUDICIAL SYSTEM

Adversarial system

In Australia we have what is known as an adversarial system of justice. It is based on the English system. The two sides to a case come before the court in an attempt to prove their story. The parties themselves (through their lawyers) have control over preparing and arguing their cases. They call witnesses, ask questions, and introduce other forms of evidence where relevant. Evidence provided by one side is tested by the other side through the process of cross-examination.

The judge is an impartial observer. A judge's role in the adversarial system is to:

- ensure that fair and proper legal procedures are followed;
- decide whether evidence is allowed to be used in court;
- decide questions of law, and if there is no jury, to decide questions of fact ie what actually happened. (If there is a jury, the jury decides questions of fact.)

The adversarial system differs from the "inquisitorial" system which is common in continental Europe. Under the inquisitorial system the judge orchestrates the case. He or she calls witnesses and examines them – the lawyers are there to assist rather than to run the case.

Criminal compared to civil

Criminal cases involve the individual and the state. Hearings determine the guilt or innocence of someone accused of committing a crime. The police (on behalf of the state) take the accused to court in attempt to prove they committed the crime. If the accused is found guilty, he or she will be punished.

A civil case, on the other hand, involves a dispute between two individuals. Civil cases arise when one person (or company) takes another to court. Usually the aim is to get an award for "damages" (monetary compensation) or similar to make up for loss suffered. Civil cases include breach of contract, neighbourhood disputes, personal injury etc.

Often one single event can result in both a criminal case and a civil case. For instance if one person assaults another they can be charged with a crime by the police, as well as being sued for damages by the victim. But success in one case does not necessarily mean there will be success in the other. This is because different procedures apply to criminal and civil cases. Generally criminal cases are harder to prove – the case must be proven "beyond reasonable doubt". Civil cases must be proven "on the balance of probabilities", which is a lower standard.

For information on the criminal court process see 5.2 Criminal Court Procedure. Civil procedure is described in 3.4 Suing and Being Sued.

THE COURT HIERARCHY

Different levels of courts exist to decide different types of disputes.

Which court a case goes to depends on how serious it is or how much money is in dispute. Generally the more important cases go to the higher courts. The reason behind such a hierarchy is that it allows courts to specialise their procedures and staff; and because it creates an appeal system.

Due to the federal structure of the legal system there are both Federal courts and State courts. The court hierarchy is most easily described by means of a diagram.

The court hierarchy

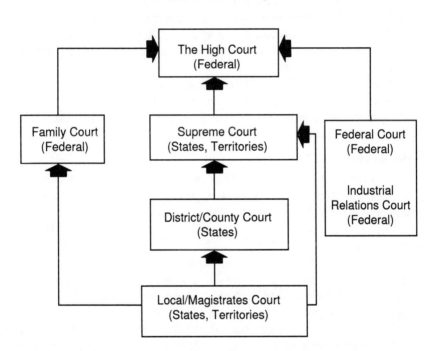

State courts

The lowest courts in the hierarchy are known as Local Courts or Magistrates Courts in some States. They exist in both States and Territories, and are presided over by a magistrate. There are no juries in Local Courts.

Local Courts hear the bulk of cases:

- all criminal cases start in a Local Court — some are determined there, others go to a higher court;
- civil cases where the amount claimed is under a certain sum are also heard in Local Courts;

7

- some family law cases are heard in Local Courts.

Special magistrates courts exist in specific areas such as the Coroners Court and the Children's Court.

Appeals can go to either intermediate courts (in States) or to the Supreme Court, depending on the circumstances.

Intermediate courts are known as District Courts (or County Courts in Victoria). They hear more important criminal cases and decide civil cases where a larger sum of money is at stake. They can hear appeals from Local Courts. A judge presides in the intermediate courts and juries are often used in criminal cases.

The highest court in the State system is the Supreme Court. It hears serious criminal cases and major civil cases. It hears appeals from the lower courts. State Supreme Courts can also hear some Federal law matters such as taxation.

Federal courts

There are various Federal courts. The new Industrial Relations Court deals with industrial matters. The Federal Court deals with Federal laws and hears appeals from the Supreme Courts in Federal matters.

The Family Court is also a Federal court (except in Western Australia where it is a State court). The Family Court deals with matters such as divorce, property settlements, custody and access. It hears appeals from State magistrates who hear *Family Law Act* matters. Decisions of single judges of the Family Court may be appealed against to a panel of judges in the same court.

The High Court of Australia is the highest court. It can hear appeals from Supreme Courts and from the Federal courts. The decision of the High Court is final, and it is binding on all lower courts. It also decides all constitutional matters and issues, such as the *Mabo* case, a recent decision on native title.

Appealing

The court that hears a case for the first time is known as the court of first instance. The case is heard in its "original jurisdiction".

If you feel that the court of first instance has made a wrong decision, you might be able to appeal. A court that hears appeals is known as an appeal court, and it exercises "appellate jurisdiction". The appeal might be made to a court higher up in the hierarchy or to a panel of judges within the same court.

The person making the appeal is known as the appellant. The person defending the appeal is known as the respondent.

You do not always have an automatic right of appeal. It depends on the nature of your case and the laws in your State. If you do have the right to appeal, you will still have to consider whether the cost, delay and stress is worth it. Factors such as the sum of money involved (in civil cases) or the severity of the punishment (in criminal cases) will have to be considered. Your lawyer should be able to give you a good indication of your chances.

Tribunals

Tribunals are bodies that operate outside the court system. Each tribunal only deals with a specific area of law, for example consumer claims or residential tenancies.

Compared to courts, tribunals are designed to be:

- faster;
- less expensive;
- less formal;
- able to consider matters that the laws of evidence would prohibit a court from hearing.

Because they only operate in one area, they build up a greater expertise. Tribunals are made up of a mixture of lawyers and non-lawyers possessing specialist knowledge.

More information about tribunals can be found in 4.3 Complaints and Tribunals.

TYPES OF EVIDENCE

Evidence can be in the form of either:

- witness testimony – usually given orally by witnesses who attend court;
- documentary evidence – this involves examining documents and their contents;
- real evidence – physical objects such as weapons or clothing can form real evidence. They can be brought into the courtroom. Other types of real evidence can include locations; the judge and jury can view a site for the purpose of examining evidence.

The rules governing witness testimony are described in 3.3 Being a Witness. In the case of documents, originals are usually required but copies might be admitted into evidence if the original is unobtainable.

Admitting evidence into court

In attempt to ensure that hearings are fair, evidence must satisfy various requirements in order to be admissible in a court case. An important rule requires that all evidence must be relevant to the case being heard. Evidence can be relevant whether it is direct or circumstantial.

Direct evidence is evidence of the actual facts being disputed in the case ("a fact in issue"). Circumstantial evidence is evidence of other facts that lead you to assume that a fact in issue exists. For instance, the fact that an accused's fingerprints were found on a gun is not direct evidence that the accused shot the victim – it is circumstantial evidence.

When there is a dispute in a jury trial over whether evidence should be admissible, the issue is usually heard in the absence of the jury.

1.2   SOURCES OF LEGAL ADVICE

Often it is difficult to know whether it is worth the time and expense of seeing a lawyer. Perhaps there is nothing they can do for you. Or maybe it will cost too much.

There is a way to find out. Many sources of free legal advice exist, but not enough people are aware of them. They are a good first source of help. If they cannot solve your problem they will be able to refer you elsewhere.

SOURCES OF ADVICE

Legal Aid Commission

There is a difference between legal assistance and legal advice.

Assistance involves helping you run a case by doing things such as representing you in court, drafting and filing documents, running negotiations. Advice on the other hand is the provision of information.

As well as providing legal assistance to people who pass the eligibility tests, the Legal Aid Commission in some States provides free legal advice to anyone, regardless of their income. In other States a fee is charged. The Commission can help you apply for legal aid if they think you might be eligible.

For information on applying for legal aid see 2.3 Legal Aid.

Community Legal Centres

Free advice is given at community legal centres on many different issues. They can help you apply for legal aid. If you are not eligible for legal aid, community legal centres may be able to provide some assistance. They can be found in the phone book or by asking any of the other advice bodies.

Legal Information Access Centre (LIAC)

The Legal Information Access Centre provides the general public with access to information about the law. It is located at the State Library in Sydney and in regional areas throughout New South Wales.

The staff at LIAC are not lawyers, they are experienced librarians. They can help you locate publications, find the meaning of legal words, and find out whether a law is operating or has been changed. They can also refer you to other appropriate legal advice services.

Aboriginal Legal Service

People of Aboriginal or Torres Strait Island descent can receive advice and often assistance at an Aboriginal Legal Service.

The Law Society

Law Societies are bodies that regulate the activities of solicitors. All practising solicitors are members.

In some States (such as New South Wales) the Law Society has a community assistance service. It can provide advice on dealings with solicitors and on other legal matters.

Private solicitors

Some solicitors offer free initial consultations, although they are not obliged to. Check when you ring up to make an appointment.

Duty solicitors

If you find yourself in a Local Court on a criminal charge without representation you can ask a duty solicitor to represent you. Duty solicitors operate in most Local Courts. If there is no duty solicitor available at that moment you can ask the magistrate to adjourn the case until you receive advice or seek representation.

Chamber magistrates/clerks

In New South Wales you can ask the Chamber Magistrate or Clerk at a Local Court for legal advice on a range of issues.

Specialist bodies

Many different bodies exist that give free advice on particular issues. They include:

- unions;
- motoring organisations (NRMA, RACV etc);
- consumer affairs;
- tenant's advice services;
- the Ombudsman (for complaints against the government);
- the Banking Ombudsman (for complaints against banks);
- some government departments.

Further information about such bodies can be found in the relevant chapters of this book.

FURTHER READING

Carvan, *Understanding The Legal System,* Montfort Press, Sydney, 1991

Crawford, *Australian Courts Of Law*, Oxford University Press, Melbourne, 1993

Griffiths, Heilbronn, Kovacs, Latimer and Pagone, *Introducing The Law*, CCH, Sydney, 1993

Nagarajan, *The Law At Work: Understanding The Australian Legal System*, Thomas Nelson Australia, Melbourne, 1990

GENERAL REFERENCES

(Contain information relevant to most chapters of this book)

Bowen, *The Macquarie Easy Guide To Australian Law*, The Macquarie Library, Sydney, 1994

Bowen, *The Reader's Digest Legal Question And Answer Book*, Reader's Digest, Sydney, 1990

Carter, *Law In Australia: The Question And Answer Book*, Blackstone Press, Sydney, 1992

Each State and Territory has a version of The Law Handbook – issues are regularly updated:

The Law Handbook (New South Wales), Redfern Legal Centre Publishing, plus Australian Capital Territory Supplement, Australian National University Law Faculty

The Law Handbook (Victoria), Fitzroy Legal Service

The Law Handbook (South Australia), Legal Services Commission of
    South Australia

Legal Resources Book (Queensland), Caxton Legal Centre

The Law Handbook (Western Australia), Sussex Street Community Law
    Service

The Law Handbook (Tasmania), Hobart Community Legal Service

The Law Handbook (Northern Territory), Darwin Community Legal
    Service

Chapter 2

LAWYERS AND FEES

2.1   LAWYERS

DO YOU REALLY NEED A LAWYER?

Not every problem is best solved by approaching a lawyer. Sometimes handling it in other ways is best – but how do you know when?

To decide, you should know as much as possible about both the legal position and your non-legal options. Ask yourself the following questions:

- what solution do you want?
- do you know what your legal rights are?
- is a large enough sum of money involved to justify paying legal fees? (for instance obtaining a refund on a relatively inexpensive product);
- will legal action jeopardise an ongoing relationship? (for instance where you have a problem with noisy neighbours).

Often it is hard to know whether you need a lawyer until after you have seen one. Many solicitors offer free initial consultations to help clarify your position. Or you could take advantage of one of the many free legal advice services: see 1.2 Sources of Legal Advice.

CHOOSING A LAWYER

Barrister or solicitor?

The word "lawyer" can refer to either barristers or solicitors.

There is a common view that barristers handle court work and solicitors only do office work such as preparing documents and seeing clients. This is not quite true. Solicitors handle a broad range of matters. They can appear in court and often do.

If you have a legal problem, the first person you usually see will be a solicitor – traditionally you cannot directly approach a barrister, although this is changing in some areas. If your case requires complicated court work, your solicitor may choose to brief a barrister to represent you in court. In some States, lawyers can practise as both barristers and solicitors. All solicitors need to have a practising certificate.

Up until recently, lawyers could not officially specialise in the sense that doctors do. But now "accredited specialist solicitors" are being introduced in some States. These solicitors have worked for several years in the field of their specialisation, and have passed rigorous exams.

Choosing a solicitor

As with most things, word of mouth is usually the best way to choose. But do not rely too heavily on this. Personalities differ, and you should feel comfortable and confident with your choice. Furthermore, solicitors have different fields of expertise and you should choose a lawyer with the experience you need.

In the past, lawyers were unable to advertise, but now the trend is reversing (within limits) in some States. Advertisements can help you determine whether the firm has experience in the area that concerns you.

If you want a solicitor with particular skills, for instance one who speaks a second language, you can call the Law Society in your State. They can suggest solicitors who meet your requirements in your local area.

The Law Society

Each State has a Law Society (called the Law Institute in Victoria). It is the solicitors' representative body, and also ensures that proper professional standards are met. All practising solicitors are members of the Law Society.

QUESTIONS TO ASK AT YOUR FIRST MEETING

Once you have found a solicitor you think is suitable, there are several questions to ask up front:

- do they charge for initial consultations?
- what do you need to bring to the consultation?
- how long will the case take?
- what are the chances of success?

- will you be kept informed of developments?
- how do they charge? (see 2.2 Legal Fees).

Keep in mind that you are employing the lawyer, and are entitled to ensure that your case is handled efficiently to your satisfaction.

CONFIDENTIALITY

A common concern that people have when they see a lawyer is the disclosure of personal information. Communications between solicitors and clients are confidential if made for the purpose of court proceedings. You should always inform your solicitor of all the aspects of your case, even negative ones, in order to avoid them being caught off guard.

Confidentiality is lost if the communication was made to enable either the solicitor or the client to commit fraud or a crime.

COMPLAINTS AGAINST LAWYERS

Lack of communication/rudeness

Most complaints arise due to a lack of communication between lawyers and clients. Clients may feel that their matter is taking too long, or they are not being kept up to date on developments.

If you find yourself in this situation, the best thing to do is to talk openly with your solicitor. Perhaps he or she was unaware of your concerns, or other factors out of their control have been delaying the work.

Clients in New South Wales can take complaints, including complaints regarding rudeness and poor communication, to the Legal Services Commissioner. The Commissioner is independent, and has powers to investigate complaints and make recommendations as to the action that should be taken. Unless the complaint is very serious (such as professional misconduct) you may be referred to mediation to help solve the problem.

Mediation involves discussing the problem with the solicitor, with the help of a neutral person. More information about this process can be found in 4.2 Mediation.

Dismissing a lawyer

You can dismiss a lawyer any time you like, but you will have to pay them for work they have already done. Remember that if you are in the middle of fighting a court case, taking on a new lawyer and starting from scratch can be time consuming and costly.

Legal code of ethics

Sometimes the complaint is more serious than a lack of communication. Lawyers are bound by a strict ethical code and breaches are taken very seriously.

Lawyers' duties include:

- duty not to break the law;
- duty not to help a client to break the law;
- duty not to mislead a court;
- duty not to influence witnesses;
- duty to apply reasonable care and skill;
- duty to account to the client.

Professional misconduct

For a person to be admitted to practise as a solicitor, they have to not only pass the educational requirements, but also be accepted by the Supreme Court of their State as a fit and proper person to be a solicitor. To remain on the Roll of Solicitors, they have to continue to be such a person.

The question of professional misconduct arises where there seems to be a failure to practise fair dealing with either a client, the court, or the general public. It does not need to be an actual criminal offence.

If you suspect fraud or intentional dishonesty you can notify the Law Society in your State. An example of misconduct is using a client's money (which is often held by a solicitor on trust) for personal purposes.

Complaints should be made in writing. The Law Society will most likely want to discuss the matter with the solicitor concerned. If your complaint is found to be justified the solicitor may be reprimanded. In the most serious cases practising certificates can be restricted or even cancelled, and a solicitor can be struck off.

If your money is misappropriated by a solicitor, you may be compensated by the Law Society's fidelity fund.

Liability in contract

The contract between a solicitor and their client is known as a retainer. In return for the client's offer to employ the solicitor, the solicitor undertakes to carry out the client's instructions. It is implicit in this agreement that the solicitor has the competence and experience to do the work.

If your solicitor fails to do the work required, or fails to use reasonable care and skill, you might have the right to sue for breach of contract.

Negligence

The relationship of solicitor and client is one that gives rise to a duty of care. This means that the solicitor has to exercise reasonable care, and this duty arises independently of the contract. You may have an action, not only for breach of contract, but also for negligence. You need to sue in court to obtain compensation.

Examples of negligence may include filing or registering a document after the allowed time period had expired. Or it could involve a failure to put an important standard clause into a contract.

Solicitors are insured against professional negligence claims.

2.2 LEGAL FEES

One thing to consider when contemplating legal action is the need to pay legal fees. Usually you need to pay your lawyer whether you win your case or not. Before you commit yourself you need to know how much you may be up for and what your chances are of winning. Then can you decide whether the risk is worth the expense.

If you are doing something straightforward that does not ordinarily involve a court battle, such as buying a house, you still need to consider whether to use a lawyer or whether to do it some other way. Take into account not just the cost of the lawyer's fees, but also what you will be up for if things go wrong.

People having difficulty affording legal fees might be eligible to receive legal aid – refer to 2.3 Legal Aid for details.

REFORMS IN NEW SOUTH WALES

The law relating to solicitor-client relationships and costs has been reformed in New South Wales. Those changes are discussed below under the appropriate headings. It is expected that similar changes will become nationwide some time in the future.

CONTRACTS WITH SOLICITORS

When you hire a solicitor to perform a legal service you are entering into a contract. Contracts between solicitors and clients are known as retainers. In return for the solicitor's promise to carry out the work skilfully and carefully, you promise to pay their fee.

Retainers do not always need to be in writing in some States, but it helps avoid misunderstandings. A retainer may simply be a letter from your solicitor confirming your instructions and noting arrangements for payment.

Statements of costs

In New South Wales potential clients must be given a written statement of costs before being taken on. If actual costs are not known you should be given an estimate. If it later turns out that a significant increase in costs is likely you must be given a written update.

If you were not given a written statement of costs, you do not have to automatically pay the bill. You can have it sent to an independent costs assessor to decide whether it is fair and reasonable: see Challenging a Bill below. Your solicitor cannot take action to recover costs from you until the assessment is completed, and they may have to pay the costs of the assessment.

A failure to disclose an estimate of costs could also lead to disciplinary measures being taken against the solicitor.

Barristers' fees

In some States lawyers can practise as either barristers or solicitors, in others they can only be one or the other. You usually deal directly with a solicitor and they may choose to brief a barrister if the work is complicated. You will be responsible for paying the barrister's fees. For more information on the difference between barristers and solicitors see 2.1 Lawyers.

HOW DO SOLICITORS CHARGE?

Different methods of charging exist. Which type is used is basically determined by the type of work being performed and the agreement reached in the retainer.

Flat fee

A simple flat fee may be charged where the work is straightforward and routine, and the solicitor has a good idea of how much effort is involved.

Flat fees are common for matters such as drawing up simple wills and dissolving marriages.

According to a scale

Cases that do not normally involve court action but still have a number of steps that need to be carried out may be charged according to a scale set down by legislation. An example is the purchase or sale of a house.

Solicitors can charge above the set scale if they inform you that they are doing so and you agree to it. Such agreements usually need to be in writing.

Reforms in New South Wales have abolished the use of scales. Instead, lawyers need to explain their charges.

Hourly rate

Where there is a court case, it can be very difficult for your solicitor to predict how much work will be involved in your case. A great deal depends on how the other side reacts. If they fight you every step of the way your lawyer will need to put a lot of time into your case, but if they are willing to compromise, less time needs to be spent.

In these situations you may be charged an hourly rate. You can ask your lawyer to keep you informed as to how costs are progressing. In New South Wales you must be informed if there are significant increases above the written estimate: see Statements of Costs above.

Out-of-pocket expenses (disbursements)

Solicitors often have to make out-of-pocket expenses when dealing with your case. These include expenses such as filing fees, ordering documents etc. A lawyer's out-of-pocket expenses are known as disbursements.

When you are sent a bill you will have to pay the solicitor's costs (their labour) plus their disbursements.

Do lawyers charge contingency fees in Australia?

Currently the answer is no. Contingency fees are common in the United States. Under such an arrangement the client pays nothing if they lose, but are charged a percentage of any winnings they may make. Often the percentage is rather high.

Some Australian solicitors will not charge you if the case is lost, particularly if they believe you cannot afford it. But if you do win you will not be charged by reference to a percentage of your winnings.

Reforms in New South Wales allow clients to enter into "conditional costs agreements" if they find a willing solicitor. Under this system you only pay if you win, but then your lawyer can charge you a premium up to 25 percent above normal fees. If you lose you do not need to pay your lawyer's costs, but you may need to pay for their disbursements. You may still need to pay the other side's legal costs. Many lawyers may be unwilling to enter such agreements unless you have a very good chance of winning.

WHAT ARE TRUST ACCOUNTS?

Your solicitor may ask you to pay some money on account – that is, before the work is completed. This money is used to pay expenses such as the solicitor's out-of-pocket expenses. It cannot be kept in the solicitor's own bank account, it usually must be kept in a trust account. Clients may be able to receive compensation for dishonest use of trust money.

CHALLENGING A BILL

What can you do if you are presented with a bill that you believe to be unreasonably high? First check it thoroughly: you may have overlooked something or the work may have been more complicated than you thought. Bills need to be fairly detailed but every single matter does not need to be itemised. Most solicitors, however, will provide you with an itemised bill if you ask for one.

If you still think the bill is too high, take it up with your solicitor or a partner of the firm. If you are unsatisfied with their response, you can:

- have the bill "taxed" or, in New South Wales, assessed;
- contact the Law Society in your State.

"Taxing" a bill

This has nothing to do with income or other forms of taxation that most people are familiar with. The process of taxing a bill involves the bill being checked by a court, usually the Supreme Court although the Family Court deals with bills in family law matters. Taxing a bill tends to be complicated and expensive, and unless a certain percentage of the bill is deducted, you will have to pay the costs.

Assessing bills in New South Wales

Clients can complain to the Legal Services Commission. Or they can apply to an officer of the Supreme Court for an assessment of the whole of, or any part of, costs in a bill. You can apply for an assessment even if you have already paid or partly paid. If you have signed a costs agreement, the bill cannot be assessed unless it is unjust or you have been charged significantly more than the amount agreed on.

Applications are made on a special form and a fee is payable. You may be able to attend a mediation session before the assessment. Mediation involves meeting with the lawyer in the presence of a neutral person in attempt to reach a solution both of you are happy with. See 4.2 Mediation for more information on the mediation process.

If you have the bill assessed, the costs assessor must consider:

- whether it was reasonable to carry out the work;
- whether the work was carried out in a reasonable manner;
- the fairness and reasonableness of the costs charged in relation to that work.

The costs assessor can either confirm the bill, or if it is unfair or unreasonable, substitute a fair sum. This can include an allowance to cover the fee you paid to have the costs assessed.

Complaint to the Law Society

Law Societies in some States have procedures for dealing with bill complaints. The Law Society is the body that governs the activities of solicitors. All practising solicitors are members. In Victoria it is known as the Law Institute.

Contact the Law Society in your State and ask them whether they have any procedures for investigating bills and resolving the problem. Even if they do not they will still be able to point you in the right direction.

COURT COSTS

If you win a court case, do you still have to pay for the legal costs?

The court may make an order for costs in your favour, but to understand what this means you need to be aware that there are two classes of costs:

- solicitor/client costs; and
- party/party costs.

Solicitor/client costs are all the legal costs involved in the case. It is what you had agreed to pay your solicitor. Party/party costs, however, might be lower. They only cover the costs that the court says were actually necessary. For instance if you brief a senior barrister or employ a senior solicitor when a junior would have sufficed, their costs may not be part of the party/party costs.

Why does this distinction matter? Because if you win the court case you may only be awarded party/party costs. Any extra costs will need to be paid by you.

Where only a small amount of money is involved, it is not uncommon for a court to order that each side pay their own costs.

2.3 LEGAL AID

The justice system should be accessible to everybody, not only those who can afford to pay legal fees. Legal aid provides help to those who may otherwise be unable to afford to assert their legal rights.

WHAT DOES LEGAL AID PROVIDE?

Legal aid provides assistance in the running of a case. This can include the drafting and filing of documents, preparing statements and court representation. Each State has a Legal Aid Commission that provides legal assistance to successful applicants. Details on applying for legal aid are provided below.

You may be aware that you have to pass a test to be eligible for legal aid. If all you want, however, is some free advice you might be able to get it without passing a test at one of the bodies discussed in 1.2 Sources of Legal Advice.

Free legal advice bodies will sometimes give minor assistance, such as making a phone call or writing a simple letter. However, if you need something more complicated and involved, you will usually need to apply for legal aid. The free advice body may help you apply.

Who will represent you?

Legal Aid Commissions employ their own solicitors. If you prefer to use your own private solicitor you might be able to do so. Your solicitor will then be paid by legal aid. Not all solicitors are willing to accept legal aid work but there are many who do. They will usually help you make the application.

Do you have to make any contributions?

Sometimes entire legal costs are covered, but in other cases you will be required to make a contribution. It all depends on your individual circumstances and the type of matter. In some States (such as New South Wales) you may be asked to pay the total legal costs at the conclusion of proceedings, depending on the outcome of the case.

APPLYING FOR LEGAL AID

Application forms

To apply for legal aid you need to fill in an application form. Forms are available from:

- Legal Aid Commission offices;
- some community legal centres;
- some Local Courts (called Magistrates Courts in some States);
- private solicitors may also have legal aid forms.

The form must be filled in carefully and accurately. Penalties exist for untruthful answers. You can ask for help with filling in the form from any of the places where forms are available, or from a free advice centre.

Tests

Generally two types of tests are used to determine eligibility:

- a means test – your income and assets (property) are taken into consideration to determine whether you are eligible to receive legal aid and whether you can afford to pay an initial contribution. If you are married or living in a de facto relationship, your partner's means may also be tested;
- a merit test – often your case must have a reasonable chance of success in order for you to receive legal aid. The Legal Aid Commission will also look to see whether you will derive any benefit from the assistance or whether you may suffer any detriment if assistance is refused.

The tests are applied differently in different jurisdictions, and you should check your position with the Legal Aid Commission in your State. For instance, in New South Wales the means and merit tests are not used for children in Children's Court matters. And the merit test does not apply in Local Court criminal matters, but it does for appeals.

Verifying your income and assets

At some stage you will be required to verify the income and assets that you disclosed on the application form. Have available:

- a recent payslip (if you earn a wage);
- your latest full tax return (if you are self-employed);
- a pensioner's benefit card (if you receive a pension);
- account statements from banks, building societies etc.

You may be asked for verification of other assets if necessary.

Some areas where legal aid is available

The availability of legal aid varies between States and should always be checked. But generally the types of legal matters where assistance is available include:

- some areas of family law;
- some civil cases such as tenancy, consumer protection;
- some criminal cases;
- some Children's Court matters;
- some social security disputes.

Some areas where legal aid is not available

Legal aid is not available for all types of cases. Different States have different rules, but generally legal aid is not available for matters such as buying and selling a house. Most traffic offences also tend not to be covered (except where there is a possibility of gaol) but members of motoring organisations such as the NRMA or the RACV may be entitled to help from those bodies.

Are you eligible to apply?

As laws vary between States and change over time it is important to contact a legal aid office, a solicitor or a free legal advice body to determine whether legal aid is available to cover your case.

FURTHER READING

Chisholm and Nettheim, *Understanding Law*, Butterworths, Sydney, 1992

Derham, Maher and Waller, *An Introduction To Law*, Law Book Co, Sydney, 1991

Disney, Basten, Redmond and Ross, *Lawyers*, Law Book Co, Sydney, 1986

See also: General references listed in Further Reading Chapter 1.

Chapter 3

GOING TO COURT

3.1   THE COURTROOM

MOST CASES GO BEFORE THE LOCAL COURT

The Local Court is also known as the Magistrates Court in some States. It hears the majority of cases, and is the court you are most likely to encounter.

All criminal cases start before a magistrate in a Local Court, and are then either decided there or sent on to a higher court. For details on the criminal law process see 5.2 Criminal Court Procedure.

Civil cases involve one person suing another; either to obtain compensation, to enforce a contract, or to get an order requiring certain action to be taken or restrained. For a more detailed explanation of the difference between criminal and civil cases see 1.1 The Australian Legal System.

Civil cases go before either a Local Court or a higher level court, depending on the sum of money involved. Local Courts only handle claims under a set figure. As this figure varies between States you should check it with a Local Court or a lawyer if you are considering taking legal action. For information on the civil court process see 3.4 Suing and Being Sued.

People involved in either civil or criminal actions should consider obtaining legal advice and/or representation. If you cannot afford to pay a solicitor there are other avenues of help: see 1.2 Sources of Legal Advice and 2.3 Legal Aid.

WHAT DOES A COURTROOM LOOK LIKE?

Part of the stress involved with appearing in court is caused by being placed in an unfamiliar and intimidating setting. To get an idea of what a courtroom looks like you may want to sit in on somebody else's case.

The following diagram may also help. It represents the floor plan of a typical Local Court room. Individual courts may of course vary in their layout but the basic elements will be the same. For a diagram of a higher criminal courtroom (where more serious cases are heard) see 5.2 Criminal Court Procedure.

Wigs and gowns are not worn in Local Courts, and the rooms are less imposing than those in higher courts. Juries are not used in Local Courts.

Local Court floor plan

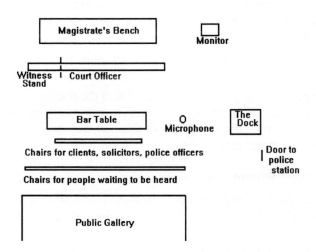

COURT PERSONNEL

Who does what in a Local Court? Knowing the functions of the major players in a court case helps make the surroundings less alien.

When you look around in a courtroom you should see:

- the magistrate – the magistrate determines what evidence can be brought before the court. He or she decides the outcome of the case;
- the monitor – the monitor operates the microphones that record the court proceedings;
- the court officer – the court officer calls people into the courtroom. You will be shown where to stand or sit;
- witnesses – witnesses usually wait outside the courtroom until they are called by the court officer. They then go into the witness stand where they will be questioned. If you are summonsed to appear as a witness, 3.3 Being a Witness can provide more information;
- the bar table – barristers sit at the bar table, and their instructing solicitors sit behind or next to them (for an explanation of the difference between barristers and solicitors see 2.1 Lawyers). In relatively simple cases solicitors often run court cases without the help of a barrister;
- a microphone near the bar table – if you are representing yourself you will be told to stand near the microphone and talk into it. Do not sit at the bar table unless you are invited to;
- the dock – this is only used in criminal trials. It is often near a door which leads to the neighbouring police station;
- the public gallery – ordinary members of the public can watch most court cases while sitting in the public gallery. People waiting for their case to be heard can also sit there, or they may be able to sit in a row of chairs nearby.

BASIC COURT ETIQUETTE

Stand when the magistrate enters or leaves. When you enter or leave a courtroom you should bow towards the magistrate's bench as a sign of respect.

When called upon to speak, do it loudly and clearly. A magistrate in the Local Court is referred to as "Your Worship". Judges in District Courts (or County Courts in Victoria) are called "Your Honour".

ARE COURT CASES HELD IN PUBLIC?

Most court cases are held in public. Anybody can sit in the public gallery to observe the proceedings. Television cameras are not allowed to cover court proceedings in Australia, but there are suggestions that this might change in the future.

The public is excluded from viewing certain types of court cases where it is believed that publicity would be harmful. Proceedings in the Children's Court are an example. When a case is shielded from the public eye it is said to be "in camera".

3.2 SERVING ON A JURY

It is likely that some day you will be required to serve on a jury. When you receive a jury service notice you will want to know whether you do in fact have to serve, and if so, what is required of you.

WHY DO JURIES EXIST?

Juries are considered to be one of the most important safeguards in our system of justice. Ordinary members of the public are chosen at random, and they represent the impartiality and common sense of society.

Initially they were used for both civil and criminal cases, but today their use in civil hearings is becoming increasingly rare. (A civil case involves one person suing another, while criminal cases involve the police prosecuting a person suspected of committing an offence.) Even in criminal cases the role of the jury has declined: they are not used for the less serious cases brought before a magistrate.

THE ROLE OF THE JURY IN COURT

Juries decide questions of fact, while the judge determines questions of law. In other words, jury members must decide which witnesses to believe, and whose versions of the facts to support.

The jury makes the ultimate decision whether the accused is guilty or not guilty after listening to any legal directions given by the judge. If the accused is found guilty it is up to the judge, not the jury, to pass sentence.

THE SELECTION PROCESS

The number of jurors

In the more serious types of criminal cases, 12 jurors are chosen. Juries might also be used in some civil matters in various States, but this is becoming less common. Where a jury is used in a civil case, a smaller number of jurors is chosen — often around 4 to 7.

Who can serve on a jury?

Anybody whose name is on the electoral roll can be randomly selected to be on the jury roll. People selected will be sent a notice informing them that they are on the jury roll.

The notice will tell you whether you can apply to be removed from the jury roll. Depending on the laws of your State, you can apply if you are:

- disqualified from serving – for instance some criminal offenders and undischarged bankrupts;

- ineligible to serve – for instance members of the legal profession, police officers, members of the clergy, non-English speakers, people who have hearing problems or are visually impaired, people who are mentally ill;

- excused from serving – for instance the elderly, pregnant women, people physically handicapped in a way that prevents them performing jury duties, people caring for young children or the elderly, doctors, dentists, pharmacists, teachers, members of parliament.

If you are disqualified or ineligible you have to notify the sheriff's office as to the fact or else you are committing an offence. If you are excused it is up to you whether you apply to be removed from the jury roll.

Summons to attend court

People on the jury roll are randomly selected for jury service. They will be sent a summons requiring them to attend court on a particular day.

If you are sent a summons and have a good reason for not attending (for instance you are in hospital) you can apply to be temporarily excused. Usually it is necessary to make a statutory declaration. Contact the Sheriff's Office without delay.

Juror's rights

Jurors are paid for each day that they attend court. They might also be eligible to receive a travelling allowance.

Employers are obliged to allow their employees to attend court for the purposes of jury service.

Empanelling a jury

Once you attend court, your name will be placed in a ballot which determines who will be empanelled. You might not get to participate in a jury ballot on your first day of attendance for some reason, for instance because existing trials are taking longer than expected.

Challenging jury members

If you are chosen to sit as a juror, you might then be challenged by either the prosecution or the defence. The lawyers have the right to challenge:

- a certain number of jurors without needing to give any reason – called a "peremptory challenge";
- any number of jurors where there is a good reason – for instance the juror might know a party or have some knowledge of the case. This is called "challenging for cause".

Jurors who have been challenged have to remain available for other trials.

Electing a foreman/forewoman

Once the final jury has been chosen they are sworn in. They will be directed to choose a foreman or a forewoman. This person is the jury's spokesperson. He or she can ask the judge questions and is responsible for delivering the jury's verdict.

COURT PROCEDURES

For details on the procedure followed in a criminal trial see 5.2 Criminal Court Procedure. Civil case procedures are described in 3.4 Suing and Being Sued.

Sometimes during a trial legal points have to be discussed in the absence of the jury. This may arise where there is a dispute as to whether a certain piece of evidence is to be allowed in court. The jury is removed from the courtroom and returned when the debate is over.

Jurors are not permitted to discuss the case, nor their deliberations in the jury room.

Jurors usually go home each afternoon. But if they are considering their verdict and it is getting late, they may be ordered to remain together overnight in accommodation arranged by the Sheriff's Officer.

Reaching a verdict

Verdicts usually need to be unanimous. If a decision cannot be reached after a certain time, the judge can dismiss the jury or direct them to try again. If the jury is dismissed the case will need to be re-heard before a new jury.

Some States allow for majority verdicts to be made for less serious matters. The judge in the case directs the jury where this is appropriate.

3.3   BEING A WITNESS

WHO CAN BE CALLED AS A WITNESS?

Generally anybody who can provide relevant evidence in a court case can be called as a witness. A witness could be:

- a party to the case;
- a victim;
- the accused in a criminal trial;
- an uninvolved person who saw the events in question or has some knowledge related to the case.

Some people, however, are unable to understand the nature of oaths and the need to tell the truth – for instance very young children (see below) and people with some types of mental disorders. As a result they are not competent to be called as witnesses.

Subpoenas

Subpoenas require witnesses to attend court to give evidence. If you receive a subpoena you must attend court on the appointed day. Failure to do so can result in arrest or punishment for contempt of court. If you have some valid reason for not attending, for instance you are in hospital, notify the court. It would be best to obtain a medical certificate stating that you are unfit for court.

Can spouses be forced to give evidence?

In most criminal trials spouses cannot be compelled to give evidence against their partners. But exceptions exist – in most States a spouse can be forced to give evidence in cases of domestic violence or child abuse. One reason behind forcing women to give evidence is that if they were given a free choice, their husbands might intimidate them into keeping quiet. For more details on domestic violence issues see 7.2 Domestic Violence.

Spouses can be forced to give evidence against their spouses in civil cases (where one person is suing another).

Can an accused person be forced to give evidence?

Anyone accused of committing a crime has the right to silence. They cannot be forced to get up in court and give evidence.

In some States the accused has the right to make an unsworn statement. This is known as a dock statement, and is not subject to cross-examination. There is a trend towards removing this right.

Child witnesses

Courts recognise that young children may not be the most reliable witnesses. As a consequence, rules have been developed to deal with evidence given by child witnesses.

Rules differ between States. In New South Wales, children over 12 can give evidence on oath. Younger children can make a declaration rather than an oath and give evidence if the court is satisfied that the child understands the duty of speaking the truth. This is known as unsworn evidence.

The age limit in Victoria is 14. Younger children can make an oath if the court is satisfied that they understand the nature and consequences of an oath. If they do not, but they do understand the duty to speak the truth and can respond rationally, they may be permitted to give unsworn evidence.

In some States the unsworn evidence of a child must be supported by other evidence. If it is not, the judge might need to warn the jury that it is unsafe to convict a person accused of a crime on the basis of unsupported evidence.

Children who are victims

An additional set of considerations apply where the child giving evidence is the victim in a sexual assault or abuse case. The child is already traumatised, and to prevent further psychological or emotional harm, some States have devised methods in which the child can give evidence in the least harmful way.

Some methods that might be used include:

- allowing a support person to stand with the child;
- barristers may be directed not to wear wigs and gowns, and to sit while the child is giving evidence;
- the child may be permitted to give their evidence out of court;
- evidence may be given by means of closed circuit television;
- screens may be used to remove the accused from the child's vision.

Children who are abused in their home may become the subject of care proceedings. For details on the law governing children in need of care, see 8.3 Children's Courts.

WITNESSES IN THE COURTROOM

Witnesses are not permitted to view the court proceedings. This prevents them from being influenced by what is going on in the case. Only the accused (in a criminal case) or the parties (in a civil case) are permitted to stay in the courtroom. Others must wait outside until they are called by a court official.

Once inside they will be directed towards the witness stand. There they will be asked to take an oath to tell the truth. If you are not religious or your religion forbids you to take an oath, you can affirm instead. To knowingly make untrue statements while under oath (or an affirmation) is a crime known as perjury.

For details of the overall court procedure, see 3.4 Suing and Being Sued for civil cases, and 5.2 Criminal Court Procedure for criminal trials.

THE EXAMINATION PROCEDURE

Witnesses generally have to give their evidence orally. There are three stages in the questioning process:

- examination-in-chief;
- cross-examination;
- re-examination.

Examination-in-chief

The lawyer who called you as a witness will be the first one to question you. He or she would have spoken to you before you give evidence, and they will explain the court procedures. They are not permitted to coach you regarding your answers.

Once you are in the witness box, the lawyer questioning you will try to put you at ease by asking simple questions – your name and address – before getting into your story. You will have to answer in your own words but the lawyer will ask you questions as you go. Generally you cannot be asked leading questions – that is, questions which suggest an answer.

Cross-examination

The purpose of cross-examination is quite different. It is carried out by the opposing lawyer and can be a stressful experience. This lawyer's aim will be to question the accuracy of the evidence you gave during the examination-in-chief, and to get you to make admissions favourable to their side.

Often this is done by attacking your competence to give evidence – for instance by saying that you could not see what you claimed to have seen, or that you have forgotten what really happened. Or they might try to attack your credibility – for instance by saying that you are biased or have contradicted yourself.

Lawyers carrying out a cross-examination are allowed to ask leading questions, but they are not allowed to be rude or hostile.

Re-examination

The first lawyer can re-examine you to clarify something said during the cross-examination. New issues cannot be raised at this point.

ANSWERING QUESTIONS

Do you have to answer all questions?

Take your time and listen to the questions carefully before answering. Generally you must answer all questions if the judge or magistrate directs you to. Sometimes a lawyer will object to a question that the opposing lawyer has asked. It is best not to answer until the judge or magistrate makes their decision.

Objections may be made to:

- leading questions – a leading question is one that hints at the answer the lawyer is trying to get; for instance "did you see the accused fighting at the bar?" is a leading question. The question should have been "what did you see at the bar?";

- irrelevant questions – questions that do not relate to the case may be objected to;

- opinion evidence – generally witnesses must confine their answers to their actual observations and not discuss their opinions. But there is an exception where the witness is an expert. An expert witness is someone with special knowledge called to give their opinion (for example a doctor giving evidence on the cause of a death);

- hearsay evidence – you can only give evidence as to what you saw and heard, not a second hand account of somebody else's story. You can say "I saw the accused carrying a knife" but to say "somebody told me they saw the accused carrying a knife" is hearsay;

- character evidence – in a criminal case the prosecution cannot ask the defendant questions to show they have a bad character or previous convictions unless the defendant's lawyer attacks the character of a prosecution witness or tries to raise the good character of the defendant;
- self-incriminating questions – you do not have to answer any questions that might expose you to criminal charges, either related to the case being decided or in a different matter.

What happens if you forget your story?

Due to delays in the court system, often a long time has passed between the events you have to relate and the actual hearing. So it is not unusual for witnesses giving evidence to sometimes forget part of their story.

If this happens you might be allowed to look at a note or document to help remind you if:

- the note was made around the time that the events occurred; and
- you either wrote the note yourself or you read it earlier and agreed it was correct.

You need to ask the court's permission before you try to refer to a note while you are giving evidence.

HARASSMENT OF WITNESSES

It is an offence for anyone to threaten or try to influence a witness. If anybody tries to prevent you from attending court or insists that you give false evidence you should inform the police. Special programs exist for protecting witnesses who have been threatened or intimidated. Ask about them if you feel you might be in danger.

3.4   SUING AND BEING SUED

Where one person (or company) sues another, the case is known as a civil case. Examples include contract disputes, debts and negligence actions. The person doing the suing is known as the plaintiff, while the person being sued is known as the defendant.

Civil cases differ from criminal cases – where the police are prosecuting someone for committing an offence. Criminal court cases are described in 5.2 Criminal Court Procedure. This discussion looks at civil issues and procedures.

DECIDING TO GO TO COURT

Which court will you go to?

Most cases go before the Local Court – also known as the Magistrates Court in some States. Your case could be heard in a higher court if a large sum of money is involved. The court hierarchy is described in 1.1 The Australian Legal System.

Costs and delays

People with legal problems often see court action (also called litigation) as a last resort. Delays in the court system could mean that months, even years, may pass before the matter is finally resolved. Local Court cases do not tend to have such large delays, but if your claim is disputed it may still take a long time. Keep this in mind when contemplating legal action.

Also take into account the fact that litigation is expensive. No matter how strong your case is, there is never a guarantee of success. If you lose the case you may be ordered to pay the other party's legal costs as well as your own. If the amount of money in dispute is high you may of course decide that it is worth taking that risk. Or, if your claim is small, you may decide to represent yourself to keep costs down.

If you are considering suing somebody it is wise to seek legal advice, either from a solicitor or from one of the free advice sources discussed in 1.2 Sources of Legal Advice. They can give you an idea of your chances of success and the costs involved.

Emotional strain

Many people find they are unprepared for the emotional strain that litigation creates. Delays can be a source of anxiety. Being cross-examined by the other party's lawyer is often stressful. The public is allowed to view most court cases, and you may find that public airing of your personal business is upsetting.

The unfamiliar surroundings of the courtroom can add to the stress. 3.1 The Courtroom shows a diagram of a Local Court room floor plan, and describes the functions of the courtroom participants.

Alternatives to litigation

Alternatives to court action exist – including conciliation, mediation, arbitration and tribunals. They are discussed in more detail in Chapter 4 Alternatives to Courts.

STARTING A COURT CASE

Fairly complicated legal procedures must be followed to commence a civil court action. Details vary depending on the type of action and the State that you live in. The following description looks primarily at the procedures used in Local Courts.

Summons

A summons is issued by the court and served on (given to) the defendant. The summons can be served in various ways (depending on specific laws) that can include:

- the summons being personally handed to the defendant by a court official or a licensed process server;
- the summons might be left with a responsible person at the defendant's home or business;
- a summons can sometimes be served by mail.

In most jurisdictions, cases for debt (where somebody owes money) only go to court if the debtor lodges a defence within 28 days of receiving the summons. If a defence is not filed in that time, an automatic judgment is made in favour of the creditor. This is known as a default judgment.

The reply to the summons

If you receive a summons do not ignore it or a default judgment may be entered against you. Once that is done, you can only be permitted to defend it later if the court gives permission. Defendants who wish to defend an action should file an official document in court – known as a grounds of defence.

The document can be obtained from court or from a solicitor. In some States the form comes with the summons. It is filed with the court and served on the plaintiff. There is only a short time limit within which this can be done, (usually 28 days) so it is important to obtain advice without delay.

Establishing the facts of the case

Each party learns the facts of the case (ie the issues in dispute) by a process known as pleadings.

Pleadings are formal legal documents exchanged by the lawyers. They may be incorporated into the summons and defence (especially in the lower courts) or they might be separate documents.

The parties exchange details on the case. The plaintiff makes a simple statement of facts upon which his or her claim is based. The defendant can defend their actions and/or come up with a claim against the plaintiff in response. This is known as a cross claim. It is heard by the court at the same time as the plaintiff's claim in order to save time. The plaintiff can make a reply and so on until all the facts are established.

Establishing the evidence

The process by which the parties learn details about evidence held by the other side is known as discovery. It ensures that neither side is taken by surprise at the hearing, and generally speeds up the court process.

Discovery can take the form of:

- listing relevant documents and describing their whereabouts;
- producing some documents for inspection and for use as evidence;
- asking questions of the other side that need to be answered on oath (known as interrogatories).

It tends to be rather limited in the lower courts.

Chance to avoid court

After the above processes have been completed, the matter may be listed for hearing. It is always possible to reach a settlement at any stage and avoid litigation. The matter might be referred by the court to a mediation service: see 4.2 Mediation. In some courts, pre-trial conferences may be ordered in attempt to reach settlement.

Pre-trial reviews exist in the Small Claims Division of Local Courts in New South Wales. Simple cases where the sum claimed is under a certain figure (currently $3000 but this may rise) can be heard in the Small Claims Division. The pre-trail review involves negotiating in the presence of a registrar or assessor in attempt to reach a settlement. If settlement is not reached, then the issues in dispute are defined to speed up the hearing. Hearings in the Small Claims Division are relatively informal.

WHAT HAPPENS IN COURT?

The court procedure

Basically the procedure followed in a civil court case is:

- the plaintiff's solicitor opens the case by explaining what the case is about and what evidence will be called;

- the plaintiff's first witness is called. The plaintiff's lawyer will question the witness – this is known as the evidence in chief;
- the defendant's solicitor can cross-examine the plaintiff's witness. The purpose of this is to pick up defects in the evidence and in the witness' reliability;
- the plaintiff may be able to re-examine the witness to clarify points raised in the cross-examination;
- the process is repeated with each plaintiff witness. For information about the types of questions that witnesses can be asked see 3.3 Being a Witness;
- the defendant's lawyer might state that there is no case to answer – in other words, the evidence called by the plaintiff fails to make out a proper case. If the court accepts this, the case is over. If it is rejected the defence opens their case;
- the defence calls witnesses and the questioning procedure is repeated;
- each side then summarises their case and the law;
- the magistrate comes to a decision "on the balance of probabilities". This means he or she must decide which version is most likely to be correct. Note that in criminal cases it must be decided "against reasonable doubt" – this is a higher standard of proof. The difference arises due to the more serious consequences of criminal verdicts.

The plaintiff usually has the responsibility of proving their case, as opposed to the defendant having to disprove it. This is known as the burden of proof. In some cases it shifts to the defendant, particularly when certain defences are used.

COURT ORDERS

Plaintiffs can seek a variety of orders, depending on the nature of the case and which court they are appearing before. The whole range of orders may not be available for your particular case.

Monetary compensation (damages)

An award of damages is a sum of money paid to the plaintiff to compensate him or her for loss suffered. Damages may be available for cases such as breach of contract and personal injury. Personal injury cases are usually heard in the District Court.

Generally the types of things considered when awarding personal injury damages include:

- out-of-pocket expenses (medical bills, hospital bills etc);
- loss of income due to absence from work;
- loss of future earning ability;
- pain and suffering;
- physical disability;
- damage to property.

If the plaintiff wins the case because their rights were infringed but they suffered no actual loss they may be awarded nominal damages. Nominal damages are very small – perhaps even just one dollar.

For some types of legal actions the right to claim damages is reduced or removed and replaced by a statutory scheme of compensation.

Debts

The Local Court hears debt cases where the sum being claimed is under a set figure, which varies between States.

Where the plaintiff claims that the defendant owes him or her a certain amount of money (for instance under a credit contract), the plaintiff can ask for a court order stating that the debt is legally owed. This is called entering judgment. Judgment can be entered following a hearing or on default (ie where the debtor failed to file a defence). If the debt is not paid the plaintiff can go back to court and request that an enforcement order be made.

Information on debts and debt enforcement can be found in 15.2 Consumer Credit.

Injunctions

An injunction requires the defendant to do something or to refrain from doing something. For instance you might get an injunction to stop somebody who continually trespasses on your land.

If you think that damage will be done by the time your case goes to court you might be able to get a temporary injunction – known as an interim or interlocutory injunction. Both the plaintiff and defendant appear before the judge. The interim injunction lasts until the hearing when the matter will be determined properly.

If the matter is very urgent you might be able to get an injunction without the defendant attending. This is known as an ex parte injunction. A longer lasting order might be made after the defendant has been heard.

Specific performance

Specific performance requires an obligation under a contract to be carried out. It is usually only granted where damages would be inadequate – that is, where the plaintiff has not actually suffered any loss.

Specific performance is most commonly used in contracts for the sale of land. Courts are reluctant to use it where ongoing supervision is required to ensure that the order is carried out – for example employment contracts.

Costs

The successful party usually asks the magistrate or judge for costs. This means that the party who loses may be ordered to pay the legal costs of the winner. For more information about court costs orders see 2.2 Legal Fees.

FURTHER READING

Bartley, *The Court Is Open*, Petty Publishing, 1987

Campbelltown Legal Centre, *Debtors Guide To Local Courts*, Redfern Legal Centre Publishing, 1991 plus 1993 supplement

Crawford, *Australian Courts Of Law*, Oxford University Press, Melbourne, 1993

Griffiths, Heilbronn, Kovacs, Latimer and Pagone, *Introducing The Law*, CCH, Sydney, 1993

McGinley and Waye, *Evidence Handbook*, Law Book Co, Sydney, 1994

See also: General references listed in Further Reading Chapter 1.

Chapter 4

ALTERNATIVES TO COURT

4.1   OUT OF COURT SOLUTIONS

For non-criminal matters, court action is often a last resort – attempted only when other methods have failed. What are these other methods? And why are they sometimes more appropriate than court cases?

COURTS – ADVANTAGES AND DISADVANTAGES

Advantages

The major advantages in going through the court system are that:

- a court's decision is legally binding and can be enforced (which is not the case for most of the alternative methods);
- compensation awarded by a court may be greater than an out of court settlement;
- if you win, the other side may be ordered to pay your legal costs.

Disadvantages

Due to the large volume and complexities of laws, litigation (court action) has developed some disadvantages:

- it is expensive;
- many delays exist in the court system, especially in the higher courts (for a description of the court hierarchy see 1.1 The Australian Legal System);
- hearings are usually held in public;

- the parties must attend court at a time convenient to the court, not to them;
- litigation can cause resentment and sour future relationships;
- decisions are not reached by the parties – rather they are imposed on them;
- in the court system one party wins but the other loses.

ALTERNATIVES TO COURT

In response to the disadvantages of litigation, alternative dispute resolution processes have developed. They are commonly referred to as ADR.

Solving it yourself

Attempting to solve a problem yourself or "take the law into your own hands" is not a recognised form of ADR. An example would involve getting a trespasser off your land yourself, rather than calling the police.

There may be some situations where solving problems yourself is best – for instance having a tactful word with a noisy neighbour. But in other cases you might be putting yourself at risk of being physically injured or of breaking the law.

Making a complaint

Special bodies exist to handle complaints in certain areas, such as consumer issues, residential tenancies, discrimination etc. They investigate complaints made by members of the public and can help find a solution.

For more information see 4.3 Complaints and Tribunals. If your complaint is about the decision of a government department see 6.2 Challenging Government Decisions.

Conciliation/Mediation

The terms conciliation and mediation are often used interchangeably. Both refer to a system where parties take their dispute to a neutral person(s) who helps them reach a solution. The neutral person is called either a conciliator or a mediator. The main difference between mediation and conciliation is that mediation involves the parties meeting face to face. Parties undergoing conciliation do not necessarily have to meet, but they can do so.

Conciliators and mediators do not impose a decision on the parties. Instead, their role is to help them discuss their problems effectively and come up with their own solution.

Conciliation and mediation are becoming increasingly popular forms of ADR. They are designed to be cheaper and faster than litigation. The parties determine their own solution – which is often preferable to one imposed on them by a court.

For information on the types of problems that are handled and the ways to access such services, see 4.2 Mediation.

Arbitration

Arbitration closely resembles litigation. It is typically used in commercial and industrial matters, or where the disagreement involves complicated technical facts. Arbitration tends to be less formal than litigation, and strict rules of evidence do not always apply.

Arbitration is also sometimes used for resolving appropriate civil cases (civil cases involve people or companies suing each other). The parties might agree to use arbitration or they may be referred to arbitration by a court.

Arbitration involves the use of a neutral person to help solve a dispute, but – unlike mediation – this person has the power to impose a solution on the parties. The arbitrator may be a lawyer or an expert in the area of dispute.

Arbitrators often have a duty to attempt conciliation before they can make a ruling. But when a ruling is made it is legally binding. Rulings made by arbitrators are known as awards. Appeals against awards exist under some limited circumstances.

Tribunal hearings

Tribunals are specialist bodies set up to deal with particular disputes – eg Small Claims Tribunals, Residential Tenancies Tribunals, Building Disputes Tribunals.

They are less formal than courts, and strict rules of evidence do not have to apply. Tribunals can be made up of both lawyers and non-lawyers who have specialist knowledge in that particular area. A tribunal will encourage the parties to reach their own solution, but if it is not reached, an order can be made.

For information about tribunal hearings, see 4.3 Complaints and Tribunals.

4.2   MEDIATION

Court action is not the only way to resolve a dispute. Often it is the last resort. An entire network of alternative dispute resolution procedures (normally called ADR) exists – but many people do not take advantage of ADR because they are unaware that it exists. Note that these methods are used primarily for non-criminal matters.

4.1 Out of Court Solutions looks at the different forms of ADR and their advantages over litigation. Mediation is becoming increasingly the most popular, so this discussion looks at it in more detail.

WHAT IS MEDIATION?

Parties in dispute may be able to refer their problem to a neutral person(s) who helps them to resolve their dispute. This process is known as mediation, and it is entered into voluntarily. Conciliation is similar, but unlike mediation it does not need to be face to face. Often the terms are used interchangeably.

The neutral person who helps the disputing parties is known as a mediator. Unlike courts, mediators do not have the power to impose a solution on the parties. Instead, they facilitate communication between the parties and help them work out their own solution.

Is mediation always suitable?

Not every dispute is best solved by mediation. It tends to be most useful when the parties have roughly equal status and power, and where there is an ongoing relationship between them. Mediation is approached cautiously or not at all where violence or intimidation has occurred. Issues of domestic violence themselves are generally not mediated – domestic violence is a crime, and it is therefore not normally a suitable topic for mediation.

Areas where mediation is commonly used

Mediation has been used to successfully resolve many different types of problems. Some of the more common include:

- family law – property settlements, child support, custody and access etc;
- employment law – discrimination, harassment, responsibilities, promotions etc;
- neighbourhood disputes – trees, fences, driveways, animals etc;
- personal injuries;

- consumers' rights;
- debts;
- landlord and tenant disputes.

ACCESS TO MEDIATION SERVICES

How do you obtain access to a mediation service? There are various different ways:

- your solicitor might suggest mediation and refer you to an appropriate service;
- many government departments and statutory authorities handle complaints from members of the public (see 4.3 Complaints and Tribunals) – often mediation is used to resolve the problem;
- a court may refer you to mediation, either of its own motion or on request by a party;
- in some States you can apply to a dispute resolution centre such as Community Justice Centre.

Community Justice Centres

Community Justice Centres are also known as Community Mediation Centres or Dispute Settlement Centres. They exist in States such as New South Wales, Victoria, Queensland, Tasmania, Western Australia and the Australian Capital Territory – and their use is spreading. Some States have special programs aimed at Aboriginal and Torres Strait Islander communities.

Community Justice Centres settle some minor disputes through mediation. The procedure is confidential and free. Mediators come from a variety of age groups, occupations, and ethnic backgrounds. Interpreters can be arranged if needed.

If you have a problem and would like to try mediation, ring or visit one of the centres. If your problem is suitable they can contact the other person and try to encourage them to try mediation. At the very least the centre will be able to direct you to other avenues of help.

If mediation is viable, a session will be arranged at a time and place that suits all concerned. Two mediators attend the meeting and help settle the argument. They do not give legal advice – rather they facilitate communications and make appropriate referrals.

Sometimes an agreement cannot be reached. When this happens you will be informed as to your options and avenues. But where an agreement is reached, it will be written and the parties sign it.

PREPARING FOR A MEDIATION SESSION

Unlike court action, mediation is flexible and informal. Usually you all sit together around a table and discuss the issues in dispute.

Preparing your case

Before you attend the session you should have a good idea of exactly what you perceive the problem to be. Know what result you want.

Also know what points you are willing to concede in order to reach a compromise. Often if you are willing to make a concession, the other person will respond in the same way. But make sure that you decide beforehand exactly what you are prepared to give away or else you may find that you have given away too much.

Should you get legal advice?

It is always wisest to know your legal position. Knowing the possible outcomes of a court case will help you with your negotiations.

Depending on the type of organisation you choose, you might wish to have a lawyer with you at the session. Even in cases where this is inappropriate, it is still best to go armed with some legal knowledge. For legal advice, contact one of the sources listed in 1.2 Sources of Legal Advice.

THE MEDIATION PROCESS

The process is flexible, but generally you meet the mediator(s) and the other party. The mediator will explain the ground rules. Each party then gets the chance to explain their story. The mediator may want to see each side privately, and then everybody gets back together again to continue discussions and hopefully arrive at a solution. This solution is written down and signed by the parties.

CAN YOU USE MEDIATION AND COURTS SIMULTANEOUSLY?

Mediation can be used at any stage of a dispute – before court action is commenced or even while it is taking place. If you go to mediation in the middle of a court case, the court proceedings will be adjourned (put on hold) while the mediation takes place. The court case can be resumed if the mediation fails.

Anything said or any documents drawn up for a mediation session are not usually allowed to be used as legal evidence if the case ends up going to court. There is an exception if there is a clause in the agreement allowing it to be shown to a court, and the agreement is signed by both parties.

ARE DECISIONS BINDING?

Generally decisions reached at a mediation session are not legally binding, even if they are written and signed. If both parties agree it may be possible to make the decision legally binding by taking it to a court and asking it to make an order in the terms of the agreement. Not all agreements are suitable to be dealt with in this way. Raise the issue with the mediator if you have any concerns.

4.3   COMPLAINTS AND TRIBUNALS

Many legal problems can be approached by making a complaint. Various bodies exist that handle complaints made against people such as employers, landlords, builders and government officials. Specialist tribunals exist that hear and resolve complaints made by members of the public.

DIRECT NEGOTIATION

First raise your problem directly with the person who caused it. Maybe there was a misunderstanding that can easily be rectified, or perhaps you can agree on a compromise solution.

You can raise the issue initially by phoning or appearing in person, but it is always best to follow it up in writing. In your letter you should:

- specify in clear terms what has caused your complaint;
- explain what result you want; and
- how you want it to be reached.

Always keep copies of the letters you write plus any replies. You can send the letter certified mail if you wish.

If this fails and if the person you are complaining about is part of an organisation you could approach their superior. For instance if your complaint is regarding a hospital doctor, you could make your complaint to the hospital administrator. Put your complaint in writing and reiterate your previous letter, as well as mentioning the fact that you approached the person concerned but without success.

Depending on the nature of your problem, they might take disciplinary action and/or rectify the situation if you are found to have a valid case. If you are still unsatisfied, you might be able to make an official complaint to a government body or tribunal.

COMPLAINTS TO GOVERNMENT BODIES

If your complaint is regarding the actions of a government official or the decision of a government body, refer to Chapter 6 Dealing with the Government.

In other areas, various government departments and statutory authorities exist which hear complaints. Examples of these bodies include:

- Human Rights and Equal Opportunities Commission / Anti-Discrimination Board;
- local councils;
- builders' registration boards;
- Consumer Affairs;
- various Federal and State government departments.

Or you could approach a tribunal that handles your type of dispute (see below).

Who do you make the complaint to?

How do you know whether a body exists that can investigate your complaint? There are various ways you can find out:

- the index to the *White Pages* may help;
- you could ask one of the free legal advice sources discussed in 1.2 Sources of Legal Advice;
- you could ask your local member of parliament;
- books such as this one describe some avenues (see under the appropriate chapter headings).

How do you lodge a complaint?

The answer depends on the formal requirements of the individual body. Usually complaints need to be in writing, but some have special forms for you to fill in. Ring the department or authority, or pay them a visit. The staff will usually be able to help you make your complaint.

Typically you will need to include all relevant details – dates, letters, receipts, documents, perhaps photographs – to support your case.

What happens when you make your complaint?

Complaints that appear to have some basis will be investigated. You will most likely be called in for an interview with an officer. The officer may then talk with or write to the person or organisation complained about.

The body will attempt to conciliate your problem. This process involves trying to get you and the other side to reach an agreement that you are both happy with. A binding decision is not imposed on you. Depending on the nature of the dispute, you might want an apology, financial compensation, or to have a decision reversed.

When conciliation fails, you might be able to take the matter to a tribunal or to court. Again, it depends on the nature of your dispute. Generally tribunals are designed to be faster and cheaper than courts – they were developed in response to the delays inherent in the court system.

TRIBUNALS

A tribunal is a specialist body set up by the government that deals with a particular type of dispute. Examples include the Small Claims Tribunal (called the Consumer Claims Tribunal in New South Wales) and the Residential Tenancies Tribunal.

Differences between courts and tribunals

Tribunals hear disputes in only one area of the law, while courts hear a broader range of disputes.

Tribunals tend to be less formal than courts. A similar procedure may be followed – each side presents their case, witnesses are called and examined. But strict rules of evidence apply in court cases, while these do not have to be followed by a tribunal.

Even the physical environment differs. Courtrooms are designed to look formal and impressive. For a diagram of the floor plan of a typical Local Court room see 3.1 The Courtroom. Tribunals, on the other hand, have a less formal look. Ordinary tables and chairs are used and the setup is less legalistic. Compare the floor plan of a courtroom with the floor plan of a typical tribunal room, reproduced below.

Tribunal floor plan

Tribunal Member

	The Parties	

Chairs for people waiting to be heard, observers etc

51

EVERYDAY LAW

The staff of a tribunal differs from that of a court. A court is made up of a judge or magistrate and various court officials. Tribunal members, on the other hand, can be but are not necessarily judges. Often people with specialist knowledge (such as engineers) will be tribunal members. There may be a chairperson and a panel or a single referee.

Generally members of the public can view court cases. Exceptions exist for certain types of matters, particularly where children are involved. Tribunal hearings might be in public or they might be confidential, depending on the rules of the individual tribunal.

How do you approach a tribunal?

You might be referred to a tribunal by a lawyer, a court, or by one of the complaint-handling bodies discussed above. Or you could ring the tribunal yourself to make inquiries.

The complaint to the tribunal will have to be made in writing, perhaps on a set form. Explain all the facts, including:

- details of the parties;
- details of the dispute;
- what steps you have already taken; and
- what solution you are after.

How are cases run?

Different tribunals have different rules. Where a case is complicated you may be allowed to have legal representation, but often you will be required to run your own case. As proceedings are informal, this is not particularly difficult. Make sure you have all your evidence ready – such as letters, receipts etc and statements made by any witnesses.

Tribunal staff can advise you as to how to prepare and present your case. You can also approach one of the advice centres discussed in 1.2 Sources of Legal Advice.

Tribunals aim to reach a decision that is satisfactory to both sides, but if this is not achieved they can make an order. A wide range of orders are available to specifically suit individual needs. Federal tribunals cannot legally enforce their own orders. This is because the Commonwealth constitution allows only courts to have enforcement powers.

Can you appeal against the decision of a tribunal?

You might have the right to appeal to a court against the decision of a tribunal or to seek a court review. These rights are rather limited.

52

If there is an appeal, a court can substitute its own decision for the tribunal's decision. If there is a review, the court can direct the tribunal to redecide the matter according to the proper principles of law. It still does not mean that you will necessarily get the decision you are after.

FURTHER READING

ADR: Family Mediation Centres, Neighbourhood Mediation Centres, Legal Service Bulletin Cooperative, Clayton, 1992

Creyke, *The Procedure of the Federal Specialist Tribunals*, Australian Government Publishing Service, Canberra, 1994

Griffiths, Heilbronn, Kovacs, Latimer and Pagone, *Introducing The Law,* CCH, Sydney, 1993

See also: General references listed in Further Reading Chapter 1.

Chapter 5

CRIMINAL LAW

5.1   DEALING WITH THE POLICE

You are judged by your manner, so when dealing with the police always try to stay calm. Acting hostile may well get you into more trouble. It is also important for you to understand your rights. Note that rights vary between States and change with time.

BEING QUESTIONED WITHOUT BEING ARRESTED

You might be asked questions by police officers investigating a crime. Generally you are under no obligation to answer, apart from providing your name and address.

In some situations, however, you do have an obligation to answer some questions. For example:

- drivers of cars involved in motor accidents must answer certain questions (for details, see 10.4 Car Accidents);
- if you know that a serious crime has been committed by somebody else you should not conceal this if questioned.

You are not legally obliged to confess to a crime – in other words, you do not have to answer questions that might incriminate you.

Do you have to go to the station to answer questions?

The police might ask you to go to the police station to "assist them with their inquiries". You can go if you wish, but in most States you cannot be forced to go unless you are actually arrested. What constitutes an arrest is discussed below.

SEARCH AND SEIZURE

What rights do the police have to search you or your property? Can they take items found?

Searching individuals

Unless you are arrested, the police generally have no right to search you. Exceptions exist, for instance if you are suspected of:

- carrying firearms without a licence;
- possessing illegal drugs;
- possessing stolen goods;
- possessing prohibited imports.

But if you are arrested, the police do have the power to search you. The manner in which they can do this is regulated. In most States a search has to be conducted in private and by a police officer of the same sex as the suspect.

If something more intrusive than an external search is necessary, for instance because the police have grounds to suspect that a drug is concealed in a body cavity, then an internal examination may be ordered. Most States require it to be carried out by a qualified medical practitioner. And in States such as Victoria, a magistrate must make an order permitting the search if the suspect refuses to consent.

Items found during a search can be seized and may be used as evidence in a court case.

Entering and searching property

Everybody has heard of search warrants. If the police want to search your house you have the right to ask to see their search warrant. Generally they cannot conduct a search without a warrant.

Some search warrants are general, while others must specify the subject of the search. Items specified in the warrant or other items relevant to the offence can be taken. The police are meant to be searching for evidence relating to a specific offence, but if in the course of that search they come across evidence related to another crime, they may be able to seize it and use it as evidence for that crime.

When police have a warrant they can use reasonable force to enter a house. This might include breaking down doors.

There is an exception to the rule that a warrant is needed for the police to enter a house. Police officers can enter without a warrant for the purposes of carrying out an arrest. They may also have special powers under statutes, for example the power to enter in cases of domestic violence: see 7.2 Domestic Violence for details.

GOING BEFORE A COURT

If you are suspected of committing a crime, there are two ways in which you can be brought before the court:

- by summons; or
- by being arrested and charged.

SUMMONS

A summons is used if the crime did not just happen, and if it is not expected that the suspect will flee. It is issued by a magistrate, usually on application by the police. It contains the name and address of the suspect plus details of the charge. The time and place of the hearing will be specified.

Do not ignore a summons. If you fail to attend then the matter may be decided in your absence, or a warrant for your arrest may be issued. It is a good idea to seek legal advice. You have the right to represent yourself in court if you wish. If you want legal representation but cannot afford it you may be able to be represented by the court's duty solicitor. For information about how a criminal court case is run see 5.2 Criminal Court Procedure.

ARREST

Suspects of serious crimes might be arrested, as might people who fail to answer a summons or skip bail. The purpose of arrest is to detain a suspect for questioning. Arrests can be carried out with or without warrants.

Arrest with a warrant

A warrant is an authority written by a judge, magistrate or authorised justice. The person named in the warrant can be arrested at any time of the day or night, at any place the police find him or her. Police can enter private residences to carry out an arrest.

Arrest without a warrant

It is a mistake to think that the police cannot arrest somebody without a warrant. Generally arrests without warrants can be made where:

- a person is caught in the act;
- a person is caught just after an offence has been committed;
- the police reasonably suspect the person committed an offence;
- the police reasonably suspect the person is about to commit an offence.

HOW IS AN ARREST CARRIED OUT?

Laws regulate how an arrest is to be carried out. To be valid it must be made clear by words and conduct that there is no choice but to comply. If you are asked to go to the police station to answer questions but there is no indication of compulsion, then generally it is not a legal arrest and you do not have to go.

The police officer has to give a reason for the arrest unless it is obvious from the surrounding circumstances. The explanation need not be specific and technical. They may not need to give an explanation to somebody who makes this impossible – for instance by trying to run away and escape.

Reasonable force can be used to carry out the arrest. What is reasonable depends on whether the suspect tries to escape and whether they are violent or dangerous.

If it later turns out that you are not charged for the offence this does not mean that the arrest was unlawful.

AFTER THE ARREST

After the arrest the suspect is taken to the police station, where he or she may be questioned and charged. The purpose of charging is to take the suspect before a court. Suspects can only be held for a reasonable length of time before being either granted bail (see below) or taken before a court.

Getting help

You should ask to have a lawyer present when you are being questioned. In some States (such as South Australia and Victoria) you have a legal right to make a phone call to a lawyer, friend or relative. In other States you may not have an actual right but the police usually allow you to make a phone call as a matter of policy.

The right may be denied if there is a belief that it will be used to warn an accomplice or to destroy evidence.

Special protection exists for Aboriginals and children. In some States the Aboriginal Legal Service is notified of the arrest of Aboriginal suspects, and they can provide assistance. Parents or guardians or adult friends should be present when children are detained. The rights of children with regards to being questioned, fingerprinted etc are dealt with under the appropriate headings.

Being questioned

You have the right to remain silent. Keep in mind that anything you say can be used against you in court. Usually you will receive a warning to this effect. You are entirely within your rights to refuse to answer questions, and it may be wise to insist on this right at least until you have received legal advice.

Children generally have the right to have an adult present when they are being questioned. It can be a family member or a friend.

If you are the adult present you should try to ensure that the child is not intimidated into answering questions and that a lawyer is called.

Written statements

A written record of the interview may be used in court if the suspect signs it or agrees that it is correct. Only sign a statement if you are certain that you understand it fully and you agree with everything it says. Again, you can refuse to sign until you obtain legal advice. If you do decide to sign a statement, ask for a copy.

Tape recordings

Interviews may be tape recorded in some States. Often the police must provide the accused with a copy of the tape.

Body searches

The power of police to conduct body searches is discussed above under the heading Search and Seizure.

Fingerprints, photographs etc

Police officers usually have the power to take fingerprints, photographs, voice recordings, writing samples etc for the purposes of identification. This also sometimes extends to more intrusive methods of identification such as blood tests and DNA testing.

Details and procedures vary between States. For instance in Victoria the police must inform a person whose fingerprints they intend to take:

- the offence they are suspected of having committed;
- the purpose of the fingerprints;
- the fact that the fingerprints may be used in court; and
- if they are not charged or the charge is dropped within a certain time, or they are found not guilty, the records will be destroyed.

In South Australia fingerprints etc can only be taken if the suspect is charged or where a magistrate provides authority. If the charge is withdrawn or dismissed, the records must be destroyed. In New South Wales the officer in charge of the police station should give permission.

Children have special rights. For instance in New South Wales it is necessary to obtain a court order to fingerprint etc a child under 14. In Victoria children under 10 cannot be fingerprinted. Children over 10 and under 15 can be fingerprinted if both the child and parent consents, or if an order is obtained from the Children's Court. A parent or guardian must be present during the request and the actual taking of fingerprints.

Identity parades

If you are asked to take part in an identity parade (also known as a line-up), seek legal advice, as rights vary between States. If you do need to submit, often you can choose any position you like. You may be able to complain if the other participants in the parade are not of similar height, build, features and age.

POLICE BAIL

Bail allows an accused person to go free until their court appearance.

After an accused person is charged at the station a senior police officer must decide whether to grant bail or keep the accused in custody until he or she is brought before the court. If you have been refused bail by the police you can apply for it in court.

For information on the factors that police and courts consider when making a bail decision and setting bail conditions see 5.2 Criminal Court Procedure.

If a person is granted bail by the police they usually have the right to telephone somebody to ask if they will help them with bail.

Where bail is breached and the accused fails to comply with any conditions or to turn up at court on the appointed day, a warrant may be issued for their arrest. If you have been granted bail by the police but are unable to attend for some reason (such as illness) be sure to notify both the police and the court you are due to appear at.

If the police refuse to grant bail then you must be brought before a court with as little delay as possible.

COMPLAINTS OF POLICE MISTREATMENT

Types of mistreatment

Police actions may be illegal if:

- you were wrongfully arrested and detained. An arrest is not wrongful merely because charges were not laid. To be unlawful, an arrest must have been carried out either without a warrant or without reasonable grounds of suspicion;
- excessive force or brutality was used;
- confessions were made involuntarily – confessions are not voluntary if they are made as the result of tricks, violence or threats;
- evidence was obtained illegally.

Steps to take

Complaints concerning police brutality and wrongful arrest should be made to the officer's superior without delay. Get a solicitor to confirm it in writing. See 4.3 Complaints and Tribunals for general information on making a complaint.

If you were injured you should arrange a medical examination to substantiate your claims. You may be able to sue for false imprisonment or assault, but a lawyer's advice is advisable.

Claims that confessions were made involuntarily are usually heard in court in the absence of the jury. If it is found that the confession was involuntary, it may be excluded from the court case.

Evidence that is unlawfully obtained might also be excluded from a court case. However, judges and magistrates usually have the power to allow it to still be used – perhaps when special circumstances exist or the value of the evidence is high.

5.2   CRIMINAL COURT PROCEDURE

There are two ways in which an accused person can be brought before a criminal court: summons and arrest. Both are described in 5.1 Dealing with the Police.

If you receive a summons or are arrested it is advisable to seek legal advice. You can act for yourself in court if you prefer, and magistrates often help people representing themselves with issues of evidence and court procedure.

But usually it is best to be represented by a solicitor, particularly in serious cases. If you cannot afford legal fees you may be able to be represented by a duty solicitor at a Local Court.

WHICH COURT DO YOU APPEAR BEFORE?

All criminal cases begin before a magistrate in the Local Court (called the Magistrates Court in some States). Whether they end up being completed there or in a higher court depends on the type and seriousness of the offence.

Types of criminal offences

When it comes to deciding which court will ultimately decide the case there are three types of criminal offences:

- summary offences – the whole case will be heard by a magistrate. No jury is involved. Generally summary offences are the least serious. Examples include some types of drug possession and some driving offences;
- indictable offences – the case will be heard initially by a magistrate in a Local Court and then in a higher court by judge and jury. Indictable offences are the most serious, such as murder and rape;
- some less serious indictable offences may be dealt with as if they were summary offences. As there are pros and cons in both systems you should obtain legal advice to help you decide whether you should have the case heard by a magistrate in the Local Court or by a judge and jury in a higher court.

Committal proceedings

Indictable cases are destined to go before a higher court, either the District Court (County Court in Victoria) or the Supreme Court for more serious offences. But first there will be committal proceedings before a magistrate in a Local Court.

The purpose of the committal proceedings is for the magistrate to determine whether there is enough evidence for a trial by judge and jury to take place in a higher court. If there is not enough evidence or if it collapses for some reason then the charge is dismissed and the accused is free to go.

The role of the Coroners Court

Doctors must report a death to the Coroner if:

- the death was suspicious;
- the death was sudden or violent;
- the deceased had not seen a doctor for a certain time before the death and the cause of death is unclear;
- the death occurred within 24 hours of being given a general anaesthetic;
- the death took place in prison or an institution.

A post mortem may be held to determine the cause of death. An inquest may be held at a Coroners Court to determine whether the death was related to a crime. Inquests have similar procedures to hearings. The Coroner decides whether there is enough evidence for someone to be put on trial before a judge and jury.

BAIL

Bail allows an accused to be at liberty during the court proceedings. You might have been granted bail by the police when you were charged at the police station. Courts also hear applications for bail. It is possible for bail to be granted by the police and refused by the courts, and vice versa.

Factors considered

When deciding whether to grant bail, the police and the court will consider factors such as:

- the seriousness of the offence;
- the penalty for the offence;
- whether there is any danger to the victim or victims;
- whether there is any danger to witnesses;
- whether evidence might be destroyed if the accused is at liberty;
- whether there is any danger to the community as a whole;
- the probability that the accused will appear for the hearing.

An accused is considered to be likely to appear before the court if they have a steady job, strong family ties, and a good past criminal history.

Bail conditions

If you are granted bail by the police or by a court you will need to sign an undertaking to appear at court. Further conditions may be imposed:

- you might be required to agree to forfeit a sum of money if you fail to appear, and you might even have to pay a deposit as security. This sum of money is known as a recognisance;
- a responsible person may have to acknowledge that you are likely to appear, and/or agree to forfeit a sum of money if you fail to appear. This person is known as a surety;
- you may have to agree to report regularly to a police station;
- you may have to sign an agreement regarding your behaviour while on bail – for instance to not drink, not approach a certain person or premises, to surrender your passport.

If you have been refused bail you can reapply, either at the same court or in a higher court such as the Supreme Court.

Breaching bail

If you do not appear at court or fail to meet the bail conditions you may be arrested. You will then be taken before the court to re-decide the matter. Penalties may be imposed, and further bail might be refused.

If you are unable to make your court appearance because of illness or some other legitimate reason you should inform both the police and the court you are due to appear before.

WHAT DOES A CRIMINAL COURT LOOK LIKE?

Unfamiliar surroundings add to the stress of being on trial. Knowing what a criminal courtroom looks like and understanding the role of the participants helps to counteract the feeling of intimidation that most people experience.

Local Courts are used for both criminal and civil cases (a civil case involves one person suing another). For a description and diagram of a Local Court room see 3.1 The Courtroom.

Criminal courtrooms in higher courts are somewhat different. They are generally larger and grander. Wigs and robes are worn by barristers and the judge – they are not worn in a Local Court. The following diagram shows an example of a floor plan of a higher criminal court. Individual courtrooms may have some variations.

Criminal Court floor plan

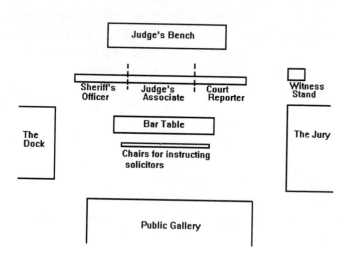

COURT PERSONNEL

Who does what in a criminal court?

Basically the court personnel consists of:

- judge – the judge decides points of law and rules on the evidence;
- jury – they decide factual issues and decide whether the accused is guilty or not guilty;
- sheriff's officer – the sheriff's officer calls witnesses and swears them in, and is responsible for maintaining order in the court;
- corrective service officer – if the accused is being held in custody, corrective service officers take him or her to and from the dock;
- judge's associate – the associate is like the judge's secretary, and attends to the judge in court;

- court reporter – records events during the trial;
- barristers – present the prosecution and defence cases, they wear robes and sit at the bar table. The defence tends to sit on the same side as the dock. In a Local Court, the prosecutor is often a member of the police force;
- solicitors – wear plain clothes and sit behind or next to the barristers (see 2.1 Lawyers for information on the difference between barristers and solicitors).

BASIC COURT ETIQUETTE

You should dress sensibly and conservatively when you go to court. Stand when the judge enters and leaves the room. If you enter or leave you should bow to the judge's bench as a mark of respect.

When called upon to talk, speak audibly, clearly and politely. Magistrates in Local Courts are referred to as "Your Worship" while judges in District or County Courts are referred to as "Your Honour".

FIRST APPEARANCE

It is unlikely that your case will be decided during your first court appearance. If you have been arrested but refused bail you will be taken to the courtroom. If you are at liberty you should attend the court early on the appointed date. Normally court commences at 10 am. A list of cases is usually displayed at the court house. The list is not necessarily in order of appearance.

Your name will be called. Accused people may be put in the dock, particularly if they are being held in custody. Or they may be allowed to sit behind their lawyer. If you do not have legal representation stand near the bar table but do not sit at it unless invited to do so.

The charge will be read out. If you do not have legal representation you can ask for an adjournment. This means that the case will be reset for another date, giving you time to seek legal assistance.

If you already have representation or wish to represent yourself you will have to decide whether to plead guilty or not guilty. If you plead not guilty a date will be set for the hearing. If you plead guilty the case might be heard then or set for a later date.

HOW DO YOU PLEAD?

It is a good idea to obtain legal advice as to whether you should plead guilty or not guilty.

Pleading guilty

If you plead guilty you are admitting to having committed the crime. Therefore there will be no hearing to decide your guilt or innocence. The only issue left is choosing a sentence. For information on the different types of sentences that might be imposed see 5.3 Sentencing Options.

You or your legal representative will bring up points in your favour in attempt to lessen the severity of the sentence. This is known as mitigating. The sort of issues that can be raised might be your previous good record and any explanations as to the circumstances that surrounded the offence.

Pleading not guilty

If you plead not guilty you are denying the charge. A hearing will be held to determine guilt or innocence. To be convicted, the prosecution must prove their case beyond reasonable doubt. You do not need to prove that you are innocent – in legal terms, the prosecution is said to bear the "burden of proof". Anybody accused of a crime is presumed to be innocent until proven guilty.

HEARING PROCEDURE

The procedure followed during a criminal hearing is:

- first the prosecution opens their case;
- the prosecution then calls a witness and asks questions (called an examination-in-chief);
- the defence may cross-examine the witness;
- the prosecution may be able to re-examine the witness;
- this procedure is repeated for each witness (for information on the types of questions witnesses can be asked see 3.3 Being a Witness);
- the defence might submit that the prosecution has not been able to prove that there is a proper case to be answered;
- if the court accepts this, the case is dismissed and the accused is free to go — if not the defence will put their case forward and call witnesses;
- the accused does not have to give evidence — in some courts the jury are not to draw an adverse inference if the accused asserts this right;

- in some States the accused has the right to make an unsworn statement known as a "dock statement" — dock statements are not subject to cross-examination. Their use is generally being removed;
- once all the evidence is completed, the prosecution will close their case and then the defence closes their case;
- if there is a magistrate alone, he or she will decide guilt or innocence and then hear argument regarding sentence;
- if there is a judge and jury the judge decides points of law, the jury decides guilt or innocence, and sentence is passed by the judge not the jury.

You may consider appealing against a guilty finding or a harsh sentence. It is best to seek legal advice for this purpose, particularly if you were convicted while representing yourself.

5.3   SENTENCING OPTIONS

Judges and magistrates have a broad range of options to choose from when passing sentence. This allows them to select a sentence to best reflect the seriousness of the crime and achieve the goals of criminal punishment.

The goals are:

- deterrence;
- protection of the community;
- punishment of the offender;
- rehabilitation of the offender (particularly in the case of young people).

Which goal is given the greater emphasis depends on the various factors taken into consideration by the court.

FACTORS CONSIDERED BY THE COURT

The sentence imposed cannot be out of proportion to the seriousness of the crime. When passing sentence, judges and magistrates can look at a pre-sentence report prepared by a probation officer. The pre-sentence report provides information on the offender's family background, education, employment and other relevant factors.

The sort of issues that a court considers include:

- the nature of the crime — where violence was involved there is a greater need to protect the community;

- the previous record of the offender – a previous good record may help reduce the sentence;
- the offender's race might be important – for instance in the case of Aboriginal offenders the court may take into account the fact that the offender's own community may inflict traditional punishment;
- the effect on the offender – their state of health and the hardship that will be caused;
- whether the offender shows remorse;
- whether the offender pleaded guilty.

A range of sentencing options exist. Which one is ultimately chosen depends on the nature of the crime and the circumstances surrounding it. The availability of the options varies between States, and the choice can reflect the attitude of the particular judge or magistrate.

IMPRISONMENT

Imprisonment is the most serious form of punishment as it involves a complete deprivation of liberty. Usually it is only considered as a last resort, where the other forms of punishment are inadequate.

Advantages and disadvantages

Prisons have the advantage of protecting the community as a whole. They also protect victims and witnesses who fear the offender may seek revenge. But prisons are expensive to run. They also have several disadvantages for offenders, who are exposed to hardened criminals. They usually lose their jobs and have difficulty finding employment when they are released. Families are disrupted and often break down.

Length of sentence

If you do receive a prison sentence, how long is it likely to last?

Most offences carry a maximum term that may be served. If more than one offence arises from the same circumstances the sentences are usually carried out together, although in some circumstances they may be served one after the other.

If you have already served time for the crime – for instance if bail was denied and you were held in custody – that time period is usually deducted from the sentence.

Parole

The court can specify a minimum period of imprisonment that must be served. An additional term may then be specified during which the prisoner might be released on parole.

While on parole, offenders must be of good behaviour and need to regularly report back to the parole officer. They may be required to undertake counselling for drug or alcohol abuse.

Periodic detention

Periodic detention is also referred to as weekend imprisonment. It allows prisoners to remain at liberty during the week, enabling them to hold down a job and keep their family together. Then on weekends they are imprisoned and deprived of their leisure time.

SUSPENDED SENTENCE

In the case of suspended sentences, a sentence of imprisonment is set. But the offender is not imprisoned unless a further offence, also punishable by imprisonment, is committed within a certain timeframe.

GOOD BEHAVIOUR BOND

Where a prison sentence is not set, offenders are often released after entering a bond (a promise) to be of good behaviour for a specified length of time. This is also known as entering into a recognisance. They usually have to promise to pay a sum of money if the bond is broken.

Conditions may be imposed on the bond, for instance:

- the undergoing of medical or psychological treatment;
- the payment of compensation to victims;
- supervision by a probation officer.

Supervision by a probation officer requires the offender to report to the officer at appointed times. The officer can also visit the offender's home and make inquiries in the community to determine whether the conditions are being met.

If the offender is convicted of a further offence during the bond period or breaks the bond conditions he or she may be given a sentence for the original crime. They may also receive a sentence for the new crime.

COMMUNITY SERVICE ORDER

As an alternative to a prison sentence an offender may be sentenced to perform a set number of hours of community service. The work is supervised and unpaid.

Community service orders are only available where the offender is suitable and community service work is available in the offender's local area.

FINES AND COMPENSATION

Fines

A fine might be the most appropriate penalty. It can be imposed instead of or in addition to a prison sentence. Offenders who are unable to pay the fine might be allowed to pay it in instalments.

Compensating the victim

The offender might be ordered to pay an injured victim a sum of money as compensation. Where death resulted from the injury the offender may be liable to pay compensation to the victim's family. See 5.4 Victims of Crime for information about compensation to victims.

NO CONVICTION RECORDED

Even if the charge is proved, the court may think that the conviction should not be recorded. The offender will not have a criminal record that may prejudice their future employment prospects.

This result may be reached because the person is a first offender or because the crime was trivial. Or it may be justified by the surrounding circumstances. The charge may be dismissed or a good behaviour bond may be set.

APPEALS AGAINST SENTENCE

It may be possible to appeal against the severity of the sentence. If you are considering appealing, seek legal advice.

AFTER-EFFECTS OF CONVICTION

Disclosure of criminal record

If you have been convicted of a crime you will normally have a criminal record. Often you are obliged to disclose the conviction and this can disadvantage you when it comes to getting a job, a loan, insurance or an occupational licence.

Can you refrain from disclosing your record?

New laws are being introduced that allow people to not disclose old minor criminal convictions in some circumstances. This does not mean that the criminal record is destroyed. Often it still exists.

The Federal Government and some States have passed laws in this area. Depending on the laws of your State and whether the offence was committed against a Federal or State law, you might not need to disclose convictions:

- where you received a pardon because you were wrongly convicted of the offence;
- where the conviction was set aside by the court;
- where the conviction is "spent" – meaning that it was a minor offence a certain number of years ago (usually 10 years but less for minors) and no further offence has been committed since that time.

You may still have to disclose a spent conviction for some purposes, for instance if you are applying for a job in child-care or law enforcement. Courts may obtain the information for the purpose of passing sentences for later crimes.

For advice about whether you have to disclose an old criminal conviction you can call the Privacy Hotline – part of the Human Rights and Equal Opportunity Commission – on 008 023 985. This is a Federal body and it can give you information about the protection you receive if the offence was against a Commonwealth or Territory law.

If the offence was against a State law you are still protected to some extent by the Federal law. It allows you to refrain from disclosing certain convictions to Federal Government bodies. You may also be protected under State laws from disclosing convictions to other bodies such as the State Government, private individuals and companies. The Privacy Hotline will either be able to answer your question regarding State offences or will refer you to the appropriate body.

5.4   VICTIMS OF CRIME

It can change your life. Crime victims often suffer great distress and trauma – and these effects can linger for many years. But help is available if you know where to turn. You might even have the legal right to claim compensation for the loss you suffered.

REPORTING THE CRIME

Do you have to report the crime?

Victims are sometimes reluctant to report the fact that a crime has been committed. Many reasons exist. The offender may be a friend or relative, or the victim might fear they will be stigmatised or that the offender will seek revenge.

Generally there is no duty placed on a victim to report a crime. Exceptions do exist, however, and the failure to report in these circumstances can have negative repercussions. For instance:

- if a serious crime has been committed you might be committing an offence yourself if you conceal your knowledge;
- drivers of cars involved in an accident have a duty to make a report in some cases, failure to do so may effect compensation claims in some States (see 10.4 Car Accidents for details);
- you need to report a burglary in order to be able to claim on your insurance (see 12.5 Home Insurance);
- you need to report an assault in order to claim under the criminal injuries compensation scheme (discussed below).

What happens if you make a report?

You will be asked to describe the event to a police officer. You may be asked questions that you find intrusive or distressing, but they are necessary if the offender is to be caught. Most likely you will be asked to sign a statement that the information given is true. If somebody is charged with the offence you may be asked to give evidence in court.

DEALING WITH BEING A VICTIM

Long after physical injuries vanish, emotional problems can still persist. Help can come from family and friends and from support groups. Some victim support groups are government run, others are made up of volunteers who have lived through similar experiences. Special rape crisis and sexual assault centres exist throughout Australia to help victims of sexual offences. Women's refuges provide emergency accommodation to victims of domestic violence.

Victim support groups offer counselling services. They can also provide practical information as to your legal rights and options. You can ask police officers, doctors or legal advice centres (see 1.2 Sources of Legal Advice) to recommend suitable support groups.

VICTIMS' RIGHTS

Traditionally victims had few rights in the legal process. But now some States such as New South Wales are adopting codes that recognise the rights of victims to:

- request to be kept informed of the progress of investigations, whether charges are laid, and the progress of the trial;
- be advised whether the accused has been granted bail and conditions have been imposed on the bail to protect them;
- have the effect that a violent or sexual crime had on them made known to the court;
- request to be notified of the outcome of the trial including the sentence imposed;
- request to be notified of the offender's release or escape from prison.

Can you insist that the police prosecute?

Victims do not have the right to insist that the police arrest, charge and prosecute a suspect. The police alone make that decision based on the evidence available to them.

Private prosecutions may be possible in some situations. Legal advice should be sought because if the accused in a private prosecution is found not guilty he or she may be able to claim damages.

COMMUNITY YOUTH CONFERENCES

Community youth conferences are being introduced in some States to deal with minor crimes. They are designed to make juvenile offenders take responsibility for their actions and face their victims. In New South Wales, the conferences are convened by Community Justice Centres.

If you are asked to attend a conference, you can ask friends or relatives to go with you for support. At the conference you will meet with the young offender and perhaps their family, and the convenors. You will be asked how you feel and what you want the offender to do to put things right. You might want an apology, compensation, or your property returned. Not everything can be put right by the conference, but it is an opportunity for you to have your say.

If the conference is successful it is unlikely that there will be need for a court case. Sexual offences and other serious offences are not handled by conferences, but only by courts.

COMPENSATION

Victims suffer financially and non-financially after a crime. There are three ways in which they may be able to receive some compensation for what they have suffered:

- as part of a penalty imposed on the offender for committing the crime;
- they might be able to sue the offender;
- they might be able to make a claim under the criminal injuries compensation scheme.

Penalty for the crime

Sometimes when an offender is being sentenced they might be ordered to pay compensation to the victim for injury or damage to property caused by the crime.

Suing the offender

There may be a right to take private action to sue the offender for damages. Theoretically damages can be higher than compensation under a government scheme, but in practice they are harder to obtain. It is more difficult to prove your case, the legal costs are higher, and the offender may either have no money or disappear while they are being sued.

The criminal injuries compensation scheme

Each State and Territory has a criminal injuries compensation scheme run by the government. Depending on the jurisdiction, it is administered by either a court, tribunal, or government official. In New South Wales it is administered by the Victims Compensation Tribunal; in Victoria by the Crimes Compensation Tribunal. Residents of other States can contact a free advice centre to determine who to make their application to (see 1.2 Sources of Legal Advice).

People who can claim under the scheme include:

- the actual victim;
- dependants or close relatives of a victim who was killed (this may include de facto spouses in some States);
- sometimes a person who sustained an injury such as nervous shock as a result of witnessing or otherwise becoming aware of the injury or death of the main victim may also be able to make a claim.

A victim might be ineligible to claim or have their award reduced if:

- their behaviour directly or indirectly contributed to the injury;
- they participated in the violence;
- they did not report the crime to the police;
- they received compensation from another source (eg workers compensation, insurance, from the offender).

Compensation under the scheme usually only covers personal injury. It must have resulted from a criminal act that is punishable by imprisonment. Note that it is not necessary that the offender be convicted: in fact, you can make a claim even if the offender is not caught or convicted.

Personal injury covers:

- physical harm;
- mental or nervous shock;
- pregnancy arising from a rape.

Claims for property damage cannot be made under the scheme, except perhaps for damage caused to clothes you were wearing when attacked.

Time limits apply for applications so it is important not to delay. The limit is about one to three years, depending on the State.

FURTHER READING

Bartley, *The Court is Open*, Petty Publishing, 1987

Findlay, Odgers and Yeo, *Australian Criminal Justice*, Oxford University Press, Melbourne, 1994

Oxley-Oxland, *New South Wales Police Law Handbook*, Butterworths, Sydney, 1988

Parks, *Crime And The Law*, Butterworths, Sydney, 1994

Wallace and Pagone (ed), *Rights And Freedoms In Australia*, Federation Press, 1990

See also: General references listed in Further Reading Chapter 1.

Chapter 6

DEALING WITH THE GOVERNMENT

6.1 Dealing with government officials
6.2 Challenging government decisions
6.3 Freedom of information
Further reading

6.1 DEALING WITH GOVERNMENT OFFICIALS

Employees of government departments and authorities often spend a lot of their time dealing with the public. It is almost inevitable that there will come a time when personalities clash and tempers fray. How do you handle it?

Furthermore sometimes complaints made by members of the public involve matters more serious than mere cross words. Sometimes government officials, in the course of their duties, have to enter homes, make searches and even restrain activities. How far can they go? And what are your rights in these situations?

This analysis explains:

- the rights you have when dealing with government officials; and

- how to make a complaint about their conduct.

For information on what to do if you are unhappy with a decision made by a government body refer to 6.2 Challenging Government Decisions.

ILL TREATMENT

Problems can arise when you make a telephone inquiry, in over the counter dealings, or when an official is trying to enter premises or restrain an activity.

Often problems arise because members of the public do not understand the procedures involved or resent them as an intrusion. Even so, you are entitled to be treated with courtesy at all times. If a government official or public servant treats you rudely or roughly you can take their name and position and make a complaint to their superior. Most government departments and statutory authorities have internal procedures for dealing with such matters.

ENTERING YOUR PROPERTY

Meter readers

Government and statutory authority employees, such as Water Board meter readers, electricity distributor meter readers etc, need identification to enter your property. You are entitled to ask to see it. They can only enter for the purposes of their work and they must leave when it is completed.

If they remain on your property when their duties are completed and without your permission they become trespassers. For information on handling trespassers see 12.7 Dealing With Trespassers.

Council officers

Council officers can enter your property at a reasonable hour for the purpose of carrying out inspections and investigations. You need to be given written notice of their intention to enter except where:

- you give your consent; or
- a meter inspection is being carried out; or
- there is an emergency.

Council officers must hold written authority to carry out the inspection and must show it to you if you require.

Council officers can do things necessary to carry out the inspection, for instance removing flooring to gain access to pipes. However, they must cause as little damage as possible and pay compensation where appropriate.

Social security field assessors

The Department of Social Security can send field assessors to your home to check that you are receiving your correct social security payment. Field assessors can call either as part of a routine review, or because they received information suggesting you are not receiving a correct payment.

Field assessors carry an official identification card and you can ask to see it. You do not have to allow a field assessor to enter your house — you can choose to be interviewed in a social security office instead.

SEARCH, SEIZURE AND ARREST

Do government officials have the right to search you or your property, or to seize documents or other items? Can they detain you without your permission? The answer depends on the type of official you are dealing with and the surrounding circumstances.

Some of the more common situations faced are discussed.

Police officers

For information on the powers of police officers see 5.1 Dealing with the Police.

Customs officers

When you are entering Australia, customs officers have the right to inspect your luggage even if they have no reason to suspect that you are carrying drugs or other prohibited imports. If such items are found they can be seized.

In order to carry out an external body search, the customs officer must have reasonable grounds to suspect that you are carrying prohibited imports. The search must be in private and carried out by an officer of the same sex.

To carry out an internal body search there must be a reasonable suspicion that drugs are hidden in a body cavity. And not just any type of drug – it must be the sort carrying a high penalty.

A customs officer can detain a person suspected of concealing drugs internally, but cannot carry out the actual search. A detention order can be sought if the suspect refuses to allow the search. If the suspect still refuses, then an order authorising an internal search can be made by a judge. The actual search must be carried out by a medical practitioner. Suspects have the right to call a lawyer.

Customs officers can search private houses for prohibited imports if they have a warrant. You can ask to see the warrant. If you try to prevent an authorised search you might be charged with obstruction. Drugs and other prohibited substances may be seized if found.

Sheriffs/bailiffs

One way that people who owe money and have a judgment against them can be forced to pay up is by a writ of execution. This authorises a sheriff or bailiff to go to their home, seize assets and sell them. Sheriffs and bailiffs cannot force entry into your home, but it is an offence to obstruct them.

More information on writs and the types of items that can be seized can be found in 15.2 Consumer Credit.

Tax inspectors

If your tax returns are questioned you will be asked to go to the Taxation Office for a desk audit. You must take all your receipts and records with you. Tax inspectors have the power to make copies but not to keep the originals.

Tax inspectors have the right to inspect a business' premises and inspect documents. This is known as a field audit. This power is unlikely to extend to private homes. If you do not attend the desk audit, penalties may apply.

Park wardens

It is an offence to remove plants or animals from national parks and reserves. Park wardens can seize plants and animals that have been removed without a permit. They have the power to search cars in the reserve if they have reasonable grounds to believe that illegally removed matter is hidden there.

If a warden catches somebody committing such an offence they have the power to arrest them if they believe that proceeding by way of summons would not be effective.

Park wardens are required to carry identification.

MAKING A COMPLAINT

Complaints are best handled by first raising the issue with the official causing the problem. If this does not help, talk to their superior. If you are still dissatisfied you should put your complaint in writing to the Chief Executive Officer of the organisation. Action may be taken within the department or authority.

You may be able to take the matter to the Ombudsman but you must have first tried to settle the problem directly with the responsible department or authority. Ombudsmen exist at both State and Federal levels, and are able to make recommendations. For information on the types of complaints handled see 6.2 Challenging Government Decisions.

6.2   CHALLENGING GOVERNMENT DECISIONS

Complaints against the government tend to fall into three categories:

- the way an individual is treated by government officials;
- the content of the law or established practice, and whether it is unreasonable, unjust or improperly discriminatory;
- the way the law is applied to an individual.

If you are unhappy with the way you have been treated by an official or want to know your rights when dealing with them, refer to 6.1 Dealing with Government Officials.

Complaints about the content of the law can be approached by organising protests, petitions, and seeking the help of the local member of parliament. The Ombudsman (discussed below) can make recommendations about changes to law and policies. Your right to vote can help change laws that are outdated or unfair. Beyond that your power as an individual is somewhat limited.

But if your complaint is based on how the law was applied to you there is a comprehensive system for dealing with complaints.

What exactly is meant by the application of the law? If a law is basically fair but is applied in one way to one person and another way to someone else, then its application is not fair. You may have been refused social security or received a deportation order. The body of law governing your right to challenge government decisions is known as administrative law.

WHO MAKES GOVERNMENT DECISIONS?

Laws made by parliament are generally administered by government departments. Statutory authorities also exist in specific areas.

Ultimately the minister is responsible for decision-making within a government department. Obviously he or she cannot personally decide every matter, so the minister's powers and duties are delegated to government officials.

Which government body?

The relevant body may be either Federal or State, depending on the type of problem. For instance, questions of deportation and social security eligibility are usually covered by the Federal Government, while education, health and public housing are State matters.

Local councils are also subject to administrative law. They play a large role in the community, and are responsible for such things as urban planning, development control, building regulation, roads, waste disposal and community services. They exist under State laws.

To find out which department, council or other body to contact, you can ask:

- your local member of parliament;
- a State or Federal Ombudsman's office (see below);
- a free legal advice centre (see 1.2 Sources of Legal Advice).

Looking in the index of the *White Pages* may also help.

MAKING A COMPLAINT

Know all the details

Where a government official makes a decision that you are unhappy with, a good first step is to raise the matter with the official involved. Try to get the name and position of the person who made the decision, and learn as much as you can about your case. This may require you to have access to your personal files or other documents. For information on obtaining such access see 6.3 Freedom of Information.

Complain to the official or the department

Write to the official first and outline why you are dissatisfied with the decision. Be concise and explain exactly what result you want. They may be able to convince you that their decision was the right one, or you may be able to get the result you wanted.

If you do not know who made the decision, or if their reply was unsatisfactory, it helps to know which department or authority is responsible. (See Which Government Body? above.)

Many government departments and authorities have their own internal review system, and you can ask them to reconsider your application.

Do you have the right to ask for reasons?

Generally there is no automatic right to ask for the reasons behind a government decision. The law had the view that imposing such an obligation would increase the cost and delay of government administration. In some cases, however, people are given the right to be told or to find out the reasoning behind decisions that affect them.

You might be able to obtain reasons in the following ways:

- under specific legislation that operates in some areas (for example reasons for refusal of or conditions imposed on building approvals or development consents);
- under freedom of information legislation, which allows you to inspect documents held by government bodies: see 6.3 Freedom of Information;
- if the decision is reviewable by the Commonwealth Administrative Appeals Tribunal or by a court (see below) you have 28 days in which to ask the decision-maker for reasons. Requests should be made in writing. The decision-maker then has a further 28 days in which to make a written reply;
- you might be able to obtain a court order to obtain access to files and other documents. This is complicated and a lawyer's help may be needed.

Reasons and documents may be refused if the information is confidential or against the public interest – for instance because they threaten security or reveal the deliberations of Cabinet. (The Cabinet is a type of committee of the key members of the government).

Can you take the matter further?

If the reply you receive from the department, authority or council is unsatisfactory and you wish to take the matter further you may be able to:

- complain to the State or Commonwealth Ombudsman;
- apply to the State (if any) or Commonwealth Administrative Appeals Tribunal; or
- seek review by a court.

Each is discussed below. Keep in mind that time limits apply. They vary between jurisdictions and they are usually not very long so it is best not to delay.

THE OMBUDSMAN

The Ombudsman investigates complaints made by members of the public in matters related to government administration. The Ombudsman is independent. Investigations are free and confidential. You do not need legal representation to make a complaint, but there is nothing to stop you seeking it if you wish.

Each State has an Ombudsman and there is also a Commonwealth Ombudsman with offices throughout Australia. Which one you complain to depends on whether the government body you wish to complain about is State or Federal.

Contact either the State or Federal Ombudsman's office and the staff will let you know which is appropriate.

Making a complaint

Before going to the Ombudsman it is necessary to try to sort the problem out directly with the responsible department or authority. If your attempts fail then you can make a complaint to the Ombudsman. Complaints can be made by mail or fax, or in person. If you need help in making your complaint the staff there will assist you.

Generally when writing a letter of complaint include:

- details of the problem;
- relevant names, dates and locations;
- what solution you require;
- copies of any letters written to and received from the relevant government body.

What types of complaints are investigated?

Complaints relating to government administration are investigated. You can complain about Federal or State government decisions, refusals and even delays. The actions of local councils can also be the subject of a complaint.

The Ombudsman will not investigate complaints concerning the actions of ministers, judges, and the employment of public servants. Complaints that are considered to be frivolous will not be investigated, neither will matters that are judged to be better handled by some other method or agency.

What action can the Ombudsman take?

If your complaint is found to be justified the Ombudsman can make a report to the relevant department or authority. Recommendations to change a decision can be made. The Ombudsman cannot insist that such recommendations are followed, but in practice they usually are.

Commonwealth and some State Ombudsmen can refer a question to the Administrative Appeals Tribunal (discussed below) for an opinion as to the legal position.

THE ADMINISTRATIVE APPEALS TRIBUNAL

The Commonwealth Government and some States, such as Victoria, have established Administrative Appeals Tribunals to deal with complaints against government decisions. Not all complaints can be brought before such Tribunals. Check your position with a lawyer or ask Tribunal staff.

Making an appeal

Appeals must be made within 28 days of the decision. If you were not provided with reasons for the decision and you are eligible to appeal, you can ask to be provided with reasons. In that case the appeal has to be made within 28 days of the receipt of the reasons. Extensions might be granted by the tribunal if there is a valid reason for the delay.

You can be represented by a lawyer or by any other person. You can do it yourself if you prefer, but some legal advice is wise as proceedings tend to be rather technical.

A preliminary conference may be held before the hearing to attempt to resolve the problem. This is usually held in private.

If the conference fails to achieve a solution the matter will go to hearing. Both sides present their case. Evidence such as government documents that would normally be barred from a court can be inspected by the tribunal. Tribunal hearings are usually in public.

Mediation might be available in some areas. For a description of the mediation process see 4.2 Mediation.

For general information about the role of tribunals refer to 4.3 Complaints and Tribunals.

What action can the tribunal take?

The tribunal can change or revoke the original decision and replace it with its own decision. This decision then operates as if the original decision-maker had made it.

If you are unhappy with the tribunal's decision you might be able to appeal on a legal point – legal advice would be necessary.

COURT REVIEW

Not everybody who disagrees with a government decision has the right to seek review by a court. Generally (but not always) you have to have a special interest that distinguishes you from other members of the public. For instance you might suffer some financial loss as a result of the decision. If you have been denied a benefit or licence it is likely that you will be able to sue.

Courts, unlike the Ombudsman or Administrative Appeals Tribunals, generally will not look at the merits of the case. The court is only interested in whether that decision was reached according to the principles of the law.

Decisions are not made correctly if:

- they are unreasonable;
- there was no evidence upon which to base the decision;
- bias was involved;
- the decision was beyond the department or authority's power to make;
- irrelevant considerations were taken into account;
- you were not given the opportunity to be heard.

Successful reviews can lead to the decision being remade according to the principles of the law. It is important to note that this does not mean that the new decision will necessarily be made in your favour.

If you are considering court review of a government decision, seek legal advice as the procedure is technical and complicated.

6.3   FREEDOM OF INFORMATION

Information held by government departments and statutory authorities can have a large impact on your life. It is used as the basis for decisions that concern you, for instance whether you are eligible to receive social security. It is being increasingly recognised that individuals should have the right to examine such information.

The Commonwealth Government has passed the *Freedom of Information Act* to give people this right. All States have passed similar legislation.

WHAT INFORMATION CAN YOU SEEK?

Under the Freedom of Information legislation you can seek access to documents concerning:

- your personal files;
- all files, notes and memos that refer to you;
- non-personal information such as policy rules and guidelines, and in fact any information held by government authorities covered by the various pieces of legislation.

How do you apply?

Applications are made to the government body concerned. They should be written; some departments have special forms that you can use.

In your application be sure to:

- make it clear that you are making a request under the Freedom of Information legislation;
- provide enough information to enable the body to identify the documents you wish to see;
- pay the appropriate fee (if any) as advised by the government body.

If you are unsure how to describe the documents you wish to view, staff members will help you with your application.

You do not need to say why you are making your application.

The decision whether to allow you access should be made within a set time period, usually 30 days but this varies between jurisdictions.

How is the information supplied?

The information you seek can be supplied in various ways. You may request:

- a copy of the document;
- the chance to inspect the document;
- a computer printout;
- the chance to hear or see taped material.

Refusal of access

Not all documents need to be released. You might be refused access for one of several reasons, for example if the material:

- affects national security;
- deals with the workings of Cabinet or internal workings of the government body;
- affects another person's personal or business affairs;
- was obtained in confidence.

AMENDING PERSONAL FILES

Information on your personal files that is:

- incomplete;
- incorrect;

- out of date; or
- misleading

may be corrected. Applications to amend personal files should be made in writing to the government body concerned. Make it clear exactly what changes should be made. It is easy to change purely factual information (such as a spelling mistake) but for some errors you may need to prove that they were wrong.

Amending your file might mean that a decision made about you will be changed, but this is not necessarily the case. If you wish to challenge a government decision that affects you, see 6.2 Challenging Government Decisions.

WHAT TO DO IF YOU ARE DISSATISFIED

You may be dissatisfied with the results of your freedom of information application. You have the right to complain or appeal if:

- you have been denied access to documents;
- there was a delay in making the decision;
- you are unhappy with the way your application was handled;
- there was a refusal to amend your personal record.

Three avenues of complaint or appeal exist:

- internal review;
- the Ombudsman (Commonwealth, Victoria, New South Wales, South Australia and Tasmania);
- the Administrative Appeals Tribunal (in the Commonwealth and Victoria) or the District Court (in New South Wales) or the Information Commissioner (in Queensland and Western Australia).

Time limits exist for each of these. The time varies between jurisdictions, so always check with the body concerned. As a general rule, however, you do not have much time – usually only a month or so. It is important not to delay.

Internal review

First you should ask the department or authority concerned to review their decision. You cannot go to an Ombudsman or to the appropriate appeal authority until you have sought internal review.

The Ombudsman

If the government body does not change or review their decision you can usually take the matter to the appropriate Ombudsman. Complaints can be lodged by mail or fax or by attending an office in person. Try to provide copies of relevant letters and other documents.

The Ombudsman can examine the government body's files. If your complaint is justified the Ombudsman can recommend a solution. Recommendations made by the Ombudsman are usually followed.

It is important to note that if you do make a complaint to the Ombudsman you will not be able to appeal to the Administrative Appeals Tribunal or District Court until the Ombudsman's investigation is completed.

More information on the role of the Ombudsman can be found in 6.2 Challenging Government Decisions.

The Administrative Appeals Tribunal / District Court / Information Commissioner

The appeal authority can review decisions and make appropriate orders. Which body you go to depends on which State you live in (see the list above). Hearings are formal and technical, and you may need to obtain legal advice.

FURTHER READING

Binkowski, *How To Deal With The Government And How To Cut The Red Tape*, Schwartz & Wilkinson, Melbourne, 1991

Harrison and Cossines, *Documents, Dossiers and the Inside Dope: A Practical Guide To Freedom Of Information Law*, Allen & Unwin, Sydney, 1993

Wallace and Pagone (ed), *Rights And Freedoms in Australia*, Federation Press, Sydney, 1990

See also: General references listed in Further Reading Chapter 1.

PART 2

PERSONAL CONCERNS

Chapter 7

YOUR FAMILY

7.1   LIVING TOGETHER

GETTING MARRIED

Engagements

No legal ties are formed by an engagement. In the past it was possible to sue somebody for breaking off an engagement (the action was called breach of promise) but this is no longer possible.

Who can get married?

To marry you must be:

- single – either never married, divorced or widowed;
- of the opposite sex;
- acting of your own free will. If you are forced to marry (forced means more than just social or parental pressure) the marriage will be invalid. If you are tricked and do not realise you are getting married or believe you are marrying another person, it will also be invalid;
- not closely related (parents cannot marry their children, grandparents cannot marry grandchildren, brothers and sisters

cannot marry each other and that includes half brothers and half sisters. Cousins are allowed to marry);

- over 18. You can marry if you are over 16 but you may need your parents' consent or court permission. The court can dispense with the need for parental consent in some situations.

Annulment

If any of the above requirements have not been met you can apply to have the marriage annulled by the Family Court. A decree of nullity is not the same as a divorce. Divorce decrees state that you were once married but the marriage is legally over. Annulment means that you were never really married in the first place.

For details on getting a divorce refer to 7.3 Separation and Divorce.

Overseas marriages

If you married overseas in accordance with that country's law your marriage will usually be recognised in Australia.

Foreign polygamous marriages are recognised for the purposes of divorce, property settlements and maintenance proceedings.

Marriage formalities

You need to fill in a Notice of Intention to Marry – available from marriage celebrants or from the Registry of Births, Deaths and Marriages. It must be given to the celebrant no earlier than six months and no later than one month before the wedding.

Also needed is:

- your birth certificates;
- your ex-spouse's death certificate if you are widowed;
- the final divorce declaration (known as the decree absolute) if you are divorced.

The actual ceremony can be religious or civil. To be valid it must be:

- performed by an authorised marriage celebrant; and
- in the presence of two witnesses over 18.

No legal requirement exists for the woman to change her surname.

Three marriage certificates are usually prepared by the celebrant and signed by the couple at their wedding. The celebrant and the witnesses also sign. The celebrant is responsible for sending one certificate to the

Registry of Births, Deaths and Marriages. The second is kept by the celebrant and the third is given to the newly married couple.

LEGAL CONSEQUENCES OF MARRIAGE

Being married gives each partner certain rights and responsibilities.

Sex

If sexual intercourse takes place without consent it is sexual assault. Marriage itself does not imply consent every time. It is possible for rape to be committed in a marriage, and this can be punished by the criminal law.

Wills

Marriage revokes a will unless it was written anticipating a specific marriage. Therefore, once a couple marry it is wisest to make new wills. If a spouse is not properly provided for in a will it might be possible for them to challenge it. Where there is no will the laws of intestacy apply – the spouse is usually entitled to a share.

For detailed information on the effects of marriage on a will see 16.1 Making a Will.

Property

No obligation exists for married couples to purchase property jointly – it is possible to have separate assets while you are married. It is only if you separate and divorce that the court will look beyond what is in who's name and begin to allocate the property: see 7.4 Property Settlements and 7.5 Maintenance for details on how this is done.

DE FACTO RELATIONSHIPS

A de facto relationship exists when two people live together in a marriage-like relationship without having gone through the formalities of a marriage ceremony.

As with marriages, to be recognised by the law de facto partners must be:

- of the opposite sex;
- over the marriageable age;
- not closely related.

What is a marriage-like relationship?

Obviously friends, acquaintances, or co-workers can live together and satisfy nearly all of the above elements and still not be in a de facto relationship. The element that distinguishes de facto relationships from others is that of a "marriage-like" relationship.

Such a relationship exists where:

- there is a sexual relationship;
- there is joint ownership of assets;
- there is joint responsibility in the care of children;
- the emotional and financial support resembles that of married couples.

No single factor is conclusive, rather it is the relationship taken as a whole that determines the matter.

DE FACTO PROPERTY SETTLEMENTS

Who gets what when a de facto relationship breaks down? The situation is more complicated than a marriage breakdown, and as a general rule de facto partners have less rights than married couples.

There are two systems determining property rights of de facto partners in Australia: common law and statute law. Common law is judge-made law while statute law is legislation made by parliament (the difference is explained more fully in 1.1 The Australian Legal System).

Which system applies?

To date, people who live in South Australia, Western Australia, Queensland or Tasmania have no choice but to rely on the common law. This might change in the future.

Legislation operates everywhere else, but in Victoria it only applies to the division of real property (ie land, houses, units). Personal property divisions are decided using the common law.

The common law

Under the common law it is important who paid for what, and whose name it is in. If there is a contract between the parties it might be taken into account: see Contracts Between De Facto Partners below. If there is no contract there is another approach that the law can take but it is complicated.

Basically the solution may be found in the law of trusts. A trust exists where somebody holds property for the benefit of another. The court can decide that one partner held property for the benefit of the other even if that was not their intention. This is known as a constructive trust. A constructive trust may be imposed where it would be unfair to allow the person who legally owns the property to keep it all. In deciding, the court will look at:

- how long the relationship lasted;
- did the breadwinner promise to support the other partner?
- did that partner rely on the promise instead of building up their own assets, for instance by working in the de facto's business, paying for property in the other's name, or by acting as a home-maker?
- how needy is the person applying? (The person applying for an order is known as the applicant);
- what is the other partner's ability to pay?

If you believe it would be unfair for your partner to keep property in his or her name for the above or other reasons, contact a solicitor for advice.

The legislation

New South Wales, Victoria and the Territories have passed de facto property rights legislation. The legislation can only be used if the de facto couple have:

- lived together for two years; or
- they have a child together; or
- the applicant is taking care of the other partner's child; or
- the applicant contributed to their income/property (ie assets), and the court believes it would be unjust to not use the property rights legislation.

If these conditions are not met the common law must be used.

The legislation was written to overcome the limitations of the common law system. It adopts similar principles to those in the Commonwealth *Family Law Act* which applies to married couples, discussed in 7.4 Property Settlements.

As with married couples, de facto property settlements are based on the contribution made to the assets by each partner, rather than whose name the property is in. Contributions can be either:

- financial (such as contributing towards a mortgage in the other person's name); or
- non-financial (such as caring for children or the home).

But it differs from married couples' property settlements because the future needs of each partner are not looked at — in other words, the person with the children does not necessarily get the largest share.

Remember that in Victoria only real property (houses, units etc) can be made the order of a de facto property settlement.

DE FACTO SPOUSE MAINTENANCE

Maintenance is available in any State if the woman is pregnant. It does not even matter whether the couple lived together or not. The mother can claim maintenance from the child's father:

- during the pregnancy; or
- within 12 months of the birth.

The mother is entitled to maintenance for herself for a period from two months before the birth to three months after the birth. Medical expenses related to the birth and pregnancy can also be claimed from the father.

Legislation exists in New South Wales and the Territories giving further rights to de facto spouses. The rights are similar to those given to married spouses (see 7.5 Maintenance) but are more limited.

De facto spouses in New South Wales can claim maintenance if they cannot support themselves because they are caring for a child. If a woman claims maintenance she must be caring either for:

- her child if the de facto partner is the father; or
- her partner's child from a previous relationship.

She cannot claim maintenance if she is supporting her own child and somebody else is the father.

Maintenance is payable if that child is:

- under 12; or
- under 16 if physically or mentally disabled.

If these conditions are not met, maintenance can only be claimed if the applicant can show that her ability to earn a living has been reduced as a result of the relationship. If she cannot earn a living for a different reason, for instance because she is ill or old, she may not be able to claim maintenance.

De facto spouses wishing to claim maintenance have to do so within two years of separation, and should seek legal advice. A claim cannot be made if the applicant enters a new relationship.

CONTRACTS BETWEEN DE FACTO PARTNERS

Note that these contracts are totally different from pre-nuptial contracts, which are often made between marrying couples in countries such as the United States. Pre-nuptial agreements are not currently recognised in Australia, but this may change.

Contracts between de facto partners defining their rights have traditionally been frowned upon by the courts and were rarely enforced. Today de facto relationships are becoming accepted by society, and a court might look at a de facto contract. In most States the contract is usually only one of many factors that will be considered and may not be followed to the letter. New South Wales is different because it has passed legislation which recognises the validity of de facto contracts.

The law in New South Wales

The *De Facto Relationships Act* allows couples who choose not to marry to come up with their own arrangements. Two types of agreements are recognised:

- cohabitation agreements – these determine how finances are to be arranged during the relationship;
- separation agreements – these determine the property division on separation.

To be valid under the Act they must be:

- in writing;
- signed; and
- each partner should have a certificate from a lawyer stating that they have received independent legal advice.

The agreements must satisfy technical requirements and are best drawn up by a lawyer. They can be drawn up at any time – before the relationship begins, during it, or on separation.

Cohabitation and separation agreements might not be enforced by a court if the terms are unjust or if circumstances have changed in such a way as to make the contract unfair (for instance a child was born).

CHILD SUPPORT

It does not matter whether the parents were married, or even whether they ever lived together – they are both still responsible for maintaining the children. Child support is explained in 7.5 Maintenance.

7.2   DOMESTIC VIOLENCE

Domestic violence is not a private family matter – it is a crime. In the past the law and the police were reluctant to interfere with household disputes but that attitude has changed. Violence in the home is recognised as being just as traumatic as street violence – perhaps even more so because of the ongoing relationship the victim has with the offender and the difficulty of escape.

WHAT IS DOMESTIC VIOLENCE?

Acts of violence

Many people incorrectly believe that the term "domestic violence" is limited to actual violent acts. It is not. The definition of domestic violence varies in its detail from State to State, but generally it covers a broad range of actions, including:

- physical abuse;
- sexual abuse;
- threats of violence;
- intimidation;
- harassment;
- molestation;
- making repeated telephone calls;
- stalking the victim with the intention to frighten her.

The offender

Most of the time the offender is male and the victim is female. The opposite can occur but it is very rare.

Offenders do not need to be married to the victim. An offender can be the victim's:

- husband;
- de facto partner;
- relative; or
- boyfriend.

FIRST STEP TO TAKE

Legal remedies take time. Women facing domestic violence need immediate help to get out of the dangerous situation. The first thing a woman should do is call the police.

If the police do not help

If the police do not attend or you are unable to call them, try to find help elsewhere. Family, friends and churches may be able to help. Counsellors, social workers, Women's Legal Services and Community Health Centres can be approached. Or you could go to a women's refuge and take the children. Women's refuges provide temporary accommodation and can help you sort the future out. They can be contacted by looking in the Index to the *White Pages*.

If the police attend but refuse to arrest and charge the offender you can take your own legal action in the Local Court (called Magistrates Courts in some States). A lawyer's help is advisable or contact one of the free legal advice services mentioned in 1.2 Sources of Legal Advice. Some States have a Domestic Violence Advocacy Service that can be approached for legal advice and court representation. Legal aid may be available: see 2.3 Legal Aid.

CALLING THE POLICE

If you are in immediate danger call the local police station or dial emergency 000. Give your name and address and be sure to stress the situation's severity. If you are unable to call the police yourself, try to get someone else to do it, perhaps a neighbour or relative. If it is safe, try to leave the house and wait for the police at a neighbour's house or go to the police station.

If you feel the police are not taking you seriously, ask to speak to the domestic violence liaison officer – many police stations have one. A great deal will depend on your attitude – if you take the matter seriously then the police should too.

Police powers of entry

Once the police arrive they have broad powers to enter private houses in domestic violence situations, but details vary between States and the following is only a guide.

To enter, the police must believe that somebody is being attacked or is about to be attacked. They can enter on the invitation of someone who appears to live in the house, even if it is a child, as long as the occupier does not expressly forbid entry. The occupier is the person living in the house whose name the house is in. Occupiers can be owners or tenants.

But what if the occupier is the person committing the offence? He is likely to try to prevent the police from entering. In this case they may still be able to enter if the victim invites them. If the victim is too frightened or is unable to give her permission the police can enter with a warrant.

Warrants can be obtained immediately by telephone or car radio, and are then called telephone warrants. If the police have a warrant they can use force to enter.

What will the police do?

Action taken by the police will depend on what occurred and on your attitude. If you need help insist that they give it to you. If you want the man charged make this clear, but it is ultimately up to the police.

The police might:

- take no action;
- reprimand the man;
- help you get a restraining order (discussed below);
- help you leave the premises and take you and the children somewhere safe;
- arrest the man if he physically assaulted you.

Arrest and bail

If the offender is arrested he will be taken to the police station and charged. For information on arrest powers and procedures refer to 5.1 Dealing with the Police.

Police can apply for a restraining order in addition to charging the offender. New provisions in New South Wales allow for police to call an after-hours justice in order to obtain an urgent interim (ie temporary) order to protect the victim immediately.

Bail must be considered. The police will look at the risk to the victim and the possibility that the offender will disappear. If bail is granted the offender will be free until the court case.

It is quite likely that conditions will be attached to the bail. Examples of conditions include orders not to:

- assault or harass the victim;
- approach the victim;
- contact the victim in any way;

- drink alcohol, particularly if the offender is more likely to hurt or approach the victim while intoxicated.

Breach of bail conditions could lead to re-arrest. If bail is refused the offender will remain in custody until the court case.

LEGAL PROCEEDINGS

Victims of domestic violence have a choice of three legal avenues:

- the criminal law;
- protection under the *Family Law Act*;
- restraining orders under State domestic violence legislation.

The criminal law

Prosecutions for assault under the criminal law may be commenced by way of summons or arrest. The decision to prosecute is made by the police, not the victim.

When it comes to domestic violence the criminal law has three disadvantages compared to the other systems:

- it can only deal with actual physical or sexual assault. It cannot deal with matters such as harassment and intimidation;
- it can only act after the event – after the assault has actually occurred;
- proving a criminal case is more difficult because a high standard of proof is required.

For details on what happens during a criminal trial, refer to 5.2 Criminal Court Procedure.

Domestic violence cases have special problems. Often the only witness will be the victim. In most areas of the law women are able to give evidence against their husbands but cannot be forced to do so. The problem with domestic violence is clear – husbands or other family members may put pressure on the woman not to testify. So with these cases the wife often has no choice, she must testify. She might be excused in certain circumstances and can discuss this with her lawyer.

Family Law Act protection

The *Family Law Act* is a Commonwealth Act and applies throughout Australia. You can apply for protection under the *Family Law Act* if you:

- are married to the offender; or

- have a child with the offender.

In Western Australia you can only get a *Family Law Act* order if you are married to the offender or have custody or access to a child of the marriage.

Unlike the criminal law, the *Family Law Act* provides remedies for intimidation, molestation and harassment – not just actual physical assault. The protection you can get is called an injunction or restraining order. It operates by ordering the offender to:

- stay away from you;
- stop the behaviour being complained of;
- refrain from hurting or threatening you.

If the order is breached the offender can be arrested, but there is a drawback. The power of arrest under the *Family Law Act* is not automatic. You have to apply to the court for an arrest order, which slows down the whole process.

Domestic violence legislation

All States and Territories in Australia have passed domestic violence legislation. Action under this system is cheaper, quicker and arguably more effective than the other two methods.

Restraining orders can be applied for where the woman is hurt, threatened, harassed, molested, stalked, intimidated etc. There is no need for actual violence to have taken place. Domestic violence restraining orders have different names in different States. In New South Wales they are called Apprehended Violence Orders. In Victoria they are known as Intervention Orders.

A complaint may be made by either the police or the victim. In States such as New South Wales, the police must make a complaint in a domestic violence situation unless the woman intends to do it herself or there is some good reason for them to not make a complaint.

If the matter is not particularly urgent the offender will be summonsed to attend court, usually in a few weeks' time. If it is urgent and you believe you are in immediate danger a warrant may be issued to arrest the offender and speed the process up. In New South Wales the police can call an after-hours justice.

Temporary orders may be made without the offender's presence in court, particularly if it is feared that the offender will become violent when he receives a summons. They are known as interim orders and begin operating as soon as they are given (served) to the offender. A summons to appear in court is served with the interim orders.

Interim orders last until the hearing, where the matter is decided in the presence of both parties. If the man does not turn up to this hearing the matter can be decided in his absence. Again, the orders come into operation once they are given to him.

Unlike Family Law orders, if a State restraining order is breached the police have the power to arrest the offender immediately. The extra protection this provides is obvious. It is also an offence to breach a restraining order and the offender faces an additional penalty.

MONEY MATTERS

Women who flee a violent home usually find themselves worrying about where to live and how to survive financially.

Social security may be available. Contact the Department of Social Security and refer to Chapter 11. The Department of Social Security can also provide social workers who can refer you to health, legal, accommodation and other support services.

Do not worry that by leaving your home you will somehow be deprived of your property rights if you divorce, because theoretically you will not. In practice, however, there are steps you can take to help prevent this. 7.4 Property Settlements gives further details.

7.3   SEPARATION AND DIVORCE

When a marriage ends it is in everybody's interests that the divorce be settled quickly with as little resentment and friction as possible.

Before the passing of the *Family Law Act* in 1975, fault such as adultery or assault had to be proved by couples wanting to divorce. The process was messy, distressing and involved a great deal of intrusion into private lives. The view that the law should not interfere gained increasing acceptance.

Since the passing of the Act the only ground for divorce is irretrievable breakdown of the marriage, and this is evidenced by a 12-month separation.

The *Family Law Act* is a Commonwealth Act and so applies to all States and Territories in Australia.

SEPARATION

It is not necessary for both parties to agree to the separation – one can leave against the other's will and the separation will still be recognised by the law. It does not make any difference to the property settlement who left or why.

To separate, there is no formal procedure to go through, no documents to fill in. Keeping a note of the date is a good idea because the party applying for a divorce will need to know the exact date.

Getting back together interrupts the separation period, but if it only happens once and lasts up to three months you will not have to start counting the 12 months all over again. Say you have been apart for six months, then try to sort things out and live together for two months, but it does not work. Another six months will have to pass before you can apply for a divorce. Getting back together means attempting to revive the marriage in every sense. Occasional sex does not interrupt the separation period.

You may have heard of couples who are separated but live together and been puzzled by it. Legally this is possible, but it makes getting a divorce harder. They will have to show that they led independent lives: slept in different rooms, performed their own housework, had separate social lives. Usually they only continued to share a home for financial reasons. No single element is conclusive, rather it is a pattern of behaviour that shows the marriage is over.

Furthermore, it is not enough for the parties to merely swear that they led separate lives. Independent evidence is needed. For instance, a friend or relative who has visited the house will have to make a sworn statement setting out their observations.

DIVORCE PROCEEDINGS

Divorce is separate from property settlements, maintenance, custody and access proceedings. (Each is discussed in detail under the appropriate headings in this chapter).

After you separate you should give thought to those other issues and, if possible, discuss them with your ex-partner. You do not have to wait until the actual divorce before you start sorting out those important aspects of your life. In fact, you should not. If you have young children you will not be allowed to divorce unless you have made arrangements for their upbringing including where they will live, how they will be supported, where they will go to school etc.

Once the 12-month separation period has elapsed, either party can apply for the divorce. The person applying is known as the applicant, and must fill out an Application for Divorce form obtainable from the Family Court Registry. Two types exist, one for people who do not have any children under 18, and another for where there are children. This type requires details to be filled in regarding arrangements made for the children.

You can do the legal work yourself or ask a lawyer to do it. You might prefer to do it yourself to save legal fees, as legal aid generally does not cover the divorce itself. If so you will need to fill in the form correctly, then file it and your marriage certificate at the Family Court Registry. If you have been living with your partner while separated you must also file a sworn statement (affidavit) made by an independent witness regarding the state of affairs.

You will then be given back the documents which must be sent to your ex-partner, who is known as the respondent. This process is known as service, and must be carried out in a particular way. You cannot simply hand them over personally. Filling in the form and serving the documents are not difficult tasks but must be carried out correctly. Ask the staff at the Registry for detailed guidance.

Joint applications are possible when both sides agree to the divorce. The requirement of sending documents to the other side then becomes unnecessary and the procedure may well be quicker.

You will be told when to attend for the appearance which will be in front of a registrar rather than a judge. Divorces are simple if unopposed and usually only the applicant need attend. The documents will be read and you may need to answer questions.

If there are no children and the divorce is straightforward, the court can deal with it without either partner having to attend.

There are three ways to oppose a divorce:

- by establishing that the separation did not last 12 months - there may be a hearing or the divorce may be postponed;
- by proving that both partners want to get together again – which is difficult if one is filing for divorce;
- by showing that arrangements made for the children are not satisfactory.

You may not be granted a divorce immediately if you were married for less than two years. Attending counselling is a prerequisite here, and it may be wise in any situation. The Family Court can arrange reconciliation counselling.

Once it is decided that a divorce should be granted an order known as a decree nisi will be made. This does not end the marriage. Usually a month will pass until the final order (the decree absolute) is made, allowing you to remarry if you wish.

THE EFFECT ON WILLS

For a description of the effect divorce has on a will, see 16.1 Making a Will.

7.4   PROPERTY SETTLEMENTS

People often wonder about the timing of property settlements. Do you have to wait until the separation period is up before you can work out who gets what? The answer is definitely no. In fact, you should start giving it some thought as soon as you are able to after the separation.

Divorces and property settlements are two separate processes. You have to wait 12 months after separation to obtain a divorce (see 7.3 Separation and Divorce) but you do not have to wait to begin property proceedings. If you delay more than one year after the divorce, you will have to ask the court to grant special permission to allow the proceedings to take place.

Property settlements can be agreed on between the partners or determined by the Family Court. The laws governing the distribution of marital property are determined by the *Family Law Act*. This is a Federal Act and so applies in all States and Territories in Australia.

PROPERTY AND MAINTENANCE

Technically property settlements and maintenance orders are two different issues, but the distinction in practice is not so clear because one often affects the other.

For a discussion on the principles governing the awarding of spousal and child maintenance see 7.5 Maintenance.

IF YOU DO NOT HAVE ENOUGH MONEY TO LIVE ON

Even if you commence proceedings as soon as possible, it will still be a long time before the court makes an order. Even then you may need to take steps to force your partner to carry out their obligations. So what can you do in the meantime?

It would have been best if you had your own bank accounts and finances during the marriage. If not, and you suddenly find yourself without any means of support, try asking your partner for help if possible. If the relationship is such that you cannot do that, you can apply to the Family Court for an urgent maintenance order or interlocutory (ie temporary) property order. Contact Legal Aid or a community legal centre for help. Also contact the Department of Social Security to discuss your eligibility to receive financial assistance.

Women who are fleeing from a violent home can go to a women's refuge and take the children. Refuges provide short-term accommodation and can help sort out something for the long term. They can be found by looking in the *White Pages* Index.

IF YOU THINK YOUR PARTNER WILL DISPOSE OF PROPERTY

As a matter of legal principle it does not matter whose name the property is in. Both partners are entitled to a share. But if it is in the other person's name there is a chance that they might sell or give away the property in attempt to frustrate a court order. And once this has happened it can be very difficult to get your fair share.

To prevent this it may be wise to not leave a house that is solely in your partner's name. But sometimes this is unavoidable, particularly if violence is involved, and you simply must leave. Seek legal advice quickly about obtaining an urgent property order. This will stop your partner from selling property until the final court order.

WHEN THE PARTIES AGREE

By far the best approach to property settlements is calm discussion with a view to reaching an agreement you are both happy with. You and your partner know your relationship best, and a mutually agreed decision may be better than one forced on you by the court – which is what will happen if you cannot agree.

You may need help in reaching an agreement, and this is available through the process of mediation. Mediation involves discussing solutions in the presence of a neutral person who will facilitate discussions. Mediation is described more fully in 4.2 Mediation.

Once you reach an agreement, getting a lawyer to draw it up is best. Do not agree to anything without first seeking legal advice. Knowing what you could get if you did go to court will give you the ability to recognise a fair division – acting out of ignorance is always dangerous. It is also a good idea to request an information session with the Family Court. It is held by a registrar and a counsellor and will help clarify the whole process.

MAKING AGREEMENTS LEGALLY BINDING

Just coming to an arrangement yourselves is not enough to make it binding, even if you write it down and sign it. It needs to be formalised by the Family Court. If it is not, either party can disregard the agreement and apply for a court order.

Agreements can be formalised in three ways:

- asking the court to make consent orders in the terms agreed by you and your partner;
- seeking the court's approval for the agreement;
- asking the court to register the agreement.

WHEN THE PARTIES CANNOT AGREE

Quite often the parties cannot reach their own agreement as to how their property should be divided. They can ask the Family Court for an order that decides the matter for them.

Even so they will still be encouraged to come to their own decision. A court conciliation conference is held with this aim. Conciliation is similar to mediation, and involves the parties working out their own agreement with the help of a neutral person. If successful the agreement will be filed in court and have the validity of a court order.

You will always have a chance to reach an agreement before the court case, right up until the last minute when a pre-hearing conference is held. If all fails there will be a hearing. You can reach agreement even on the day of the hearing.

HOW DOES THE COURT DECIDE?

It does not make any difference who left the relationship nor whose "fault" it was that the marriage broke down. Neither is there a pre-determined formula (such as a 50-50 split) that will automatically be applied. Pre-nuptial agreements (where partners agree before the wedding what the property separation will be if there is a divorce) are currently not recognised by Australian law, but this may possibly change.

All that a court will consider at a property settlement is the contributions you made during the marriage and your present and future needs.

107

Contributions

Who contributed what? The court will look at who paid for family assets, but contributions are not only financial. Non-monetary contributions such as raising children and looking after the home can be of equal value and are recognised as such by the court.

Needs

To determine your present and future needs the court will look at:

- whether maintenance orders have been made;
- how long the marriage lasted;

and at both parties':

- age and health;
- income;
- ability to earn a living in the future (for example women caring for young children have a reduced ability to support themselves, as might older women who spent their entire life as a home-maker);
- need to support children under 18;
- current expenses.

Often the person looking after the children will receive the largest share because their needs are greater.

WHAT CAN BE DIVIDED?

All family assets can be made the subject of a court order.

Property owned before the marriage

In short marriages, property owned by each partner before the marriage may tend to remain theirs. This is not definitive, however, and the court will look at how the property has been treated and maintained during the marriage. For instance, if the husband already owned a house but the wife helped clean and renovate it and they both lived there, that pre-marriage asset may have become part of the family property. The longer the marriage, the more likely it is that such a conclusion will be drawn.

Gifts and inheritances

Here it is the intention of the person making the gift that matters. If the gift was given to the couple because they were a couple (for example money to buy children's furniture or spend on a family holiday) then it is likely to be part of the family assets. But if it was given specifically to one person (for instance giving the bride an heirloom with the intention that she will pass it on when her daughter marries) then it may remain the property of the wife.

The family home

The wife often wants to remain in the family home, particularly if she gets custody of the children. The court may allow this if there is enough money over all for it to still be fair to the husband. If there is not, it will have to be sold and the proceeds divided.

The family business

This is also a family asset, and the court will look at contributions made by both parties in financing and running it.

Superannuation

Superannuation poses difficulties because it will not be received by the employee until an often much later date. Its ultimate value cannot be predicted at the time of the hearing because it depends on when the employee retires, whether he or she will go through long periods of unemployment, how much they earn etc.

Different judges have different approaches to superannuation. Some try to estimate what the payout will be worth and make an adjustment out of present assets. Others treat it as a future resource. It is possible that legislation will be passed to clarify the law.

ARE PROPERTY ORDERS FINAL?

Yes. Settlements should be final to allow both parties to leave their old relationship behind and start on their new lives. If, however, you think that the settlement was wrong, you have 28 days to appeal. You will need a lawyer's advice as to whether this is worthwhile.

Decisions might be altered if one party later suffers unexpected hardship, if it can be shown that property was hidden to frustrate the court order, or if the order becomes very difficult or impossible to carry out.

ENFORCING AN ORDER

Court orders must be carried out. If either party does not do so, the other should see a lawyer about taking steps to enforce compliance.

DE FACTO RELATIONSHIPS

Property settlements when de facto relationships end are not governed by the Commonwealth *Family Law Act*, but by State legislation. Generally you take out what you brought in, and it matters who paid for the property and whose name it is in.

States such as Victoria and New South Wales have legislation giving similar rights to those held by married couples under the *Family Law Act*, but their rights are much more limited. 7.1 Living Together gives further details.

7.5   MAINTENANCE

Many people who have just separated, particularly women, are anxious about being able to support themselves and their children. They may be able to claim social security, and should contact the Department of Social Security for advice. Chapter 11 outlines what is available and gives details on eligibility.

But the law prefers the father to be responsible if possible by paying maintenance. There are two types of maintenance orders you can seek:

- maintenance for yourself, known as spouse maintenance, although this has become rather uncommon;
- child maintenance, also known as child support.

SPOUSE MAINTENANCE

Eligibility to apply

Spouse maintenance is not awarded automatically when you separate, you have to apply for it. It is usually women who apply for maintenance but there is no reason that men cannot if all the conditions are met. Applications can be made after separation – you do not have to wait until the divorce. The latest you can apply is 12 months after the divorce, unless you have valid reasons which convince the court to give you special leave to apply.

The rules governing spouse maintenance come under the *Family Law Act*, a Commonwealth Act that applies throughout Australia. The court that decides the matter is the Family Court.

Under the Act you have to show that you cannot support yourself for any of the following reasons:

- you are looking after young children;
- you have been married so long without working that you have lost your ability to find a job;
- you are too old to get a job;

- you have a disability;
- there is some other valid reason preventing you from earning a living.

You also have to show that your partner can afford to pay. He will not be forced to make maintenance payments if he is unable to.

Every case is different and the court will consider all the relevant facts. Maintenance orders are unlikely if you remarry or enter into a de facto relationship. Similarly, if your husband remarries and has to support new children, he may not be able to afford to pay spouse maintenance and may be relieved of his obligations. Orders are most likely to be made where the husband is well off and the wife is unable to earn a living.

How much will be awarded?

If you and your partner can reach a maintenance arrangement that you are both happy with you can apply to make it legally binding by asking the court for consent orders. Agreeing is better than having an order imposed on you and is less likely to lead to enforcement problems. Mediation services can help you reach an agreement, and can be arranged by the Family Court or by other mediation services: see 4.2 Mediation. If you cannot agree on maintenance you can ask the Family Court to decide for you.

There is no set formula that a court will follow. In deciding how much to award, the court will consider:

- the length of the marriage;

and both partner's:

- age;
- health;
- responsibility to support children;
- standard of living;
- income;
- property ownership;
- ability to work;
- intention to retrain or pursue further education;
- involvement in new relationships.

It is difficult to make generalisations as to how much will be awarded as no two cases are alike. Solicitors experienced in this field can give you a good idea of what you can expect.

If you receive social security and are then awarded maintenance your pension or allowance may be reduced.

How is maintenance paid?

It can be paid periodically or in a lump sum. Periodic payments may be changed as your circumstances change – for instance if you remarry or get a job, or if your ex-partner dies or becomes unemployed.

Lump sum payments tend to be final. They are paid once and generally cannot be varied if circumstances later change. They may be awarded as part of a property settlement: see 7.4 Property Settlements.

If you need the money urgently

Applications for maintenance orders take time and if you do not have your own finances you can apply for an urgent maintenance order to keep you going until final orders can be made.

De facto spouses

Under the *Family Law Act*, women who have separated from their de facto partner and are pregnant can claim maintenance while pregnant or within one year of the birth. Reasonable medical expenses may be covered. That is as far as the Federal Act goes. Other women have to rely on the laws of their State, and these vary significantly.

In New South Wales, de facto women can claim maintenance if they have lost the ability to support themselves because of the relationship or if they are supporting either the de facto's child or a child of the relationship who is under 12.

The law in this area is changing throughout the country, with the trend toward giving greater rights to de facto partners. Advice should be sought for up-to-date information. See also 7.1 Living Together.

CHILD MAINTENANCE/(CHILD SUPPORT)

Parents are expected to support their children. It does not matter whether they were married to each other or even if they lived together. Maintenance can be claimed for children under 18 if they are not married or self-supporting, and for children over 18 if they are studying or disabled.

There are two different ways to apply for child maintenance and the type you choose is determined by when you separated and when the child was born.

Birth/separation before 1 October 1989

If you separated before 1 October 1989 or the child was born before that date, maintenance proceedings are brought under the *Family Law Act*.

It is best if the parents can reach their own child maintenance agreement. As with spouse maintenance discussed above, mediation services run by the Family Court can help you reach a satisfactory agreement. Consent orders may then be made by the court to make the agreement enforceable – meaning that legal steps can be taken if the paying parent does not fulfil their obligations.

If no agreement can be reached, the Family Court or a Local Court (called Magistrates Courts in some States) can be asked to decide the matter.

People who can apply for a court order are:

- a parent;
- the child;
- somebody with an interest in the child's welfare (such as an aunt, uncle, grandparent).

The court will consider:

- each parent's income;
- whether the father has children from a different relationship to support;
- the children's needs;
- the children's income or financial resources.

All child maintenance orders or agreements can be varied at any time where:

- there has been a change in circumstances – for instance if the father loses his job;
- the cost of living has changed considerably;
- facts were withheld from the court or false evidence was given. In the case of agreements, they can also be changed where the amount agreed on was not proper or adequate.

In the past the sum awarded was often too low. Enforcing payment was time consuming and expensive. The Child Support Scheme was introduced from 1 October 1989 and removed the need for a court battle.

Birth/separation after 1 October 1989

If you separated after 1 October 1989 or have a child born after that date you can apply for child maintenance under the Child Support Scheme. You can apply for all of your children, even if some were born before that date.

To apply you must be the parent who has custody of the child or cares for the child on a daily basis. You need to be separated but you do not have to wait until you are divorced. In most States it does not matter whether you were married or in a de facto relationship. Step-parents usually cannot apply for maintenance themselves but may be able to if the natural parent has died and they have custody of the child.

If you are the parent looking after the child and are entitled to seek maintenance, you must apply for it or else you may lose your ability to receive social security.

How does the child support scheme differ from court proceedings?

The Child Support Agency, a government body, has taken over the court's role. It decides how much maintenance shall be paid, but rather than requiring an expensive and protracted court battle, it decides the matter by using a formula set by law.

The formula takes into account both parents' taxable income, living expenses, and responsibilities to care for other dependants. The Child Support Agency can provide further details on the amount that may be paid.

An application form must be filled in and is available from the Child Support Agency or the Department of Social Security. You will need to provide details regarding the children's birth dates, the date of separation, who has custody and who the father is. If you were married, your ex-husband is assumed to be the father. If he adopted the child he will also be considered to be the father. Otherwise you will need to prove it, for instance by showing his name on the birth certificate or asking him to sign a declaration. If he refuses, you can go to court and ask for a parentage testing order.

You can still come to your own agreement as to maintenance payments and ask the Child Support Agency to approve it. The agency can register the agreement and then they will collect the payments.

Collecting the money

The Child Support Agency arranges for the collection of child maintenance – a vast improvement on the old system of enforcing obligations through the court system.

On registering with the agency, maintenance is payable to the agency rather than the mother. It is then paid into her bank account. The agency can direct the father's employer to deduct the sum owed from the father's salary, making it much more likely that it will be paid.

If you are receiving maintenance under the pre 1 October 1989 system you can apply to have the Child Support Agency collect payments for you.

Changing the amount of child support

Both parents can appeal to a court if they believe the assessment was wrong, for instance because incorrect information was used. This must be done within 28 days of the assessment, and a lawyer's help would be needed.

Child support is reviewed every year to ensure it keeps up with changing circumstances.

7.6   CUSTODY AND ACCESS

One of the hardest decisions that must be made when a marriage breaks down is who gets the children. Custody and access battles can be traumatic, so the law encourages parents to make their own arrangements. If they cannot the case will be decided by a court. It is important to realise that if there is a hearing the children's welfare will be the judge's highest priority – higher, in fact, than the parents' feelings.

TERMINOLOGY

Children

In every State and Territory except for Western Australia, orders can be sought under the Federal *Family Law Act* for children that are:

- children of the marriage;
- children of a previous marriage;
- a de facto couple's children;
- foster children;
- children born using artificial conception.

At the moment, Western Australian children who are not children of the marriage are covered by State law.

Custody

The person with custody of the children is responsible for their day-to-day care and control, such as feeding them, protecting them, sending them to school. Children live with the custodial parent.

Guardian

Guardians have the right to make long-term decisions for the children, such as choice of schooling, medical treatment, religious upbringing. If the parents are divorced both usually remain guardians of the children.

Access

Children have the right to continue good relationships with both parents. Access is the children's right to see the non-custodial parent.

CHILDREN AND DIVORCE

Unless suitable custody arrangements are made for children under 18, a divorce will not be finalised by the court. 7.3 Separation and Divorce provides details on obtaining a divorce.

WHEN THE PARENTS AGREE

Parents are better placed than the court to know what is best for their children. Court action is expensive and stressful, and is best avoided if possible.

Family Court counsellors are available to help you and your partner reach an agreement satisfactory to you both. Anything said to a Family Court counsellor is confidential and will not be used if the matter goes to court. Sessions are free and can be attended at any time – contact the court for details.

It is a good idea to seek legal help when drawing up the agreement. Any agreement you make will have to be approved by the court in order to make it legally valid. Courts are unlikely to change arrangements that you are both happy with. If you belong to a particular religious or ethnic group your customs will be respected by the court if you wish to follow them.

The court can make the agreement legally enforceable by:

- making consent orders; or
- registering the agreement under the *Family Law Act*.

WHEN THE PARENTS CANNOT AGREE

If you cannot agree on custody and access arrangements you can ask the Family Court to decide for you. Legal procedure is moving away from the traditional adversarial system (where one person wins and the other loses) to minimise emotional damage to the children. The movement is towards mediation.

Mediation

Mediation involves discussion between the parents with an independent third person who helps them reach an agreement. 4.2 Mediation explains the process in more detail.

Pre-filing mediation takes place before the court case begins. It is advisable to ask for it because at this early stage disagreements have not yet become entrenched. In deciding whether to allow it, the court will look at issues such as:

- whether there is any violence or abuse towards the children or the other parent;
- whether the request is really just a delaying tactic;
- whether one party intimidates the other and tries to bully them into a situation they are not happy with.

If it believes any of these are present it will not be inclined to order mediation. Mediation works best when both sides have equal strength.

Counselling

The court will make an order for confidential counselling with a Family Court counsellor. Possible choices will be discussed, with an emphasis on how they will effect the children. Information sessions are held by the Family Court, providing details about counselling and other procedures.

Family Reports

The court needs to have a good understanding of each family's individual circumstances – how the parents and children relate to each other. To get this information it can order a Family Report. This will be prepared by a Family Court Counsellor, but not the same one who carried out the confidential session. The counsellor writing the report will interview you, your partner and the children and make observations. The report will be discussed with you before it is sent to the judge.

Who can apply for an order?

Anybody who has an interest in the children's welfare can apply for a custody order. Usually it is a parent but grandparents, step-parents, other relatives and even family friends may be able to apply and should seek legal advice as to their position.

You can do the application yourself but it is complicated and a lawyer's guidance is recommended. Legal aid may be available if you have a reasonable chance of success and pass the means test – contact Legal Aid in your State if you think you may be eligible. 2.3 Legal Aid provides further details.

The child's representative

To ensure that the children's needs are given paramount consideration, the court is able to order separate legal representation for the children. Usually they are appointed in cases of abuse.

The children's lawyer will be present at the court making sure that all the evidence relevant to their welfare is raised. He or she makes all the relevant inquiries and obtains material such as teachers' reports, medical reports, family reports (prepared by the court counsellor or a child psychologist).

This lawyer is not employed by either parent but is independent, and is paid by legal aid. A child or either of the parties can ask the court to appoint a representative or the court may do it of its own motion.

CUSTODY AND GUARDIANSHIP ORDERS

Where do you apply?

You can apply for custody, guardianship or access orders at either the Family Court or Local Court (called Magistrates Courts in some States).

What will the court consider?

Decisions are made with the children's welfare in mind. When coming to a decision a court will look at each parents':

- age;
- health;
- income and property;
- relationship with the children;
- ability to provide a secure loving environment.

Both parents are heard by the court.

The effect that separation from either parent will have on the children is also considered. Parents' conduct such as living in a de facto or homosexual relationship will only be considered to the extent that it effects the children's welfare. Otherwise the court will not make a moral judgment on the applicant's lifestyle.

The children's wishes will be taken into account. How much weight the court gives them depends on each child's age and maturity.

Brothers and sisters

Courts are unwilling to separate brothers and sisters. All of the children usually end up with the one parent, but if the parents and children have decided otherwise a court is unlikely to interfere.

What types of orders can be made?

Mothers do not automatically get custody, the father also has a chance of obtaining a custody order. This is particularly so if the children are not very young.

Parents who are married or live together automatically have joint custody and joint guardianship of their children. When the parents separate this changes, and the court may order:

- sole custody and joint guardianship – one parent has the daily responsibility, and both share long-term decision-making. This is the most common order;
- sole custody and guardianship – only one parent has both short and long-term responsibility. This may be ordered if the other parent does not wish to have any rights over the children, or where there was abuse;
- joint custody and guardianship – the children spend equal time with each parent. This is only likely if the parents live close to each other and have a good relationship.

Changing custody orders

Custody orders are never final. They can be changed by a court or by an agreement between the parents. Changing orders is unsettling and the court will not do this unless there has been a significant change that affects the children's welfare.

When does the order end?

Orders cease when the children turn 18 or earlier if:

- the court changes the order;

- the children marry; or
- are adopted (for example by a step-parent).

ACCESS ORDERS

The principles determining access orders are similar to those that determine custody and guardianship.

Again, it is best if parents can reach their own agreement, preferably by consulting their children if they are old enough. The agreement can be formalised by the court. If you are unable to agree you can ask the court to make an order.

The court may order:

- reasonable access – it is left up to you to work out what is reasonable. This is the most common access order;
- specific access times may be set by the court;
- supervised access – another adult must be present during visits. This may be ordered if there is a fear that the child might be abducted or hurt.

Total denial of access is less common. This might be ordered if there is a fear that the child will be physically or sexually abused. Evidence is needed to convince a court that the risk is real rather than a strategy designed to cut off the relationship.

Changing or ending access orders

The same principles apply to changing and ending custody orders discussed above.

EFFECT OF ADOPTION

Once a child is adopted the adoptive parents take over all the rights and responsibilities of a natural parent. If you remarry and want your new partner to adopt your children you generally will need the consent of their real father (or mother as the case may be). They will no longer have access rights. If that person is untraceable and takes no interest in the children then you may not need their consent.

It may help to talk to a lawyer or one of the advice centres discussed in 1.2 Sources of Legal Advice.

IF CUSTODY OR ACCESS ORDERS ARE BREACHED

Breaching an access or custody order can be punished by fine or imprisonment. Courts are reluctant to do this as it is usually not in the children's best interests. In practice it is often difficult to solve such problems using legal sanctions.

Fathers who have unlawfully been denied access are still responsible for paying child support (child support is discussed in 7.5 Maintenance).

Children in danger

Legal advice should be obtained urgently if you believe your children are in danger of being abducted or assaulted by your partner. If threats have been made call the police.

If the children are taken but you do not yet have a custody order, you can apply for an order in the absence of your partner. This is known as an ex parte order. Once you have a custody order the police can be issued with a warrant to take the children and return them to you.

Bringing them back from overseas is obviously much more difficult. If you suspect your children will be abducted overseas and you have a custody order, you can:

- ask the court for an order stopping anyone from taking the children out of the country – a temporary order can be made very quickly;
- ask the passport office to not issue passports to your children;
- if they already have passports they cannot be cancelled, but the Federal Police at airports and seaports can be notified;
- ask the court to order your partner to surrender his/her passport and the children's passports;
- ask airlines and shipping lines to stop them boarding.

You will need legal help to do this as the passport office and air and shipping lines require documents such as custody orders and sworn statements.

If the worst has happened and they are gone there are two things you can do. If the country they have gone to is part of an international convention on child abduction you may be able to arrange an order for their return. This can be arranged in Australia. But if the country is not part of the convention you will have to go there yourself to try to get a custody order. The laws of that country will apply and tragically you may find yourself facing a long and difficult battle.

FURTHER READING

Bowen, *Child Support the Essential Guide*, Jacaranda Wiley, Sydney, 1992

Bowen, *Divorce: A Guide For Australian Women*, Mandarin Australia, Melbourne, 1991

Graycar and Shiff (ed), *Life Without Marriage: A Woman's Guide To The Law,* Pluto Press, Sydney, 1987

Pearl Watson Foundation, *A Guide To Family Law*, Bay Books, Sydney, 1991

Roxburgh, *Taking Control: Help For Women And Children Escaping Domestic Violence*, Greenhouse Publications, Melbourne, 1989

Seddon, *Domestic Violence in Australia: The Legal Response*, 2nd edn, Federation Press, Sydney, 1993

Women's Legal Resources Centre, *Law And Relationships: A Woman's A to Z Guide*, Redfern Legal Centre Publishing, 1991, Sydney

See also: General references listed in Further Reading Chapter 1.

Chapter 8

CHILDREN AND THE LAW

8.1   Parents' rights and duties

8.2   Children's rights

8.3   Children's courts

Further reading

8.1   PARENTS' RIGHTS AND DUTIES

Discussions often centre around children's rights and tend to neglect parents' rights. It is easy as a parent to feel anxious about your legal position. The law recognises that parents have basic legal rights that they can insist on. Coupled with this are many legal duties owed to the child.

WHO IS A PARENT?

This may sound like an obvious question but it is not. Are step-parents included? What about guardians? And what are the rights of unmarried parents?

Step-parents

Step-parents do not have the same legal rights as parents, although they do have some rights – for example they might seek to intervene in a custody battle, particularly where they had a long standing relationship with the child.

For a step-parent to be in the same legal position as a parent, they would have to either adopt the child or obtain a custody or guardianship order.

Guardians

A guardian may be appointed if the parents are dead or unable to take care of the child. Guardians can be appointed in a will or selected by a court. If court appointed, the court will look at the prospective guardian's age, relationship to the child (if any), character, health, financial position etc.

The child's wishes are also taken into account, and the older the child the greater impact their say will have.

Guardians have the same rights and duties as parents.

Unmarried parents

Children who are born when their parents are unmarried are referred to as ex-nuptial children. The old term "illegitimate" is not used much today. Note that a child is not ex-nuptial if his or her parents subsequently marry.

The father of an ex-nuptial child may still have a responsibility to contribute to the cost of raising the child, but the extent of his rights may be limited depending on the laws of the State the child lives in.

Unmarried fathers wanting to object to the mother's actions (such as putting the child up for adoption or changing the child's surname) can seek advice from one of the free advice centres described in 1.2 Sources of Legal Advice.

PARENTS' RIGHTS

The child's upbringing

It is up to you what religion your child follows, if any at all. You decide what values to give your children and how they are to be brought up.

The child's education

Which school you can send your child to depends on the laws of your State. It may depend on where you live, where you went as a child, and your child's intellectual abilities. Non-government schools have their own criteria (often based on religion or academic ability) and can be contacted to discuss entry requirements and fees.

If you do not want your child to attend certain classes, such as sex education or religion, discuss the matter with the school principal. Contact the Department of Education if you are unsatisfied with the response.

Medical matters

Parents need to give consent for their children to receive medical treatment. You have the right to refuse, but the child may be treated without the need for your consent if his or her life is in imminent danger.

Discipline

Parents have the right to use physical or non-physical methods of discipline, as long as the punishment is moderate and reasonable. What is reasonable depends on:

- the child's age;
- the behaviour that caused the punishment;
- the method used;
- if the child was hit, it matters where and how often, and whether any injury resulted.

The right to discipline can be granted to people who also stand in the parents' place such as school teachers. Anybody else who punishes a child may be liable for assault.

A school's authority to punish a child depends on the laws of the State. See 8.2 Children's Rights.

Taking legal action on the child's behalf

If your child has been injured, you have the right to take legal action to secure compensation on the child's behalf.

PARENTS' DUTIES

You do not need anybody to tell you that being a parent requires responsibility. Your views are determined by your upbringing and your moral outlook. But what responsibilities are placed on parents by the law?

Registering the child's birth

All births must be registered with the Registry of Births, Deaths and Marriages. The time in which you have to do this varies between States but is generally between one and two months. You can ask the hospital, midwife, or Registry for details.

Maintaining the child

Children must be fed, clothed and sheltered. Theoretically this legal obligation lasts until they are 18 or, if they marry at a younger age, until they marry. But in practice if a child is around school leaving age (about 15), and can care for him/herself, the parents' obligations diminish.

Parents who fail in their duty to maintain their children are committing an offence. Prosecutions are most likely to be made in the more serious cases, which involve physical or sexual abuse, or severe neglect of very young children.

Care proceedings in the Children's Court might be commenced if the neglect or abuse is bad enough: see 8.3 Children's Courts.

The duty to make provision for your children even survives your death. If you do not make adequate provision for them in your will they might be able to challenge it: see 16.1 Making a Will.

Sending the child to school

Parents are responsible for ensuring that their children attend school until they reach a certain age, usually 15 (sometimes 16). Failure to attend without good reason is known as truancy.

Government permission is needed to educate the child from home. It may be granted where the child is ill or disabled, lives too far from the nearest school, or has some other special reason. Contact the Department of Education if you strongly feel that your child should not attend school.

PARENTS' LIABILITY FOR THE CHILD'S ACTS

If your child has legal responsibilities and fails to meet them, can you be held responsible?

Criminal offence

Parents are not responsible for a crime committed by the child unless they helped or encouraged the child to commit the crime.

The child's negligence

Negligence refers to a failure to take care – for instance hurting another child in play or damaging fragile items in a store. You are not responsible unless you were negligent in controlling the child.

The degree of control that you are reasonably expected to have over the child depends on the child's age. Obviously a younger child needs to be closely controlled to prevent inadvertent injury to other people and property.

Liability under contract

If your child breaches a contract are you liable to pay?

You cannot be made responsible unless your child borrowed money and you acted as guarantor. Guarantors promise to personally pay back money if the borrower defaults. The sum can be quite large, causing the guarantor to lose their home to repay the loan. If you are asked to become a guarantor, seek independent legal advice before agreeing.

8.2   CHILDREN'S RIGHTS

Children and young people under 18 do not have the same legal rights as adults. They are restricted in their rights to drink, vote, work and have sexual relationships.

This is because the law believes that children need more protection than adults; not only from other people but also from their own mistakes. But it is increasingly being recognised that children and young people are individuals who have rights that should be respected.

The United Nations passed a Convention on the Rights of the Child. It has been ratified in Australia, meaning that laws can be developed here in line with its principles. The Convention states:

- children have a right to express themselves and be taken seriously;
- children should have a say in decisions affecting them;
- the child's best interests should be the focus in any such decision made.

STUDENT'S RIGHTS

School plays such a large role in shaping a young person's future that it is important that they understand the rights they have as students. Some of the more common concerns expressed by students include:

- can they be searched by teachers?
- do teachers and principals have the right to inflict physical punishment?
- on what grounds can they be suspended or expelled from school?

Answers vary between States but it is possible to make the following generalisations.

Searches

Can teachers search you or your bag? Basically the answer is no, unless you consent. They can look in your desk as that is school property. If they spot a weapon or other dangerous object on you they can remove it.

Punishment

Different forms of punishment exist, such as:

- taking away your privileges – such as excursions;
- being sent out of class;
- detention – as long as it is not unreasonable in length nor makes your journey home difficult or dangerous;
- physical (or corporal) punishment.

Physical punishment arouses the strongest debate. In New South Wales the school decides if it is to be allowed, but parents can write a letter forbidding its use on their children. Only the principal or a senior teacher can administer it, and it can only be a last resort. Guidelines specify exactly how the punishment is to be carried out. Only a light caning on the palm is permitted.

Corporal punishment is forbidden in Victoria. In Queensland corporal punishment is only permitted in accordance with regulations but is not to be used for minor offences nor on very young children.

If you have been punished in a way you believe is unfair, talk to a teacher you trust or the principal and ask your parents for their support.

Suspensions and expulsions

You cannot be suspended or expelled due to your political or religious views, but only for serious misbehaviour – which can include violence, insolence, carrying weapons or drugs, or persistent disobedience.

Getting more information

The National Children's and Youth Law Centre has published a "Know Your Rights" kit for school students, available in most States and soon to be published in the rest. Kits should be available at all school libraries. If you have difficulty finding one, contact the Centre.

Community legal centres and other sources of free advice can also help: see 1.2 Sources of Legal Advice.

LEAVING HOME

If you are under 18 and you want to leave home, then you need to be able to show that proper provision will be made for your accommodation and other needs.

Parents can ask the police to pick up runaways. Court proceedings can be taken asking the court for a ruling that the child must stay at home. But if you are nearly 18 and do leave, it is unlikely that a court would force you to go back home.

In making its decision a court would take into account:

- how mature you are;
- whether you have found alternative accommodation;
- whether you have a job;
- the environment at home, including problems of abuse or neglect;
- the attitude of your parents.

Young people living on the streets can be picked up by police or welfare officers if they appear to be under a certain age (usually 16) and in need of care. These children may be either returned home or placed in care: see 8.3 Children's Courts for information on care proceedings.

THE RIGHT TO WORK

Employing a child under 15 without a licence is a criminal offence. Licences allow children to perform in advertisements or work for the purposes of entertainment. Their health and education must be adequately maintained for them to continue working.

Working in the parents' business without pay (for instance in a shop) is allowed as long as the workload is reasonable for the child's age and the child is not being exploited. Some after-school work, such as newspaper runs, is permitted but the hours are restricted. Contact the department of employment in your State for details.

ENTERING INTO A CONTRACT

You may have heard that children cannot enter into a contract, but this is not strictly true. Children enter them every day – buying something from a store is a type of contract. What the law is trying to do is to protect young people from entering into contracts that may exploit them.

Generally a contract made with a child cannot be legally enforced unless it is for the basic necessities of life, such as food and clothing. The law in New South Wales goes further, and states that a contract cannot be enforced unless it is for the benefit of the child.

If you have entered into a contract that you later believe to be unfair and someone is threatening to sue you or refusing to return your money, do not simply ignore it just because you believe it cannot be enforced. It is best to seek legal advice to prevent the problem escalating.

TAKING LEGAL ACTION

Children cannot take legal action in their own name. The action must be brought by an adult on the child's behalf, known as a next friend. The next friend is often a parent or another close relative. However, when it comes to matters such as custody and access, children are able to make independent applications.

ALCOHOL

Young people under 18 do not have a legal right to buy alcohol or to drink on licensed premises. Anybody who sells alcohol to a minor is committing an offence.

Generally minors are not even allowed to enter licensed premises, but the law is starting to change in this area. In New South Wales children may enter licensed premises (but cannot drink alcohol) provided they are under the supervision of a responsible adult.

SEX

The age at which young people can consent to sexual relationships is known as the age of consent. The term "sexual relationship" is quite broad, including not only intercourse but any type of penetration or oral sex.

Anybody having such a relationship with someone under that age is guilty of a criminal offence, regardless of whether the under-aged partner was willing. The severity of the punishment reflects the age of the child. There may be a defence where the child was near the age of consent and the offender honestly believed he or she was older.

Incest is always a crime. Sexual relationships with parents, grandparents, brothers or sisters are prohibited by law regardless of age or consent. The only defence is where the couple did not know of their familial relationship.

The age of consent varies between States and for different types of sexual relationships but is usually 16. Currently in New South Wales the age of consent for boys and girls to have intercourse with the opposite sex is 16. For a girl to have a sexual relationship with another girl the age is also 16, but for a boy to have sex with another boy the age is 18.

Young people have the right to know about and obtain contraception. There is no problem once they have passed the age of consent, but at an earlier age they should find a sympathetic doctor or chemist if they intend to have a sexual relationship anyway. The safe sex campaign has made it easier to obtain suitable protection.

MARRIAGE

Under a certain age couples need their parents' consent to marry. Both boys and girls can marry without parental consent when they are 18. Between the ages of 16 and 18 they need their parents' consent. The court may have the power to allow a marriage even if the parents disagree. A court will look at:

- the couple's maturity;
- the length of the relationship;
- whether they have children or are expecting;

- the couple's ability to support themselves;
- whether adequate accommodation has been arranged.

8.3 CHILDREN'S COURTS

Children can become involved with Children's Courts either because:

- they are the subject of care proceedings (ie orders are sought to supervise the family or impose conditions like counselling, or in the last resort to remove the child);
- they have been charged with a crime.

CARE PROCEEDINGS

Parents are responsible for looking after their children properly. The nature of their duties are covered in 8.1 Parents' Rights and Duties, but basically they must feed, clothe and shelter their children, ensuring that they receive medical treatment when needed and an education.

If parents are unable or unwilling to take this responsibility then it must be taken up by others in the community. In other words, if a child becomes the subject of care proceedings, they might need to be looked after by somebody other than their parents.

Whether this is done, and if so, how it is done, is determined by a magistrate of the Children's Court in care proceedings.

Children in need of care

Children who are in need of care may become the subject of care proceedings in the Children's Court. A child may be found to be in need of care if:

- they are neglected – neglected children do not have their basic physical and emotional needs met;
- they have been abused – child abuse can be either physical, sexual or psychological.

Care proceedings generally are commenced by State welfare officers, although in some cases they may be commenced by police or parents.

Some States, such as New South Wales and Victoria, have laws stating that a child may also be in need of care if their relationship with their parents has broken down. In Victoria children themselves can make an application for care proceedings in this situation. Conciliation is attempted to resolve such problems by talking them through before court proceedings are begun.

Often children need to be removed from their home or taken off the street before the court hearing. In cases where the child is in immediate danger of abuse they can be removed from their home by police or welfare officers without a warrant. A warrant would be needed to remove a child not in imminent danger.

Court proceedings

Children needing care have already led traumatic lives and unfortunately care proceedings can be emotional and highly distressing. The law tries to reduce the stress involved by making the court proceedings relatively informal.

One way it does this is by making the physical environment less threatening. Children's Court rooms are similar to normal courtrooms (see 3.1 The Courtroom) but they tend to be smaller and the magistrate's bench is less intimidating.

Care proceedings are closed to the public to protect the privacy of the child and remove the feeling of being on display. The media has a right to attend but cannot publish the names of the children in their reports.

Strict rules of evidence do not apply – evidence that would be excluded in other court cases may be admitted in care proceedings as long as it is relevant. The most important consideration in care proceedings is the child's welfare, not legal technicalities.

If you become the subject of care proceedings you will be represented in court by a solicitor. Often this will be the duty solicitor who normally attends the court on certain days. Or you can approach a solicitor from Legal Aid or a community legal centre.

The magistrate will hear evidence from witnesses, including welfare officers, doctors, and the police. Parents also have the right to give evidence, and the child can if he or she is mature enough.

The child welfare department (whose name varies between States) will prepare a report, which you can see. The court and your solicitor can also order independent reports.

Do not feel that you have to sit through it all if you find it too distressing. Your solicitor can ask the magistrate that you be excused.

Court orders

After hearing all the evidence and taking your wishes into account, the court's aim is to make a decision that is in your best interests. It has a range of options:

- undertakings – you will remain at home with your parents if they make certain promises, such as to attend counselling and family therapy. A welfare officer may, if the court orders, supervise the arrangement to make sure you are being looked after properly;
- you may be placed with friends, relatives or neighbours;
- you may be placed with a foster family;
- you may be made a ward – this is a last resort. It means that your parents are no longer responsible for you. Instead, the minister responsible for child welfare becomes your guardian, meaning that he or she will be responsible for your upbringing. Welfare officers will be responsible for finding a placement for you.

All of these orders expire when you turn 18 or even earlier where the court so orders or circumstances change enough for the court to alter its decision. If you are unhappy with the new arrangements you can ask the court to change the order.

CHILDREN AND CRIME

The age of criminal responsibility

Under a certain age a child cannot be held guilty of committing a crime, because the law does not believe that such a young child is able to recognise that they have done wrong.

The age at which children do become responsible varies between States but is generally between seven and ten. However, children under the age of criminal responsibility who repeatedly commit crimes may be viewed as being in need of care. They may become the subject of care proceedings (discussed above).

Dealing with the police

Adults have basic rights when they are questioned by the police or arrested: see 5.1 Dealing with the Police. Children have all of these rights plus more.

All States and Territories require that children should not be questioned by the police unless an adult that they trust is with them – be it a parent, lawyer or friend. The extent of the protection varies, and is at its strongest in New South Wales where statements made without an adult present are not admitted as evidence in court proceedings.

At the most you should give your name, age and address. Being polite often helps prevent further trouble.

In some States there are some types of questions that will need to be answered. For instance anybody driving a car involved in an accident may have a duty to make a report or answer questions. It depends on the circumstances of the accident and the State laws.

It is wise not to engage in an interview with police unless you have received legal advice. If you request the presence of a lawyer, the police are required to suspend any interview while you attempt to contact one. The police should also provide you with the means to contact a lawyer – ie a phone and a phone book. If a lawyer is not available, then you might be allowed to come back some other time after you have seen one, provided, of course, that you are given bail.

Do the police have the right to take fingerprints? Again, the answer varies. Court orders or the consent of parents are required in some States: a court order is required for children under 14 in New South Wales. The taking of fingerprints highlights the need for a lawyer's presence.

If you did commit the crime and admit it, you might be given an informal on-the-spot caution by the police officer. More formal cautions may be made at the police station where a record is kept.

Children can be brought before the court by way of summons or arrest. If the offence is only minor, the police will normally issue a summons. With more serious offences, the child will be placed under arrest, and must then be taken to a Children's Court as soon as possible. Usually they are not to be held in police cells or prison but in a welfare institution.

Which court are children taken to?

Most cases are heard in the Children's Court. Specialist Children's Courts exist in major cities, but in the country Local Courts (called Magistrates Courts in some States) also sit as Children's Courts. Cases are heard by a magistrate, and are closed to the public. Sometimes if the offence was very serious, such as murder or rape, the child may be tried in an adult court, particularly if they are nearly 18.

If you are summonsed to appear in a Children's Court or arrested, you should seek legal advice. If you have not done so by the day of your first court appearance, arrive early and see the duty solicitor who can represent you.

134

On your first appearance you are likely to have to wait a long time to be called. Once called the court has to make sure that you understand what you have been charged with, and that you understand what can happen if you are found guilty. You will be asked whether you plead guilty or not guilty.

Pleading guilty or not guilty

If you plead guilty this means that you are admitting the crime and there will be no hearing. Your lawyer will raise matters in attempt to reduce the sentence – such as pointing out your previously good character, or mentioning extenuating circumstances particular to your case. This is known as mitigation. You should not plead guilty without legal advice. The court may make a decision on the same day or it may prefer to think it over and seek more information such as welfare reports.

Pleading not guilty leads to a hearing. It is unlikely to happen on that first day, rather a later date will be set. The court will decide whether you are to be released on bail. Bail may be refused if the court fears that you will abscond, commit further offences, threaten witnesses or destroy evidence.

If you have not had a chance to seek legal advice and are unrepresented, you are permitted to ask the court for an adjournment to give you a chance to do so.

Court procedure

When it comes to the actual hearing the same procedure is followed as for adult criminal court cases, which are described in 5.2 Criminal Court Procedure.

Sentencing

If you have been found guilty, either because you pleaded guilty or because the case went to hearing but you lost, the issue of the sentence then arises.

When sentencing a child, the court keeps in mind that children should continue their education if possible and remain in their own home if the conditions there are suitable.

Magistrates have a range of orders they can make. In deciding, they will take many factors into account: the nature of the offence, whether it is a first, your age and maturity, whether you show remorse, and the mitigating factors your solicitor will bring up to plead for a lesser sentence.

Possible orders include:

- a dismissal – if you have no previous record and the offence was minor, you might be warned not to repeat the crime and dismissed. No conviction will be recorded, a great advantage as it will not harm your future employment prospects;

- a fine – this is rare unless you are earning an income;

- release on bond – you may be told to be of good behaviour for a set period of time. If you are not, you will then be punished for the original offence and for the new one as well. Often there are conditions attached – for instance you may be required to attend counselling;

- probation – this is similar to a bond but requires supervision by a welfare officer;

- community service order – you might be required to do unpaid work for the community for a certain number of hours;

- committal – there are different types. Committal may involve being in the control of a relative or refuge, or being made a ward of the State. Or it may involve being sent to a detention centre;

- prison – children are rarely sent to an adult prison. It may be ordered where further offences are committed in the detention centre particularly if they are violent. Once a child reaches 18 they might be transferred from a detention centre into an adult prison.

Appealing against a guilty finding or sentence may be possible. It is important to seek a lawyer's advice if you wish to appeal.

Community youth conferences

In some States, juvenile offenders may be given the opportunity to attend a community youth conference instead of going to court. This involves meeting with the victim (and any support people the victim requires) to discuss the situation and work out a solution. The offender's family is encouraged to attend. In New South Wales, community youth conferences are convened by Community Justice Centres.

At the conference, the victim is given a chance to tell their story and explain the impact it has had on them. You can work out how to make amends, perhaps by an apology, and/or giving back what was stolen or damaged or paying some compensation. If everyone agrees, an outcome plan will be written up, stating what each person will do to make their plan work.

Not all types of offences are suitable to be dealt with by a conference. Matters such as the seriousness of the offence, whether violence was used, the attitudes of the offender and victim, and the age of the offender will be taken into account.

If you are asked to attend a conference, you can seek legal advice to help you decide. If you want to attend, work out who you want to go with you, and what you can do to make amends to the victim. If you do not attend, the matter is referred to court.

These conferences provide young offenders with an opportunity to stay out of court and not get a criminal record.

FURTHER READING

Chisholm, *Teachers, Schools and the Law in New South Wales*, New South Wales University Press, Sydney, 1987

Gamble, *Law For Parents and Children*, Law Book Co, Sydney, 1986

National Children's and Youth Law Centre, *Know Your Rights Kit*

O'Connor and Sweetapple, *Children in Justice*, Longman Cheshire, Melbourne, 1988

Spender (ed), *Kids and the Law: A Guide Book For Parents, Youth Workers And Teachers*, Redfern Legal Centre Publishing, 1991

White and Alder, *The Police and Young People in Australia*, Cambridge University Press, Melbourne, 1994

Women's Legal Resources Centre, *Girls and the Law: A Practical Guide*, Redfern Legal Centre Publishing, Sydney, 1990

See also: General references listed in Further Reading Chapter 1.

Chapter 9

YOUR JOB

9.1   EMPLOYEES' RIGHTS AND DUTIES

WHO IS AN EMPLOYEE?

Employees are obviously different from independent contractors, but why does the distinction matter?

Both are governed by general contract law. However, employees are covered by the rules of employment law, independent contractors are not. Employment law determines the rights and duties of both employers and employees. As a general rule, employees have more rights and legal protection than independent contractors.

Distinguishing between the two is usually simple but some people seem to be a mixture. Courts have devised tests to cover these situations. You are likely to be classed as an employee if:

- the employer can tell you what work to do and how to do it;

- you work at the employer's premises using their equipment;

- you work during set hours;

- you are paid regular wages rather than a fee based on how much work you have performed;

- tax is taken out of your pay;

- the employer makes compulsory superannuation contributions on your behalf;

- you are not permitted to work for other employers at the same time.

No single issue determines the matter on its own, rather it is a combination of factors that is important.

For the purposes of workers' compensation, people who are not normally classed as employees may be counted as such to enable them to claim compensation. They are known as "deemed" employees. For the ability of employees and deemed employees to claim workers' compensation see 10.3 Accidents at Work.

Similarly, for the purposes of superannuation, the definition of employee is broader than normal.

THE EMPLOYMENT RELATIONSHIP

The relationship between workers and employers is heavily regulated in Australia. Your rights and duties are derived from various sources, including:

- common law (contracts);
- legislation;
- awards;
- enterprise agreements.

Common law (contracts)

If you are an employee there is a contract between you and your employer, even if it is not written down. Basically the contract provides that you will perform work in return for an income. If either side breaches the contract the other can take legal action.

Historically the law did not interfere with the contents of contracts. Employers and employees were supposed to be free to bargain as they wished. But as a result, the weaker party was often unable to adequately protect its interests. The common law developed to provide the parties to an employment contract with basic rights and duties; such as the employee's duty to follow lawful instructions and the employer's duty to provide a safe place of work.

Common law is judge-made law as opposed to parliament-made law. The concept is described more fully in 1.1 The Australian Legal System. If no award, legislation or enterprise agreement covers a particular matter, the common law can deal with it by looking at implied rights and the intention of the parties.

Legislation

Both Federal and State parliaments have passed legislation which modifies the employment contract. Rights such as sick leave, maternity/parental leave and annual leave are provided by legislation.

Awards

Federal and State industrial tribunals make awards that cover particular industries. Awards establish basic conditions such as hours of work, minimum wages and overtime. Your industry may be covered by either a Federal or a State award. Most jobs are covered by awards, but not all. If you are covered, your working conditions cannot be less than those prescribed in the award.

Copies of awards are usually pinned up at the workplace. If you cannot find it or do not know which award you are covered by, contact your union, the government department responsible for employment, or ask your local member of parliament.

Enterprise agreements

Australian employment law has always focused around awards but there is a current shift to enterprise bargaining. The extent to which it is replacing awards varies throughout Australia, but generally awards are being kept to operate as a safety net.

Enterprise bargaining means that negotiations for work conditions can occur within a specific workplace rather than across the whole industry. Employees (or a union on their behalf) negotiate directly with their own employer.

The employment terms and conditions agreed on during the bargaining process are set out in an enterprise agreement. Enterprise agreements have safeguards and must conform with minimum standards concerning matters such as wages and leave.

Using the Federal law as an example, under the Commonwealth *Industrial Relations Act* there are two types of enterprise agreements:

- certified agreements – made between unions and employers in a single workplace;
- enterprise flexibility agreements – made between employers and employees without union involvement, on the condition that a majority of employees agree.

Both types of agreement must be approved by the Australian Industrial Relations Commission. To gain approval they must meet certain conditions, such as upholding anti-discrimination laws. Apart from these conditions it is up to the parties to work out the content of enterprise agreements.

EMPLOYEES' RIGHTS

The rights you have as an employee are derived from a combination of the above sources. Details may vary between jurisdictions, but the general principles are similar.

Payment

You are entitled to be paid wages in return for your work, but generally there is no obligation for the employer to provide you with work. There may be exceptions:

- for workers paid purely on a commission or piece work basis;
- for workers who need continual exposure to maintain their ability to work eg actors.

Minimum wages exist in most industries, and it is an offence for an employer to pay less than that rate.

If you have not been paid money owed to you it may be possible to take legal action to recover it.

Safety

Employers must provide workers with a safe place to work, maintain equipment properly and provide a safe system of work. If you are injured you may be able to sue your employer or claim workers' compensation: see 10.3 Accidents at Work for details.

Leave entitlements

Generally, employees have the right to:

- four weeks' annual leave – usually you have to work for a year before you become eligible;
- sick leave – this varies but is on average around eight days per year;
- family leave – sick leave has recently been expanded in some jurisdictions to cover caring for ill family members. A few extra days of sick leave per year will cover this;
- parental/maternity leave – either the mother or (in most States) the father can take 12 months unpaid leave to care for the child if they worked for the employer for at least a year. In some jurisdictions (such as the Federal law) parents can share the 12 months leave.

141

Generally parents are entitled to get their previous job back when they return if it still exists. If it does not they may get a similar one, but different laws apply in different States;

- long service leave – if you have been working for the same employer continuously for 10 or 15 years (depending on the State) you are entitled to paid long service leave, usually three months.

Superannuation

Superannuation schemes are based on monetary contributions made while a person is working. On retirement, the worker receives either a lump sum payout or periodic payments.

Employers have to contribute a percentage of an employee's wages towards superannuation. If they do not they can be fined. The definition of employee is wide under superannuation laws and includes some contractors.

The right to strike

Traditionally there has been only a limited right to strike in Australia. Workers who took such action sometimes faced the threat of dismissal.

But with the movement towards enterprise agreements it is being recognised that the right to strike is a part of the bargaining process. In some jurisdictions strikers might be protected during the negotiation stage of an agreement, but not while an agreement is in force. Requirements must be met, for example appropriate notice must be given.

To be reimbursed for expenditure

If you have to pay money in the course of your employment on the employer's behalf you are entitled to be reimbursed by your employer.

Anti-discrimination

Employees and people seeking jobs have the right not to be discriminated against. For a description of the law, see 9.2 Discrimination.

Dismissal

For details on whether a dismissal is lawful and what your rights are, refer to 9.3 Losing Your Job.

WHAT TO DO IF YOUR RIGHTS HAVE BEEN DENIED

The steps you can take depend on the action complained of and whether you are covered by a Federal or State law, an award or an enterprise agreement. For help contact:

- the union;
- a free advice centre (see 1.2 Sources of Legal Advice);
- a private solicitor;
- the Arbitration Inspectorate – if you are covered by a Federal award and you believe it has been breached;
- your local member of parliament for advice on who to contact;
- the Federal or State department responsible for employment;
- industrial relations commissions or tribunals.

EMPLOYEES' DUTIES

Details may vary between jurisdictions, but in general workers have the following duties.

To work

You have to go to work at the agreed hours and carry out your job with reasonable skill and competence.

To follow instructions

Do you have to do everything your boss tells you? Generally employees have a duty to carry out their employer's instructions. However, you do not need to do something that is:

- unreasonable – what is reasonable depends on the nature of your work and the standards that are typically expected in that field;
- unsafe – you are within your rights to refuse to carry out a task which you have reason to believe is unsafe or dangerous;
- unlawful – your employer cannot ask you to make false statements on its behalf or do anything against the law;
- outside the scope of your job – the scope of your job would have been discussed at your interview and you may have a written statement of duties. You do not have to do something that is clearly beyond that. For instance a clerk would not be expected to fix a blocked pipe.

Confidentiality

Confidential information picked up in the course of employment cannot be disclosed. Sometimes this duty persists even after you have left the job, particularly if the information was a trade secret.

Duty not to harm the employer

This is known as the duty of fidelity. Employees cannot act in a way which would hurt the employer's business, for instance by:

- being negligent or incompetent;
- being dishonest in business dealings;
- committing crimes such as bribery, embezzlement;
- using the employer's property to make a secret profit.

Money etc received during employment

If you receive money or property belonging to your employer you have a duty to account for it.

Duty not to compete

Employers sometimes try to stop workers who resign from working for a competitor, starting up a new business, or taking customers away. This is usually done by inserting a "restraint of trade" clause in the employment contract.

Courts are unwilling to enforce such clauses if they are unreasonably broad. There must be both a time limit and a geographical restriction. What is reasonable depends on the nature of the business. For example a hairdresser might be able to prevent an assistant from setting up a business in the same suburb within a year or two, but could not stop him or her from ever setting up in the same city.

9.2 DISCRIMINATION

As long as you can do the job, that is all that matters.

Discrimination involves being treated unfairly because you happen to be a member of a particular group. If you are discriminated against in the workplace there are steps you can take to remedy the situation.

DISCRIMINATION AT WORK

Discrimination at work is unlawful at any stage of the employment process:

- the job advertisement;
- the interview;
- work conditions;
- work opportunities (eg training courses);

- promotions/transfers;
- pay;
- termination of employment.

It does not matter whether the discrimination was intentional or not. You can still seek justice where you have been discriminated against unconsciously.

Direct and indirect discrimination

Sometimes discrimination is direct and obvious, such as advertising a job for men only.

But discrimination can also be indirect. Indirect discrimination occurs when something at first appears to apply equally to everyone, but on closer examination the requirement excludes a particular group of people. For example if a job advertisement states that only people over six foot will be employed, most women will be unable to qualify. If the requirement is unreasonable, and people under six foot can in fact do the job, then indirect discrimination occurred.

Is discrimination ever allowed?

Discrimination is not always unlawful. It might be acceptable to restrict employment to a particular group where the job genuinely requires it. For instance, if a Chinese actor was needed to authentically play the part of a Chinese character in a play, a Greek actor could not complain about not being hired.

It would also be acceptable for a private householder seeking a babysitter or cleaner to advertise to employ only a woman.

TYPES OF DISCRIMINATION

Discrimination laws exist at both the State and Federal level. Not all forms of discrimination are unlawful in every State. Each jurisdiction has variations on:

- the types of discrimination prohibited;
- the aspects of employment covered; and
- the extent of the employee's right to seek a remedy.

If you are not covered by a State law the Federal laws may apply.

To clarify the position in your State, you can contact an anti-discrimination agency, such as the Human Rights and Equal

Opportunity Commission. New South Wales residents can also contact the Anti-Discrimination Board.

As a general guide, the following may be unlawful.

Race discrimination

Treating somebody unfairly because of their race or ethnic background is against the law. As well as not being able to deprive you of equal work conditions and opportunities, employers cannot:

- insist you speak English fluently or without an accent unless it is necessary for the job;
- insist that you do not speak your own language at work unless it interferes with your work performance.

If you are an Aboriginal person or a Torres Strait Islander you can contact an Aboriginal Legal Service. Anti-discrimination agencies usually have an Aboriginal Officer that you can ask to speak to.

Age discrimination

Jobs should be open to people of all ages. Employers generally cannot refuse to employ you because you are over or under a certain age, unless the age restriction is necessary for that particular job.

Employers are able to advertise for junior positions without breaching age discrimination laws, and they can pay them junior rates.

Compulsory retirement is seen by some as a form of age discrimination. In New South Wales it is against the law to compulsorily retire most employees in both the public and private sectors.

Sex discrimination

Treating somebody unfairly because they are either male or female is unlawful. Sexual harassment in the workplace is a type of sex discrimination. Your rights if you are sexually harassed are described below.

Marital status and family responsibility

It is against the law to discriminate against a person for being married, single, divorced, widowed, or in a de facto relationship.

In some States it is also unlawful to discriminate against someone for having children. Discriminating against pregnant women can also be unlawful in some situations, but there are some types of work that pregnant women cannot do because they are medically hazardous.

Generally pregnant women are entitled to be given back their pre-pregnancy job after they return from parental leave if that job still exists. If not, then women should seek advice as different States treat this problem differently.

Homosexual discrimination

In some States it is unlawful to discriminate against a person on the basis of their homosexuality, regardless of whether they are male or female.

Discrimination against people with HIV and AIDS

In States such as New South Wales it is against the law to treat someone unfairly because they are living with HIV or AIDS or because someone thinks they are.

Discrimination against people with disabilities

Discriminating against people with physical or intellectual disabilities may be unlawful. If a person with a disability is best for the job, he or she should get it. Employers may be obliged to install special facilities such as wheelchair ramps to ensure that a worker with a disability can do the job. They are not, however, obliged to make modifications that are unreasonably high in price or impractical.

Workers who develop disabilities after they have already started working are entitled to remain in their job unless the disability prevents them from performing properly. Employers cannot insist that such workers carry out non-essential tasks, and cannot use their inability to perform non-essential tasks as an excuse to dismiss them.

SEXUAL HARASSMENT

Sexual harassment is a form of sex discrimination. It occurs when somebody at work makes unwelcome sexual advances. If the advances are welcome there is no harassment.

Women are usually the victims of sexual harassment but this is not necessarily the case. Both men and women are protected by sexual harassment laws. The offender can be either of the opposite sex or the same sex as the victim.

Employers have an obligation to ensure that sexual harassment does not take place not by supervisors, fellow work mates nor business clients.

What amounts to sexual harassment?

Sexual harassment can cover a broad range of conduct. It depends on the surrounding circumstances, but the following acts could amount to sexual harassment:

- leering;
- making rude and offensive jokes;
- sexual insinuations;
- sexually offensive gestures;
- displaying pornography in the workplace;
- asking personal questions about sexual experience;
- making propositions;
- offering a promotion in return for sex;
- threatening dismissal if sex is refused;
- groping/touching/kissing.

What can you do about it?

Make it clear to the person harassing you that you do not welcome their behaviour. If they do not take you seriously point out the consequences of their conduct and that you intend to lodge a complaint if they do not stop it.

If this fails see a supervisor or manager. Insist that you be taken seriously. Keeping written records of events as they occur can back up your story. Enlist the help of any witnesses. Employers have a duty to listen to both sides and to treat the matter confidentially.

If you find that you are not believed or you are unsatisfied with the response you can complain to an anti-discrimination agency (discussed below).

EQUALITY OF TREATMENT

The effect of the anti-discrimination laws is that everybody in the workforce has a right to be treated fairly – they should be judged by their work performance and not by irrelevant factors. The following policies have been developed to help achieve this goal.

Equal opportunity

Employers that call themselves equal opportunity employers uphold anti-discrimination policies. Some go further and implement programs to ensure this is achieved.

Affirmative action

Anti-discrimination laws are aimed at remedying present inequalities. Affirmative action strategies provide special help for groups of people who have been disadvantaged in the past. An example would be a training course run only for migrants, giving them the skills to compete equally with the rest of the labour force.

Affirmative action policies are usually aimed towards women. Under Federal law, all employers with 100 or more employees are required to implement an affirmative action program to promote equal opportunity for women.

Note that affirmative action is not the same as reverse discrimination. Reverse discrimination involves giving a job to a person in a minority group purely because they belong to that group, and refusing to give it to a better qualified person who does not belong to a minority group.

Equal pay for equal work

The principle of equal pay for equal work means that people doing the same job should be paid the same, regardless of differences such as sex. But it is not as fair as it sounds.

Problems arise because some industries employ mainly women, and they tend to be lowly paid. For instance most nurses, receptionists and cleaners are women, and they are all typically poorly paid.

Equal pay for work of equal value

This policy tries to be fairer than the "equal pay for equal work" policy. Equal pay for work of equal value means that people in comparable jobs (rather than people in the same job) should be paid the same. Difficulties arise, however, in comparing the relative worth of different types of jobs.

Under the Federal law, the Australian Industrial Relations Commission can hear unequal pay complaints. It can order that equal pay rates apply if it finds that the jobs are comparable and the only difference in pay arises from gender. Applications to the Commission can be made by an employee, a union, or the Sex Discrimination Commissioner.

The Commission will not make an order if alternative avenues exist, such as State laws. It can order equal pay immediately or it can phase it in gradually. The Commission will not approve any enterprise agreements that are inconsistent with the equal pay for work of equal value principle. For information on enterprise agreements see 9.1 Employees' Rights and Duties.

DEALING WITH DISCRIMINATION

If you have been the victim of discrimination at the workplace there are various avenues of assistance:

- a sympathetic supervisor or manager at work;
- the union;
- free legal advice centres (see 1.2 Sources of Legal Advice);
- private solicitors;
- anti-discrimination agencies.

Dealing with the problem personally

Handling the problem personally is usually the best first step. Talk to the person causing the problem calmly and confidently, and make your views clear. It may be the case that they did not consciously intend to discriminate against you, and they may be willing to make amends.

If this fails go higher up the hierarchy, talk to a supervisor or manager and try to get their support. Make sure that you can point out exactly what the problem is and what solution you are after. You may want to be given:

- the job, pay rise or promotion you believe you are entitled to;
- compensation;
- your job back if the discrimination led to your dismissal.

Unions can help you with the negotiations.

If you are still unsatisfied or if you would rather not raise the matter personally you can make a complaint to an anti- discrimination agency.

Complaints to anti-discrimination agencies

Anti-discrimination agencies handle complaints. Usually the complaint must be made in writing, and there may be a set form to use. Anti-discrimination agencies can be State or Federal. Ring either and they will be able to inform you as to your best avenues.

Do not delay making your complaint as time limits may apply. It will not cost you anything to make a complaint and the matter is treated confidentially. It is unlawful for employers to victimise you because you have made a complaint.

An anti-discrimination officer will investigate the complaint. Both sides of the story are listened to. You may be required to attend a conciliation conference where you, the person causing the problem, and the officer will attempt to reach a satisfactory solution. No solution is forced upon you by the officer, rather you are encouraged to come up with a decision that both you and your employer are happy with.

Failure to reach a solution can result in a tribunal hearing. Very few cases go to court.

Tribunal hearing

Tribunals are less formal than courts. Proceedings are meant to be quicker and cheaper, and tribunals do not have to follow strict rules of evidence. Some tribunals allow legal representation – you are not compelled, but it may be wise to seek it. In a court case, the party that loses might have to pay the winner's legal costs, but in tribunals each party usually pays its own costs. For more information about tribunals generally, see 4.3 Complaints and Tribunals.

Tribunals encourage the parties to come to a mutually satisfactory arrangement, but they have the power to make binding orders. The tribunal can order that:

- you be paid monetary compensation;
- the discriminatory action not be repeated;
- any discriminatory agreements be cancelled;
- steps be taken to put the situation right.

Failure to follow the orders of some tribunals can result in a large fine. You may be able to appeal to a court if you are unhappy with the tribunal's decision. If you intend to appeal it is a good idea to seek legal advice.

9.3   LOSING YOUR JOB

Employment relationships are based on contracts between employees and employers, even if the contracts are not written. Like any other contract, the employment contract can be terminated, but if it is done unlawfully the innocent party may have a legal remedy.

TERMINATING EMPLOYMENT

Employment relationships can be ended in a number of different ways.

Completion

Some employment contracts last for a set period of time or until a particular job is completed. When the period lapses or the work is finished the contract automatically ends. The parties can renegotiate to enter into a new contract.

Death of employer or employee

If either the employer or employee dies the employment relationship is at an end. Note that if the head of a company dies the company does not die with him or her – it continues to exist as a separate legal entity, and so employment relationships continue.

Liquidation or bankruptcy

If the employer goes bankrupt or is wound up then performance of the employment contract becomes impossible. Employees may be entitled to some wages earned before the winding up.

Resignation

You can resign at any time you like for any reason as long as you give proper notice. If you are employed under a fixed-term contract, however, you generally have to wait until the period has expired unless the terms of the contract provide otherwise.

If you are not employed under a fixed-term contract, how much notice do you have to give? The period might be fixed by a law or an award. If not, there is a requirement that reasonable notice be given. What is reasonable varies depending on the industry and your position. Usually giving one pay period's notice is considered to be reasonable. It may be longer for highly skilled and responsible positions.

Theoretically if you leave without giving proper notice you might be sued by the employer for breach of contract. If they have suffered loss they may be entitled to monetary compensation, but it is often difficult for the employer to show loss. They may have a good case if they spent money training you, particularly if you had promised to stay with the employer after completion of the training course.

A court would not normally be willing to order you to go back and work during the notice period. In practice if you leave without proper notice an employer may refuse to give you a reference or to pay you for the unworked notice period.

Retrenchment

During periods of recession workers are vulnerable to being retrenched or made redundant. They are dismissed, not because of their performance, but because their job has been superseded by technology or because the company cannot afford to pay their wages.

Retrenched workers have rights under most awards, which can include severance pay and time off during their notice period to look for other work.

Dismissal with notice

Employers wishing to dismiss an employee must give proper notice. The notice period may be determined by agreement or by an award.

Under the Federal *Industrial Relations Act* there is a sliding scale of minimum notice periods. Employees covered by the Act must be given the following minimum notice where they have worked for:

- one year or less – one week's notice;
- one to three years – two weeks' notice;
- three to five years – three weeks' notice;
- over five years – four weeks' notice.

If an employee is over 45 and has worked with the same employer continuously for two years, the minimum notice period is increased by a week.

If there is no set notice period, then "reasonable" notice must be given. Often a reasonable notice period equals the pay period, but if you are working in a skilled senior position it is likely that the notice will have to be longer.

You do not have to stay in the job after you have been given notice, but if you leave you may be giving up the right to be paid during the notice period. Employers often choose to pay a dismissed employee his or her entitlement instead of requiring them to work during the notice period.

Wrongful dismissal

After reading the above discussion you may get the impression that employers can dismiss anybody for any reason as long as they give appropriate notice. This was the case in the past, but now there are legal restrictions on the employer's ability to do so.

Different laws exist in different jurisdictions, but generally workers cannot be dismissed purely because they belong to a union or a minority group.

Recent amendments to the Federal *Industrial Relations Act* have introduced new rights for workers. Employers must not dismiss employees without a valid reason. The reason must be connected to the employees' capacity or conduct, or the operational requirements of the business. A reason is not considered to be valid if the sacking is harsh, unjust or unreasonable.

Some reasons for termination are never valid under the Federal law. In other words, employers cannot dismiss employees because of:

- temporary absence from work due to illness or an injury;
- union membership;
- taking part in legitimate union activities;
- acting as an employee representative;
- non membership of a union;
- race, sex, sexual preference, age, marital or family status, maternity or parental leave, political or religious beliefs, physical or intellectual disability – unless termination is based on the inherent nature of the job (see 9.2 Discrimination).

Where there is a valid reason for dismissing the employee, they should usually be warned first and given the chance to remedy the problem.

Workers on probation and casual workers employed for less than six months are currently not covered by the Federal law.

As this law is relatively new, workers should consult a solicitor if they believe they have been unfairly dismissed and wish to take legal action.

Dismissal without notice

Can you be sacked on the spot, without notice and without pay in lieu of notice? This is known as summary dismissal, and employers do have the right to summarily dismiss employees in certain situations.

Summary dismissal can be legally permitted where the employee has committed serious misconduct. Serious misconduct is action that is deliberate rather than accidental, and it indicates that the employment relationship has broken down. Examples of serious misconduct may include:

- being drunk at work;
- physical violence at work;

- stealing from the employer;
- fraud or dishonesty in the course of employment;
- breaching confidentiality in an important matter.

Less serious misconduct can also lead to summary dismissal if it occurs often enough, such as:

- missing work without a valid reason;
- incompetence;
- rudeness to staff or business clients;
- refusal to obey the employer's orders (for information on whether you are obliged to follow all your employer's instructions see 9.1 Employees' Rights and Duties).

You will have noticed that all these examples occur at the workplace or in the course of employment. Can an employer summarily dismiss you for something done outside of work hours?

It depends on the circumstances. If an employee wearing a company uniform gets drunk and fights in a bar, this may be serious misconduct, particularly if the company image is important to the company's business. If an employee commits a crime they might be dismissed summarily, particularly if there is a relationship to the work – for instance a bus driver being convicted on a charge of dangerous driving.

LEGAL REMEDIES

What can you do if you lose your job? You have various legal options, and it is a good idea to enlist the help of:

- the union;
- a private solicitor;
- a free advice centre (see 1.2 Sources of Legal Advice);
- an anti-discrimination agency if you were sacked due to your age, race, sex etc.

Suing for compensation

If you have been unlawfully dismissed you may be able to sue for compensation (also called damages) because the employer breached the contract of employment. Unpaid wages can be recovered. If you were not given the appropriate notice you will be able to recover the money that should have been paid during that period. If you are employed under a fixed-term contract you may be entitled to wages due for the remainder of the contract.

Sacked employees have a duty to keep their loss low. This is known as the duty to mitigate. Basically it means that employees have to take reasonable steps to find another job. If they do not, the damages they receive in a court case could be reduced.

Generally the amount an employee would receive is rather low and often not worth the trouble, expense and delays of litigation.

But in recent years a court awarded substantial damages to an unfairly dismissed worker. The court took account of the income the employee lost by not pursuing his career with that particular employer. The sum was then reduced to reflect the fact that he may have left in the future anyway, perhaps of his own free will or due to death or illness.

Even so, the payout was very large. Courts in the future may make similar orders, but as this area of the law is complicated and changing it is important to seek a lawyer's advice.

Getting your job back

Some employees want monetary compensation when they are unfairly dismissed, others want to be reinstated.

Several States such as New South Wales and South Australia have laws that provide for reinstatement where the dismissal was unfair, harsh or unreasonable. The extent of the protection varies between jurisdictions.

Using the Federal law as an example, employees can apply to the Australian Industrial Relations Court for either compensation or reinstatement. The application can be made by the employee personally or by a union on behalf of its member. The application should be made within 14 days of receiving written notice of the dismissal.

Before the complaint is heard by the court, the Australian Industrial Relations Commission will attempt to solve the problem using conciliation. Conciliation involves the parties reaching their own solution with the help of a neutral person – the neutral person facilitates discussions but does not impose a solution. If conciliation fails the court will decide whether the dismissal was lawful. If it was unlawful it can order reinstatement or compensation, perhaps both.

Note that if alternative adequate remedies apply, such as under State laws, the Federal system may not be available.

Unfortunately, in reality reinstatement rights are not as beneficial as they sound. If an employer really wants somebody to leave they can make work unpleasant and stressful, effectively forcing them to resign. Due to the ongoing and personal nature of the employment relationship, a mutually satisfactory solution worked out by conciliation is often better than one imposed by a court.

FURTHER READING

Macken, *The Employment Revolution*, Federation Press, Sydney, 1992

McKenna, *The Labour Council's Easy Guide To Your Rights At Work*, Pluto Press, Sydney, 1993

Moorhouse and Punch, *Termination Of Employment: The New Federal Law*, CCH, Sydney, 1994

Ronalds, *Affirmative Action And Sex Discrimination*, Pluto Press, Sydney, 1991

See also: General references listed in Further Reading Chapter 1.

Chapter 10

YOUR HEALTH AND SAFETY

10.1   MEDICAL RIGHTS

When you are ill you see a doctor, they make a diagnosis and suggest a treatment. End of story? It should not be. To make the most of the doctor-patient relationship you need to know your medical rights and responsibilities, and what to do if something goes wrong.

THE MEDICAL PROFESSION

Doctors qualify by completing a university degree and then working for a few years in a hospital. After that they can undertake further study to become a specialist or they might decide to go into general practice.

All doctors need a licence to practice – anybody falsely representing themselves to be a registered medical practitioner is guilty of an offence.

The relationship between a patient and their doctor is an important one, and is governed to some extent by the law.

PATIENTS' RIGHTS

Patients have various rights in their dealings with the medical profession:

Right to information

You have a right to be told what is wrong with you. Doctors can, however, use their discretion and withhold information if they have reason to believe that disclosure would cause further serious harm. Relatives do not have the right to demand that the doctor withhold information from the patient.

If treatment is required patients should be given all the relevant details in terms that they can understand. Information regarding side effects of medication, risks of operations, and appropriate alternatives should be discussed.

This responsibility works both ways. If you are on medication or have a pre-existing condition, it is in your interests to inform your doctor as it may influence their treatment. Women on the oral contraceptive pill, for instance, should not take certain antibiotics because they can render the pill inoperative.

Medical files

A general practitioner's medical files are the doctor's property, and you do not have the right to see your file. Of course you can ask to see it, and your doctor may consent, but some are reluctant because files are full of medical terminology and difficult to understand. If you change doctors your new doctor can ask the old to forward your files. Most are willing to comply in these circumstances.

The situation with government hospitals may differ, and you may have a right to see your medical records under freedom of information legislation: see 6.3 Freedom of Information.

Right to refuse treatment

Consent is usually required before treatment can be carried out (see Consent to Treatment below). You have the general right to refuse treatment, and it is possible to withdraw consent after you have given it.

Right to leave hospital

Patients cannot be forced to remain in a hospital unless they have certain types of infectious diseases or psychiatric conditions. You can check out even if you are advised not to, but it is likely that you will be asked to sign a form agreeing that you are leaving against advice. If your condition then worsens as a result, you cannot take action against the hospital for letting you go.

Staying with a child

You have the right to ask to stay with your ill child in hospital. This is usually granted unless there are medical reasons preventing it.

Right to die?

Euthanasia is a controversial area of the law, arousing strong emotions for and against. Basically the law is that euthanasia, also called mercy killing, is currently illegal. The law has recently changed in the Northern Territory, but elsewhere doctors that help a patient die may be liable to prosecution for murder. Uncertainties exist, particularly in cases where life support systems are used.

Rights concerning autopsies

Relatives are often disturbed when an autopsy is performed. Autopsies are not up to the doctor, but are a legal requirement in certain situations.

CONSENT TO TREATMENT

Treatment without consent is a form of assault. In order for consent to be valid, it must be freely given. It also must be based on full information, in other words, it must be informed consent. The procedure including risks and other options must be explained to the patient before treatment commences.

Consent can be given orally or it can be implied by the patient's conduct, particularly for simple routine matters. For more serious procedures, such as an operation under a general anaesthetic, the consent should be written.

If you are asked to sign a consent form, read it to ensure that you know exactly what you are consenting to. Are you allowing another doctor to step in if yours cannot attend? Are you consenting to further surgical procedures while still under the anaesthetic?

Can you refuse treatment?

You are under no obligation to consent to medical treatment, and you can withdraw your consent at any time.

Children and some types of psychiatric patients cannot consent to medical treatment. In some States it is necessary for specified relatives or bodies such as the Guardianship Board to give consent for them.

Unconscious patients obviously cannot consent – the nearest relative should be contacted. If there is no time and a life threatening condition is involved, the hospital will most likely be able to act without obtaining consent first.

CONFIDENTIALITY

Doctors cannot discuss your case with anybody else unless you give permission.

Confidentiality is implied into the usually unwritten contract that exists between doctors and patients. If your doctor breaches this, you may be able to sue for breach of contract or perhaps for defamation. Usually it will not be worth your while as you will have to show that you suffered some loss (eg you lost your job) rather than merely wounded feelings.

Exceptions

Exceptions exist to the duty of confidentiality:

- where the information is needed for court proceedings;
- where public safety is threatened;
- the health department must be notified of certain infectious diseases;
- in most States, the child welfare authorities must be notified if child abuse is suspected.

DOCTORS' LEGAL DUTIES

Legal duties include the requirement to be licensed and to use care and skill. An act or omission that causes further harm or injury to the patient may result in a legal action for negligence.

Negligence

Medical practitioners must exercise a reasonable standard of care. The standard is measured by comparing the competence of other doctors of the same level of training and experience.

In order to commence legal proceedings for negligence against a doctor you would have to show:

- that the medical service was below standard – evidence by other doctors is needed to establish this unless it is very obvious, for instance if the wrong leg was amputated; and
- that the failure caused the damage – for example where an incompetent use of forceps during birth caused brain damage.

Proving negligence is difficult as most treatments involve some degree of risk.

Successful legal action awards a sum of money (called damages) to the patient to compensate them for problems caused by the negligence. Pre-existing problems and later arising conditions unrelated to the negligence are not taken into account in calculating the sum of damages.

DOCTORS' ETHICAL DUTIES

Ethical duties require a doctor to be of good character. They involve issues which are not necessarily against the law but which could result in the doctor being struck off. Having a sexual relationship with a patient is an obvious example of a breach of ethics.

Professional misconduct

Professional misconduct arises where there have been departures from accepted procedures in a way that would attract serious criticism by fellow practitioners. Examples include seeing patients while intoxicated, and failing to attend without a valid reason.

The situation may not have been enough to amount to negligence, particularly if no harm resulted. But if these departures recur often enough they may amount to misconduct.

COMPLAINTS

Problems regarding medical treatment usually involve incompetence, misconduct, or a breach of ethics. They should first be discussed with the doctor involved – the problem might be the result of a misunderstanding. Complaints arising in a hospital can be taken to the hospital administrator. Many hospitals have a patient's representative that you can talk to.

If you are still unsatisfied, there are further avenues that can be pursued:

- Medical Boards in each State issue doctors with licences. Complaints may lead to an investigation and disciplinary proceedings if the allegations are serious;
- the Health Department in your State may also have an avenue for complaints;
- the New South Wales Health Care Complaints Commission is an independent body that hears complaints. It can refer complaints for investigation or conciliation (ie discussions to help work out a mutually satisfactory solution);
- the Australian Medical Association is a body representing the interests of doctors. It demands a high standard of its members. If the doctor involved is a member, a complaint can be made to the Association. It may investigate the matter and help reach a settlement. Not all doctors are members.

Patients that suffer harm due to a doctor's negligence wishing to sue for compensation should consult a lawyer.

10.2   ACCIDENTS IN PUBLIC PLACES AND HOMES

After an accident an injured person can be frightened and in pain, and legalities will be the last thing on their mind. If you witness an accident or are involved yourself, knowing what evidence to look for before it is gone for good would help if a personal injury claim arises.

But what if somebody hurts themselves on your property? Not every accident that occurs on your property is your responsibility. It depends on factors that include whether you knew about the danger, and whether steps were taken to warn the person before they were injured.

Assuming the injured person does have the right to sue, it is the occupier who is liable. Occupiers are not necessarily owners – occupiers are in possession of the property and therefore include tenants.

WITNESSING AN ACCIDENT

Passers-by are sometimes reluctant to offer assistance at an accident scene due to the misconception that they can be sued if something goes wrong. In fact, you are unlikely to be sued unless you intentionally or recklessly worsen the situation – eg by claiming to be a doctor when you are not, thereby obstructing proper care.

Taking steps that an ordinary inexperienced member of the public would take is unlikely to lead to legal liability.

Is there a duty to rescue?

Passers-by are not legally obliged to rescue somebody in a perilous situation. Your moral views may differ, but the law does not expect the general public to put themselves in a dangerous situation that they cannot handle.

WHAT IS A PUBLIC PLACE?

For our purposes, a "public place" can include streets, stores, restaurants, sports grounds etc, occupied either by the government or privately. The legal principles that apply to occupiers of public places also basically apply to you as a home occupier.

Not all accidents that occur in a public place are discussed here. Car accidents are governed by a different body of law – see 10.4 Car Accidents. Information on work-related accidents is provided in 10.3 Accidents at Work.

Generally negligence needs to be established to make the occupier liable for the injury.

NEGLIGENCE

The person causing the accident may have either done something that caused the accident (such as digging a hole) or may have failed to take action to remove the danger (such as not replacing worn carpet).

Keep in mind that laws can vary between States, but generally proving negligence involves three things:

(i) Was there a duty of care?

(ii) Was the duty breached?

(iii) Did the breach cause the injury?

Was there a duty of care?

The person responsible for the accident must have had a duty to take reasonable care to prevent the injury. Occupiers of premises have a duty to take reasonable steps to protect entrants. "Premises" include buildings and surrounding land.

The duty owed depends to some extent on the circumstances under which the person entered – if you entered to provide the occupier with a financial gain (for instance if you bought something in a shop) then the occupier has a higher duty than if you were merely passing through (for instance if you took a short cut through a car park).

This mirrors the duty that you as an occupier owe to people who enter your house. For a description of the duties owed to different types of entrants see Accidents in your Home below.

But what if the accident did not take place in a building or on somebody's property? What if it took place on the footpath? Is the local council liable?

It may be if the danger was caused by the council's actions – for instance if they dug up the footpath and did not put up an appropriate barrier. But if the danger was the result of ordinary wear and tear it is unlikely that the council would be liable.

Was the duty breached?

Establishing that a duty of care exists is not enough – it must have been breached.

The duty was breached if there was a failure to use reasonable care. The word "reasonable" is important. It means neither super-human nor sub-human; it lurks mysteriously somewhere in between. A court hearing a personal injuries case would ask itself whether the risk was reasonably foreseeable, and what would a reasonable person have done in similar circumstances.

Did the breach cause the injury?

Damage must be caused by the breach to give rise to liability. For example, a woman who slips in a store because she was in a hurry or because her shoes had worn out might not be able to sue (or the amount she could recover may be reduced).

DEFENCES TO NEGLIGENCE

Even if the above elements of negligence can be established, the person responsible may have a legal defence. That could mean that the injured person loses the case or has their compensation award reduced.

Where their own negligence contributed to the injury

This defence is commonly known as contributory negligence. If the injured person carelessly walked into the danger, the compensation that they receive could be reduced to reflect the degree to which their own negligence was to blame.

Where they voluntarily assumed the risk

Legally this is known as the voluntary assumption of risk defence. This can be raised if it can be shown that they knew about the risks involved but were willing to accept them.

But what risk did they accept? Sitting in the stands at a cricket match might mean someone accepts the risk of a ball being hit into the stand, but it does not mean they accept the risk that the stand will collapse due to poor maintenance.

STEPS TO TAKE IF YOU HAVE BEEN INJURED

Gathering evidence

Personal injury cases often fail due to a lack of evidence. It is important that somebody at the accident scene keeps their wits about them and knows what to look for. A woman fell in a shopping centre – did she slip on spilt water, or were her shoes dangerously worn? Look for physical signs that may have caused the accident, such as spillages, worn carpets, broken tiles, poor lighting.

Was there anything to suggest that the store knew about the potential danger but failed to remove it? Previous complaints made can indicate that the store should have taken steps to make the premises safe.

It is necessary to find out who is responsible. Who occupies the building? Who is the manager in charge? If the accident was on a footpath, which local council's area is it? If it was on transport such as a bus, is it a government bus or privately owned?

Take witnesses' details. If the matter goes to court, the solicitor may need to obtain statements from them.

Seeing a solicitor

Do not let too much time lapse before seeing a solicitor. Legal action is barred by statute if you wait too long – three years in some States, six years in others. Delaying also makes the solicitor's job more difficult because chasing up evidence becomes harder.

Your solicitor will want a full chronological account of what happened. He or she may want photographs or a plan of the accident scene. Official records such as police reports will be obtained. Medical examinations are needed to ascertain the extent of the injury.

Settling out of court

If you have a good case, you might be offered a sum in settlement before the court case begins. In deciding whether to accept, consider:

- whether the sum is adequate (an experienced solicitor will be able to give their opinion);
- whether you want to go through the disruption of a court case;
- what the risk of losing the court case would be – no matter how strong your case is, you never have a guarantee of success;
- whether you can afford the legal costs if you lose (if you win, you might be able to recover your costs from the other party).

Accepting an out of court settlement usually involves releasing your rights to go ahead with a court case.

In cases where there is not enough evidence to support court action but you feel strongly that you should receive some compensation, you could always try appealing to the occupier. It is not unknown for large department stores to pay a customer's medical bills for the sake of customer goodwill and to avoid adverse publicity.

Court action

After balancing up all the considerations, you might decide to go ahead and sue for negligence. Obtaining legal advice is advisable. For a description of the court process, see 3.4 Suing and Being Sued.

ACCIDENTS IN YOUR HOME

Are you responsible if somebody hurts themselves on your property? You might be if your negligence caused the injury.

Your duty to take reasonable care to prevent injury to entrants depends to some extent on who the entrant was. Traditionally, entrants were classed into different groups depending on the circumstances under which they entered.

Today the classification is still used by courts but it is only one of many factors that will be looked at. Understanding the traditional classifications may help us anticipate what a court's decision might be. In this area of the law, as in many others, there are no cut and dried answers.

Invitees

This sounds like someone you merely invited in, but an invitee has a higher status. Technically, an invitee is someone invited onto the premises who provides the occupier with some sort of financial gain. Customers in shops are invitees. If you work from home or have business meetings with clients in your home, the clients would be invitees.

Licensees

Licensees enter with the consent of the occupier, but they differ from invitees because the occupier receives no financial gain. Social guests are an example.

Traditionally a greater duty was owed to invitees, but today courts also consider:

- whether you knew or should have known of the danger;
- whether you warned the entrant;
- whether the danger was obvious;
- whether the injury was foreseeable.

Trespassers

Anybody entering your land without permission or official authority is a trespasser. In the past trespassers could not sue for injuries sustained while on land without the occupier's knowledge or approval.

But the law has changed. A duty to take care does exist, but its extent depends on the circumstances. Certainly occupiers are not permitted to set traps with the deliberate intention of harming the trespasser. The court would also consider whether the occupier knew of the trespasser's presence, and whether the trespasser had entered the property before.

For details on removing trespassers, see 12.7 Dealing with Trespassers.

Where children are injured

Not surprisingly, a greater duty is owed where children are involved. Very young children have to be protected against themselves.

Signs that warn of danger are of no use if the child is too young to read. And children trespassers are more likely to be awarded compensation than adult trespassers. Most occupiers realise that children are attracted to dangerous objects, such as piled up rotten boards, and steps should be taken to lessen or remove the danger.

Injury caused by animals

Similar considerations to those above apply to injury caused by animals. Generally trespassers will not be able to sue for injury caused by a guard dog.

If an animal that you do not own enters your property and hurts somebody, it is likely that the animal's owner will be liable. For information on the responsibility of animal owners, see 13.3 Animals.

Insurance

Home occupiers can protect themselves from personal injury claims by taking out public liability insurance and/or domestic workers compensation: see 12.5 Home Insurance.

MONETARY COMPENSATION (DAMAGES)

If a personal injuries action succeeds, how much compensation will be awarded? Courts assess damages by considering various issues:

Financial loss

Out-of-pocket expenses incurred in seeking medical treatment (including hospitalisation and physiotherapy costs) can be compensated.

Lost earnings resulting from being unable to work can also be covered. If the injury is such that it reduces the injured person's future capacity to earn a living, they may be paid a sum to reflect this loss of earning potential. They will not be paid the wages they will miss out on, but a smaller sum reflecting the uncertainties inherent in anybody's working life (eg future illness, unemployment, early retirement or death).

Non-monetary issues

Often more difficult to handle than financial loss is the traumatic impact that accidents have on the injured person's life. Pain and suffering and the loss of enjoyment of life are examples. Obviously it is difficult to work out a monetary figure to compensate for such issues, but a court will award a sum of money that it considers to be fair in all the circumstances.

Interest

Court procedures are lengthy, and most likely a considerable time will have passed between the date of the injury and the court's decision. Interest on the damages may be awarded to make up for this.

Compensation to relatives

Where the accident resulted in death, the relatives of the deceased may have the right to claim compensation if negligence was involved.

10.3 ACCIDENTS AT WORK

Work-related injuries often result in financial loss both from actual expenses (such as medical bills) and from a reduced ability to earn an income. Employees who suffer loss as the result of a work injury are entitled to some form of compensation. Various sources of compensation exist, but generally you can only recover from one.

SOCIAL SECURITY PAYMENTS

Most work injuries result in a workers compensation claim (discussed below), but financial problems may arise if the claim is not paid promptly. Applying for social security may help solve the problem in the meantime. Contact the Department of Social Security to see if you are entitled to any payments.

Benefits received may need to be repaid once the compensation claim comes through.

Chapter 11 provides an overview of the different types of social security benefits and allowances, and discusses eligibility requirements.

EMPLOYMENT ENTITLEMENTS

Ill or injured workers have sick leave rights. Some awards go further than this and make a provision for accident pay, which works by topping up workers compensation. For a general discussion on employment law, awards and the rights of employees, see 9.1 Employee's Rights and Duties.

WORKERS COMPENSATION

Workers compensation law is rather complex. While it is possible to express the main concepts in simple terms, keep in mind that each State has variations on the basic principles. Generally the law of the State where the injury occurred is followed. Commonwealth public servants, however, are covered by a specific Federal Act establishing the Comcare Authority.

So when can you claim workers compensation?

Employees are entitled to workers compensation where the injury arose out of or in the course of employment. Quite a lot is packed into this seemingly simple statement. Breaking it up into its three basic parts makes it easier to understand:

(i) Who is an employee?
(ii) What is an injury?
(iii) The course of employment.

Who is an employee?

If you have a regular job working for an employer in a situation where you use their equipment and follow their instructions in return for a wage, it is no surprise to learn that you will be classed as an employee.

But under Workers Compensation legislation, people who are not normally employees may be deemed to be so in order to be entitled to compensation. It varies between States, but typically "deemed employees" can include independent contractors and people paid on a commission basis.

What is an injury?

The range is very broad. An injury can be internal or external. It includes conditions such as deafness or blindness, burns, wounds and even death. Diseases contracted in the course of the job (such as lung cancer) may also be classed as injuries.

Pre-existing injuries that are aggravated by the work can be covered. A person with a bad back who worsens it lifting a heavy load as part of the job should still be entitled to workers compensation.

Even psychological problems caused by the stress of work may be covered. As with all injuries, the link to the job has to be proven. It tends to be more difficult in this area as psychological problems typically develop due to several factors in the person's life.

The course of employment

To be compensated, the injury must arise out of or in the course of employment. This does not mean you actually have to be working at the time the accident occurred.

Activities normally authorised by the employer, such as using the tea room or toilet, are still considered to be in the course of employment. Even recreational activities, such as sporting events, may be covered, particularly if the employer arranged the activity or knew of its existence and did not object.

Journeys between home and work are usually covered, but here the situation becomes more complicated.

Using the New South Wales law as an example, compensation may be paid for injuries incurred between the boundaries of the worker's home and the workplace (or some other place related to work) unless the injury was wholly or partly due to the worker's fault. However, if the risk increased due to a work-related factor (for instance if the worker was asked to deliver a package and by the time it was done it got dark), compensation is payable even if the injury was due to the worker's fault. Conversely, if the worker deviated from their normal journey (for instance to shop for groceries), compensation would only be payable if the interruption did not materially increase the risk.

Must the employer be at fault?

Unlike suing for negligence (see below) it is irrelevant whether or not the employer was to blame for the injury. In fact, workers are entitled to compensation even if the accident was their own fault (except in the New South Wales journey cases described above).

One exception exists – if the injury was caused by the serious and deliberate misconduct of the worker, they may lose their entitlement. As you can imagine, this is not ordinary negligence, but something rather extreme. What amounts to serious and deliberate misconduct depends on all the surrounding circumstances.

New South Wales limits this exception further by requiring that the misconduct must have been the sole cause of the injury in order for it to disentitle the worker.

The exception does not apply at all if the injury resulted in death or serious and permanent disablement – in other words compensation would still be paid.

Making a claim

If you need to make a claim you should obtain a workers compensation claim form from your employer, complete it and return it to your employer together with an appropriate medical certificate. Penalties exist for false claims.

How much would you get?

Compensation is paid to injured workers while they are unable to perform their original job. The amount paid depends on whether the incapacity is total or partial.

Partial incapacity means that the worker can still perform suitable duties. The employer should put the employee on suitable duties if this is at all possible. Total incapacity means that the injured person cannot work at all.

Generally, for the first six months a totally incapacitated worker would receive their pre-injury pay, then they would get a lesser amount. This lesser amount would be determined by various factors, including the number of dependants.

The amount that a partially incapacitated worker on suitable duties would receive is worked out differently in different States. It may be reached by deducting their current pay from their pre-injury pay, or by working out a percentage of the maximum amount payable to reflect the severity of the injury.

Lump sum payments as a substitute for the above are discouraged and most States heavily restrict them. But all workers are entitled to receive a lump sum for the loss of the use of a certain part of the body. Set amounts exist for fingers, arms etc. This is paid in addition to the weekly loss of earnings payments.

Medical and related expenses (such as travelling to the doctor) are compensated. Personal items damaged in the accident, such as clothes, are also paid for.

Payments to dependants

Where the worker dies as a result of the injury or disease, a person dependent on the worker may claim benefits. Dependants include members of the worker's family who rely on the worker for financial support. De facto spouses may be included in some States.

What if your employer tries to sack you?

Under Federal legislation, an employer cannot dismiss an employee purely because they receive compensation. Some States have similar laws prohibiting dismissal. 9.3 Losing Your Job looks at the issue in more detail.

Even if you are dismissed, you do not lose your entitlement to claim workers compensation.

Employer's insurance

It is compulsory for employers to take out insurance to cover workers compensation claims. Failure to do so does not mean the worker will miss out on their rights. The worker can claim the money from a fund, which will then recover it from the employer.

SUING FOR NEGLIGENCE

Injuries caused by the employer's negligence may give rise to a right to sue for monetary compensation (damages) at common law. Damages are different from workers compensation. The term "common law" is described more fully in 1.1 The Australian Legal System, but for now it is enough to say that common law is law developed by courts as opposed to workers compensation law which is spelled out by parliament.

Damages are generally higher than workers compensation payouts, but they are harder to obtain because it is necessary to prove that there was a breach of the employer's duties.

The employer's duties

Employers must take reasonable care to prevent injury to employees. This includes providing safe premises, maintaining equipment, and providing appropriate supervision.

If you are injured by the actions of a fellow worker the employer is still responsible. The legal term describing this is vicarious liability.

Workers should be guarded against reasonably foreseeable risks – employers cannot be liable at common law if something utterly unpredictable occurs. If oil spills on the floor, it is foreseeable that somebody will slip and fall.

Employers may not be liable if the worker steps outside their normal field to carry out duties that the employer has no knowledge of.

The worker's negligence

Unlike workers compensation, if the worker caused or contributed to the accident, the amount of damages that can be claimed would be reduced. The reduction would be in line with the extent of the worker's negligence (called contributory negligence in these circumstances).

How much would you get?

Damages include compensation for both monetary and non-monetary loss.

Monetary loss can sometimes be given an exact figure. It includes out-of-pocket expenses such as medical bills and loss of income. Future loss of earnings due to a decreased capacity to work are also compensated, but this figure has to be estimated because it is not possible to predict future earnings. The possibility of early retirement or future injury must be considered.

Non-monetary loss cannot be given an exact sum either. Pain and suffering and loss of enjoyment of life are examples. The court will estimate a sum of money that in its opinion is a fair attempt to address the problem.

A description of the general laws of negligence and damages assessment can be found in 10.2 Accidents in Public Places and Homes.

Restrictions in different States

Most States are restricting the right to sue employers at common law. Some have abolished it completely, while others retain it. Others such as New South Wales, Victoria and South Australia keep the common law but restrict access to it. For example, in New South Wales the common law has been restricted to only allow claims for non-economic loss such as pain and suffering, unless the injury is serious or results in death.

Even in the States where you can sue, you cannot receive both compensation and full damages. You can apply for workers compensation while you seek legal advice to consider whether you should sue. It is usually only worth it for serious injuries. The damages that an employer would have to pay would be reduced to reflect the compensation payout.

REHABILITATION

All States encourage employers to rehabilitate seriously injured workers. Rehabilitation involves doing what is reasonably possible to return the employee to work. It may require switching to suitable duties, retraining, or even modifying work procedures.

The laws of New South Wales and Victoria go further. In those States rehabilitation programs are required by law. Guidelines are issued by the WorkCover Authorities that must be followed.

10.4 CAR ACCIDENTS

A momentary slip in concentration can have traumatic results. Car accidents have become such a common feature of modern life that they are seen as almost inevitable. It is important for drivers involved in car accidents to know what to do.

THE ACCIDENT SCENE

People involved in accidents often experience a sense of unreality – it is not until much later that it all sinks in. Staying calm reduces the chance of further danger and helps rectify the situation.

Drivers have various duties:

Duty to stop

After an accident all drivers involved have to stop. You should stop even if your car was not damaged but your actions caused others to crash – for instance if you had to brake suddenly and the car behind you stopped in time, but the car behind that didn't.

Pulling away from the flow of traffic is wisest. You should do this as soon as possible – once you have checked for injuries, and ensured that witnesses and drivers are available to give statements when the police arrive. Do not cause a further hazard by waiting until the police arrive, they should be able to reconstruct events by hearing witness accounts and examining the damage.

Duty to offer assistance

The first thing you should do after stopping is to see if anybody is hurt and needs assistance. If somebody is hurt ask one bystander to call the ambulance, and get others to divert the flow of traffic. Unconscious victims need instant attention – especially if something is blocking their airway and preventing them from breathing. But be very careful. If you do not know how to assist you could harm the injured person further.

Exchange particulars

You have a legal duty to give your name, address and registration details to other drivers involved in the accident. If you are not the car's owner, you need to provide the owner's name and address as well.

What happens if the driver of the other car is absent – for instance, if you hit a parked car? Then you need to write your details and attach the paper to the windshield.

If you do not comply with this obligation you could be summonsed by the police. The courts take the obligation to stop and exchange particulars very seriously and the penalties can be as severe as those for drink driving (including loss of licence).

Duty to report

If the police do not attend the accident you may need to visit the nearest police station to file a report. Whether you have this duty depends on the circumstances and the laws of your State. In New South Wales you must make a report if any of the following occur:

- a driver involved in the accident failed to stop or exchange particulars;
- somebody was injured;
- a car needs to be towed away;
- a driver was intoxicated;
- the damage exceeded a certain sum.

You must answer police questions about the details of the accident and if the police do not attend, you must report the accident within 24 hours to the police station nearest to the accident. You are not required to answer questions that could lead to you being charged with a criminal offence.

In other States the duty depends on various factors including the extent of the damage. But it is difficult to estimate the cost of the damage yourself. Repairs are often more expensive than you would expect, particularly if more than one panel is involved. So if in doubt, it is best to contact the police to ask them if you need to make a report.

This duty is doubly important in some States, because a failure to make a report to the police may effect compensation claims (discussed below).

In the report itself, you will need to outline the time, place and nature of the accident. Provide the police with the registration number of the other car and, if possible, the names and addresses of witnesses.

How long do you have to make the report? It varies between States. In some States it is not a specific period – the requirement is that the report be made as soon as possible. In other States such as New South Wales it must be made within 24 hours.

Do not admit liability

Even if you believe that the accident was your fault, you should not admit this as it could invalidate your insurance policy.

MOTOR VEHICLE INSURANCE

Accidents can result in personal injury or property damage or both. Different types of insurance policies exist to cover claims in both areas.

Third party

Third party insurance is compulsory – you cannot register your car without it. It covers claims for injuries caused to others where you were at fault. The driver at fault is not covered for their own injuries in some States, but his or her passengers are able to make a claim.

Third party property

Damage caused to another person's property is covered by this type of insurance. If your car is not particularly valuable you may prefer to save on the premiums by taking out third party property insurance rather than comprehensive.

Although this is not compulsory it is a wise choice. Even if you drive an old, inexpensive car, there is always a chance you will hit a Rolls Royce some day.

Comprehensive

Damage to your own vehicle is covered by comprehensive insurance, even if you were at fault. Comprehensive insurance can also cover matters such as theft, hail and flood damage – read the policy's information booklet to check.

Losing your cover

Claims may be refused by the insurance company if any of the following occurred:

- you admitted liability at the scene of the accident;

- the driver did not have a licence;
- the driver was intoxicated;
- the vehicle was in an unsafe condition;
- the accident was not reported to the insurance company and/or police as soon as possible;
- the claim is suspected to be dishonest or fraudulent;
- the vehicle was being used for an illegal purpose.

These exclusions vary between policies. Contact your insurance company or read your policy's information booklet to determine which apply in your case.

PROPERTY DAMAGE

If your car is damaged in an accident, there are various ways to deal with it. Your decision will depend on who was at fault, the insurance cover, and the extent of the damage.

If you have comprehensive insurance

It is often best to let your insurance company deal with it. If you were not at fault and can identify the other driver, you might keep your no claim bonus. Some insurance companies will even recover the set amount usually paid by claimants (called an excess) from the party at fault, so you might not even need to pay that.

If you were at fault, you will lose your no-claim bonus and be required to pay the excess. Do your sums to determine if the damage caused to your car is high enough to justify this. Remember that it takes more than one year to recover the percentage of no claim bonus lost by making a claim.

Third party property insurance

Where the other driver has third party property insurance, damage to your vehicle will be covered.

Where there is no insurance

You will have to bear the costs yourself unless you are prepared to sue the other driver for damages (see Suing For Damages below).

Making a claim

Notify the insurance company as to the accident as soon as possible, even if you are not sure that you intend to make a claim.

To make a claim you need to obtain a quotation from a repairer and fill in a claim form. Most repairers hold claim forms from the insurance companies and the quote and claim form can be done together. Answers must be accurate and complete – the company can refuse payouts where false or misleading information was given.

The damage will be inspected, and if your claim is substantiated the insurance company will agree to pay for the repairs. They may allow you to choose your own repairer or they may prefer to choose the repairer themselves.

Suing for damages

When considering legal action, remember that you may have to pay legal costs even if you lose. And initiating proceedings may cause the other side to also make a claim (known as a cross claim). Generally it will only be worth the risk if the sum of money at stake is high.

Doing your own legal work to save money is possible. Obtain at least two repair quotes. Write a letter to the other driver demanding payment and stating your intention to commence proceedings if payment is not made by a given date. If this fails to achieve any result, visit your Local Court (also called Magistrates Courts in some States) and ask the staff for further information. The general court process is described in 3.4 Suing and Being Sued.

Seeking a solicitor's assistance is advisable, particularly if the other driver files a defence or a cross claim.

PERSONAL INJURY

Compulsory third party insurance will cover you if you are hurt and not at fault. In some States everybody is covered regardless of fault.

Two different systems exist for making personal injury claims in Australia – the right to sue at common law and the ability to make claims under a statutory scheme. (Common law is judge-made law while statutory schemes are developed by parliament. Further details on the general differences can be found in 1.1 The Australian Legal System).

Which system applies to you? It depends on the laws of your State. Some States have both systems. In New South Wales common law claims were initially abolished but have more recently been returned in a restricted form. South Australia retains the common law. Victoria has a statutory scheme, but allows limited common law claims if the injury is serious and the Transport Accident Commission determines that the degree of impairment is high enough.

As the law in this area is complicated and continually changing, anyone injured in a car accident should obtain legal advice without delay. The following discussion is merely an introduction to the types of issues that may arise.

Common law

To sue at common law you must be able to prove that the driver causing your injuries was negligent.

Establishing negligence requires three things:

- a duty was owed by the driver to take care;
- the duty was not fulfilled;
- that breach of duty caused the injuries.

For a more detailed description of the general laws of negligence see 10.2 Accidents in Public Places and Homes. Applying it to car accidents – drivers owe a duty of care to people who it is reasonable to expect may be injured if there is a failure to take care. Therefore passengers in the driver's car, people in other cars and people on or near the road are all owed this duty.

What actually is the duty of care? Drivers of vehicles have a duty to:

- drive at an appropriate speed (which may even be below the speed limit if it is dark, raining etc);
- obey road rules;
- keep a proper lookout for danger;
- give proper signals;
- keep the vehicle in good condition.

Bystanders may also be owed a duty. Personal injury damages can include becoming ill due to the shock of witnessing an accident, particularly if a family member was involved.

The damages that you can claim will be reduced if the court decides that you are partly to blame for your own injuries. This is known as contributory negligence. Situations such as these arise when both drivers were responsible for the accident to some degree, or where your injuries were aggravated by your own actions, for example the failure to wear a seat belt.

Statutory schemes

Each State is different and the law is constantly changing, so always check your current situation. The current scheme in New South Wales provides an example.

New South Wales introduced the Motor Accidents Scheme to replace the earlier TransCover. To claim under this compulsory third party insurance scheme, you must have made a report to the police within 28 days of the injury. You might be excused if the injuries were so serious that they prevented this.

Where possible, you need to identify the vehicle at fault. Then find out who the compulsory third party insurer is, either by asking the owner or the Motor Accidents Authority. Contact the insurance company and ask them to send you a claim form.

What happens if you cannot identify the vehicle or if it is not insured (for instance because it is unregistered)? You are entitled to claim against the Motor Accidents Authority. The Motor Accidents Authority is known as the nominal defendant in these situations.

Fill in the claim form and send it to the insurer. The form itself provides detailed instructions on how to do this. Severe penalties exist for false claims. The claim must be made within six months of the injury, and the person at fault must be notified within six months.

Claimants have a duty to cooperate with the other party. They must comply with reasonable requests for information and medical examinations.

The person at fault should notify their insurance company without delay if they believe a claim will be made.

If the accident was partly your fault, you might still be able to claim, but the amount you receive may be reduced.

FURTHER READING

Australian Consumers' Association, *Your Health Rights*, Random House Australia, Sydney, 1992

Guidebook to Workers Compensation in Australia, CCH, Sydney, 1988

Luntz, *Assessment of Damages for Personal Injury and Death*, Butterworths, Sydney, 1990

Motor Accidents: Drink Driving And Beyond, Legal and Accounting Management Seminars, Sydney, 1994

See also: General references listed in Further Reading Chapter 1.

Chapter 11

SOCIAL SECURITY

11.1   Claiming social security
11.2   Types of payments
Further reading

11.1 CLAIMING SOCIAL SECURITY

People who are unable to support themselves may be eligible to receive financial assistance from the Department of Social Security (DSS). The DSS is a Commonwealth government department with offices throughout Australia.

ARE YOU ELIGIBLE?

It is not enough that you cannot currently earn a living – to receive a social security payment you must establish that you are eligible for payment. If you do not meet the requirements you may be able to receive a one-off emergency grant from a charity or community agency. The DSS will be able to identify these bodies for you.

Social security tests differ depending on the type of payment sought, but general requirements include residency and age. Even if you are entitled to a social security payment you may receive a reduced rate. The amount paid will depend on factors such as:

- income;
- asset levels;
- marital status;
- number of children.

Australian residency

Generally to claim social security you need to be an Australian resident and in many cases you must be present in Australia. Exceptions exist, however, and some people living overseas can be paid certain types of pensions if they are in a country that has a reciprocal agreement with Australia. The rate of payment would depend on how long they lived in Australia and when they left.

Recently the residency rules for refugees have changed. Refugees granted permanent residence no longer need to satisfy the standard length of residency requirements, and should contact the DSS for details.

Income and assets test

"Income" refers to money you earn such as wages, interest, and rent. "Assets" refers to property you own.

The DSS will assess your income and asset levels – most social security payments are affected by the result. If you are unhappy with the department's assessment you can ask for a review. If you are assets rich and income poor you may be entitled to a social security payment if you make a hardship claim.

Couples

If you are married or live in a "marriage-like" relationship, your ability to claim social security may be affected.

A marriage-like relationship is one between two people of the opposite sex that is similar to the relationship between a legally married couple. To determine this, all the circumstances of the relationship are considered, including whether the couple:

- live together;
- have a sexual relationship;
- share financial resources;
- share the same social life;
- see themselves as being in a committed and long-term relationship;
- are bringing up children together.

If you are married or in a marriage-like relationship and your partner has an income, your pension or benefit may be reduced or cancelled. If you were living in a marriage-like relationship during a time where you were receiving social security payments, you may owe money to the DSS. If your partner dies you may be entitled to a widow pension.

MAKING A CLAIM

Claim forms

To claim social security you need to fill in a claim form. Different forms exist for each type of social security payment. You should explain your circumstances carefully to ensure you are given the correct form.

Claim forms are available at DSS offices and at post offices. Read the form carefully and answer all the questions. Ask for help if you are unsure of something. Making untrue or misleading statements can lead to a penalty. Married or de facto couples need to fill in separate forms. Once completed, the form should be lodged at a DSS office.

Interviews

You might be required to attend an interview at a DSS office. At the interview you will be given information regarding payments, your rights and obligations. Interpreters are available if needed.

You will be required to prove who you are by using three different documents. They should be originals, not photocopies. The types of documents you can use include:

- birth certificate;
- passport;
- citizenship or naturalisation certificate if applicable;
- marriage certificate if applicable;
- driver's licence;
- motor vehicle registration form;
- bank accounts;
- taxation notice.

It may also be necessary to take documents to show what income and assets you own. Take details of:

- any income that you receive (wages, superannuation etc);
- all your financial accounts (bank, building society etc);
- any other investments;
- maintenance and child support.

You will also be required to provide your tax file number.

How are payments made?

Payments are made directly into your bank, building society or credit union account. In limited circumstances you can ask for payment by cheque. Most payments are made fortnightly – Family Payments are made in the alternate week to the payment of a pension or allowance. Payments tend to be raised each year in line with increases in the Consumer Price Index (a measure of inflation).

INVESTIGATIONS/REVIEWS

The Department regularly reviews your entitlement to payment. They may do this by asking you to complete and return review forms or by arranging an interview with a DSS officer either at your home or at a DSS office.

Field assessors employed by the DSS check that people receiving benefits are in fact entitled to them. Field assessors are required to carry an official identification card, and you can ask to see it. They may call as part of a routine review, or because they are following up information suggesting you are not receiving your correct payment. You can ask to be told the reason for the call, but they cannot tell you who (if anybody) gave the information.

If a field assessor knocks on your door you do not have to let them in or answer questions straight away unless you received formal written notice stating that you have to. Usually you can choose to be interviewed at a later date at the department office. The field assessor should give you a pamphlet about your rights.

You can take somebody with you to the interview, such as a lawyer or friend. If you do not attend an interview your payment may be cancelled or suspended.

The Department may investigate your entitlement to payment by contacting your employer(s). If they do this they must send a written notice to that person listing the questions, and detailing the time in which a person must respond and the punishment that can be imposed for failure to respond.

CHANGED CIRCUMSTANCES

The DSS must be advised of any changes in your circumstances that might affect your eligibility or the rate of payment. The sorts of things you must notify them about include:

- changes of address;
- getting married or living in a de facto relationship;

- any receipt of income;
- finding a job;
- having a child;
- when your child grows up/marries/gets a job/moves away from home.

YOUR PERSONAL FILE

Checking your file

You may want to check your personal DSS file for any number of reasons, perhaps because you suspect it contains an error, or because your entitlements were refused or reduced. Usually there is no charge for gaining access to your file.

Some documents you can look at simply by phoning the DSS and arranging to go in. These can be:

- details of payments;
- details of requested repayments;
- papers sent to you by the DSS;
- papers you sent them.

Other documents may require that you make a formal Freedom of Information application. Contact the DSS first and they will be able to advise you. For details on Freedom of Information applications see 6.3 Freedom of Information. As the DSS is a Federal government department, complaints regarding these applications should be directed towards the Commonwealth (not State) Ombudsman.

Changing your file

Applications to amend personal files should be made in writing. Simple factual errors (such as wrong dates or spelling) are usually corrected readily. For other matters you may need to convince the DSS that you are correct.

If the DSS refuses to change information held about you, you can complain to the Privacy Commissioner or appeal the decision. Your rights of appeal should be explained in the letter telling you of the Department's decision.

REVIEWING REFUSED CLAIMS

If you have been refused social security, had your entitlement reduced or suspended, or have been ordered to pay back some money, you can have the decision reviewed.

6.2 Challenging Government Decisions describes general principles; this discussion looks at the process from the viewpoint of social security claimants.

Payment pending review

In some cases the payment can continue while the decision is being reviewed. You should not delay your request for this if you are seeking a review.

Review within the DSS

Your first step is to ask the DSS to have the decision reviewed. You can ask for the review to be carried out by an authorised review officer. The review officer was not involved in the original decision, and he or she may change the decision if they think it appropriate.

The Social Security Appeals Tribunal

If the first step failed you can appeal to the Social Security Appeals Tribunal. The tribunal is independent of the DSS. Appeals should be made within three months of the DSS' decision if full arrears are to be paid.

Appealing to the tribunal is free. You can obtain an appeal form from the tribunal or from a DSS office. The actual hearing is informal, and you may be helped by a friend or social worker. The tribunal has the power to change decisions, and orders made are binding.

Information on tribunals in general can be found in 4.3 Complaints and Tribunals.

The Administrative Appeals Tribunal

Decisions made by the Social Security Appeals Tribunal may be able to be appealed against before the Commonwealth Administrative Appeals Tribunal. Appeals should be lodged within 28 days of receiving the Social Security Appeal Tribunal's written decision.

See 6.2 Challenging Government Decisions for more information on the Administrative Appeals Tribunal.

11.2   TYPES OF PAYMENTS

If you need financial assistance you might be eligible to receive a social security payment. See 11.1 Claiming Social Security for details on eligibility and claims.

Note that the types of social security payments available change fairly often. The following information is therefore only a general guide – you should always check the situation with the Department of Social Security (DSS).

PENSIONS, BENEFITS AND ALLOWANCES

Social security can come in the form of a pension, benefit or allowance. The differences are related to the eligibility requirements and the sum paid, and how long the payment is designed to last. For example, pensions are designed to be a long-term source of income, while benefits and allowances are only meant to be sources of short-term assistance.

TYPES OF SOCIAL SECURITY PAYMENTS

Family Payment

The Family Payment is paid for dependent children up to 16. It can also be paid for full-time high school students over this age up until the end of the school year in which they turn 18.

There is a basic allowance (known as Basic Family Payment) and an additional allowance (known as Additional Family Payment). Both are subject to income and assets tests.

Home Child-care Allowance

This provides assistance to the parent who stays at home to look after the children. Applicants need to:

- have a dependent child;
- be part of a couple;
- have little or no income of their own;
- be an Australian resident.

Sole Parent Pension

This is available for people who are:

- caring for a dependent child;
- neither married nor living in a de facto relationship;

- not receiving any other pension.

Residency and income/assets tests apply.

You must try to get child support from the father: see 7.5 Maintenance. Child support can affect entitlements to receive social security.

Carer Pension

This is designed to assist people who are caring full-time for somebody who is old or is living with a disability, requiring constant care at home. It does not need to be a relative, but you need to either live with them or very close to them. You have to meet residency and income/assets tests.

The person you are caring for must need supervision for at least six months, or less if he or she has a terminal condition. They must either be receiving a pension, or if they do not, the reason for that must be based only on residency criteria.

Age Pension

You may be entitled to an Age Pension if you are:
- a man aged 65 or over;
- a woman aged 60 or over (over the next 20 years this age requirement will increase gradually to 65); and
- an Australian resident of 10 years.

Exceptions to the residency rule exist, because Australia has agreements with some other countries which may allow people living overseas to still get an Australian pension. The laws have recently changed for refugees who have been granted permanent residence – they no longer have to satisfy the standard length of residency requirements to receive a pension.

Mature Age Allowance

The Mature Age Allowance is different from the Age Pension. The allowance exists to help older people who are out of work.

Applicants must be:
- 60 or over, but unable to receive the Age Pension;
- unemployed for at least 12 months and registered as such with the Commonwealth Employment Service (CES);
- the recipient of financial assistance for at least 12 months;
- an Australian resident for 10 years.

The amount paid under the Mature Age Allowance is generally higher than that paid for other unemployed people (discussed below). The rates and benefits of the Mature Age Allowance are similar to the Age Pension.

Widowed Person Allowance

This is a short-term allowance for men or women whose spouse or de facto spouse died recently. To qualify they must:

- have been living with their partner just before their death;
- have no dependant children;
- not be receiving any other social security assistance.

Survivors of pensioner couples do not need to claim this as they automatically receive a Bereavement Allowance.

Disability Support Pension

People who are unable to work because of a long-term health problem or because they are living with a disability may be able to claim the Disability Support Pension. They must be over 16 but too young to receive the Age Pension.

Impairment ratings measure the degree of disability. To receive the pension you must establish that you have an impairment rating of 20 percent or more, and because of that disability you cannot work.

If you were in an accident and you receive compensation for your injuries (eg workers compensation, insurance payout, court damages) then your ability to receive this pension might be affected.

Sickness Allowance

People who fall ill might be able to claim the sickness allowance if they:

- are working but have used up their work sick leave entitlements;
- are self-employed;
- are unemployed and already receiving social security assistance (eg Jobsearch).

The allowance is not paid to people who are able to work, even if they can only perform light duties.

Proof of illness is of course necessary – you should obtain an adequately detailed medical certificate.

Young Homeless Allowance

Young people may be entitled to this allowance if they are:

- under 18;
- single;
- not living at home, either because they have been kicked out or because it has become impossible to stay at home (eg for reasons such as sexual or physical abuse);
- not receiving help from their parents or guardians;
- already receiving an allowance such as the Job Search Allowance or Austudy if they are students.

Job Search and Newstart Allowance

The Job Search Allowance is designed for unemployed people. Recipients must be:

- unemployed;
- actively seeking work;
- over 16 and under the age pension age;
- registered with the CES for under 12 months; and
- an Australian resident and living in Australia.

The Newstart Allowance is also for unemployed people, but has different requirements to the Job Search Allowance. Applicants for the Newstart Allowance must be:

- unemployed;
- actively seeking work;
- over 18;
- registered with the CES for more than 12 months; and
- an Australian resident and living in Australia.

Applicants for either type must register with the CES as soon as they can. Once you start receiving the allowance, you must keep the DSS informed as to your efforts to find work every fortnight. If you have not looked for work or undertaken any approved related activity, you will not be paid for that fortnight and may incur a "deferment period".

A deferment period will mean that you cannot receive a social security payment for a number of weeks. The length of the deferment period will depend on how long you have been unemployed, the reason why the deferment period was imposed, and whether or not you served a deferment period in the last three years.

Special Benefit

A Special Benefit might be paid to people who cannot receive assistance in any other way if they are:

- in severe financial hardship (ie cannot afford food and shelter);
- unable to earn a living for some reason out of their control;
- allowed to remain in Australia.

Veteran's Pensions

Ex-servicemen, women and their dependants may be entitled to assistance provided by the Department of Veteran's Affairs. They are similar to the DSS age and disability pensions, and war widows may also be entitled to a pension. Contact the Department of Veteran's Affairs for details.

Often you cannot receive both a Veteran's pension and a DSS pension simultaneously.

Austudy/Abstudy

Austudy payments can be made to assist students. Abstudy applies specifically to students of Aboriginal descent. The payment can be made whether you are living at home or independently, but the rate differs.

These payments are administered by the Commonwealth Department of Employment, Education and Training.

SUPPLEMENTARY ENTITLEMENTS

In addition to the actual social security payment, some recipients are entitled to supplementary benefits.

Some examples are:

- Pensioner Concession Cards – providing health and transport concessions (Seniors Cards also exist in States such as New South Wales to provide discounts for people over 60 who are not working full-time – income/assets tests are not applied);
- pensioners may be entitled to rebates on local government rates and water rates;
- people with disabilities may be eligible for taxi subsidies, travel concessions, parking concessions and some sales tax exemptions under State and Federal laws (laws vary between States and should be checked).

Contact the DSS for information about these entitlements. For State and Federal government benefits, contact the relevant government department (eg Department of Transport, Roads and Traffic Authority, Australian Taxation Office).

DO YOU HAVE TO PAY TAX?

Many forms of assistance are taxable. But if social security is your only form of income it is unlikely that you will have to pay tax. You might have to pay tax if you already earn income from another source (eg wages, rent, interest, superannuation) – it is best to check with the Australian Taxation Office. You can also refer to the Tax Pack for information.

Tax may be paid as a lump sum, or you can arrange to have it deducted from your social security payments.

Also check whether you need a tax file number, and whether you need to quote it to employers, banks, building societies etc. Failure to use a tax file number where necessary results in being taxed at the highest rate.

FURTHER READING

Carney and Hanks, *Social Security in Australia*, Oxford University Press, Melbourne, 1994

Information Handbook: A Guide to Social Security Payments and Services, Department of Social Security, Sydney, 1990

Welfare Rights Centre, *The Independent Social Security Handbook*, Pluto Press, Sydney, 1994

See also: General references listed in Further Reading Chapter 1.

PART 3

PROPERTY CONCERNS

Chapter 12

YOUR HOME

12.1 RENTING A HOME

Paying money to a landlord gives a tenant the right to live in the landlord's premises. Each party's rights and responsibilities are governed by a residential tenancy agreement (also called a lease) and by statute law.

TYPES OF TENANCIES

Two basic types of tenancies exist: fixed term and periodic.

Fixed-term tenancies are just that – they exist for a set period of time. At the end of that time:

- a new agreement may be entered into; or
- the tenancy may end; or
- the tenancy may turn into a periodic tenancy if the tenant continues to live in the premises and the landlord continues to accept rent.

Periodic tenancies have no set end date. They exist for recurring periods of time, for instance from week to week or month to month. The length of the period coincides with how often rent is paid.

It is important to know which type of tenancy you have, as it determines issues such as how much notice must be given to end the tenancy. Check the agreement or ask your agent if you are unsure.

BEFORE YOU SIGN THE AGREEMENT

Unexpected costs

Renting a home involves many initial outlays that tenants may not have anticipated. Make sure that you obtain an itemised list of expenses from the landlord or agent. Typical expenses include:

- costs for preparing the residential tenancy agreement;
- rent in advance – usually two to four weeks;
- bond – a sum paid as security for failure to pay rent or for causing damage – it usually cannot exceed four weeks' rent.

You will have to pay to have a telephone connected. You may also need to pay gas and electricity deposits which should be refundable when you leave, unless you have fallen behind on payments. Normally the landlord is responsible to pay council rates and water rates.

The building should be insured by the landlord, but you should take out home contents insurance to protect your personal belongings. For further details on insurance see 12.5 Home Insurance.

Condition reports

Condition reports are required to be prepared by the landlord and given to the tenant. These reports detail the state of cleanliness and repair of the premises as at the time that you move in.

When you receive a condition report, check it in minute detail to ensure that you agree with it. Test all the windows, locks and doors. Turn on all the taps and flush the toilet. Check walls and floors for stains and cracks. Are there any holes in the carpet? Any defects not listed in the report could be blamed on you, and may result in you losing the bond when you move out.

If you did not receive a condition report ask for one. In the meantime draw up your own list and have it witnessed. Send a copy to the real estate agent. You may also wish to take photographs of any defects.

The Residential Tenancy Agreement

The residential tenancy agreement gives you the right to live in the landlord's premises. It also governs your duties, such as paying rent and keeping the place clean.

In some States, such as New South Wales and Victoria, the form and content of the agreement is dictated by law. In other States, residential tenancies legislation sets minimum conditions which cannot be overridden by the landlord.

Wherever you live, make sure the agreement that you sign is the one published by the Real Estate Institute in your State. Read it through thoroughly before you sign – most residential tenancy agreements are in plain English and not too hard to understand. If you are uncertain, consult a tenant's advice service, particularly if any deletions, alterations or additions have been made to the standard form.

Tenant's advice services

Tenant's advice services can provide free legal information for tenants who are unsure of their rights. Some services are part of government departments such as the Department of Consumer Affairs. Others are bodies like unions. The bodies in 1.2 Sources of Legal Advice may be able to help you, if not they can direct you to appropriate advice services.

BONDS

A bond is money paid by a tenant before moving into the premises, usually equal to four weeks rent. A bond is given to a landlord or agent to cover a breach of the tenancy agreement.

You may be wondering what stops the landlord from simply keeping the money. In some States the money has to be lodged with a government authority, such as the Rental Bond Board in New South Wales or the Rental Bond Authority in Queensland. If the landlord tries to claim the money without the tenant's agreement, the tenant will be notified.

In other States, such as Victoria, the landlord must lodge the money in a trust account with an approved institution. In Western Australia, the money can be either paid to the bond administrator or placed in a trust account. A receipt must be given to the tenant in all jurisdictions.

Receiving a bond refund

When you move out, you are entitled to get the bond back if:

- you have paid the rent up to date;
- you have left the place in a similar condition to when you moved in, not counting reasonable wear and tear; and
- you gave proper notice that you were leaving.

The procedure for claiming a refund varies between States. Where there is a bond authority, a joint application is made by the landlord and tenant. Where there is a trust account, the landlord must either refund the money or else give notice to the tenant of their intention to claim the money.

Disputes as to who is entitled to keep the bond money are heard by the Residential Tenancies Tribunal, or the Small Claims Tribunal in States such as Western Australia and Queensland. You will need your copy of the condition report or your witnessed list of defects to defend any claims by the landlord that you have damaged their property.

RENT INCREASES

Whether the landlord can increase the rent depends on the type of tenancy you have and the laws of your State.

Landlords cannot raise the rent during a fixed-term lease. For periodic tenancies, the number of times that the rent can be raised is usually restricted. For most States, it cannot be increased more often than every six months and 60 days notice is required.

Excessive rent increases can be discussed with the landlord. If that does not help, you may wish to complain to consumer affairs or the Residential Tenancies Tribunal. Do not delay, as time limits for challenging increases are quite short. You will have to show that the rent is high compared to similar properties in your area.

THE LANDLORD'S RIGHT TO ENTER

Your most important right as a tenant is the right to the "quiet enjoyment" of the property. This legal expression does not mean that the landlord must ensure that the premises cannot be noisy. Rather, it means that you are protected from unnecessary intrusion by the landlord or real estate agent. It also means you have the same right as owners to complain about noise (see 13.2 Noise and Odours) and to deal with trespassers (see 12.7 Dealing with Trespassers).

The landlord can enter at any time if you give your consent, but otherwise their right to enter is restricted to the terms of the residential tenancy agreement. Generally, a landlord can enter:

- where urgent repairs are required in an emergency;
- in order to carry out routine repairs and maintenance;
- to inspect the premises;
- to show the premises to potential buyers or tenants.

Unless there is an emergency, the landlord must give notice and can only enter at a reasonable time. The period of notice differs depending on the purpose of the visit and the particular laws of your State.

THE STATE OF REPAIR

When you move into a residence, it should be in a condition fit for human habitation, and it is the landlord's duty to ensure this.

Tenants' obligations

Tenants are obliged to keep the premises clean. You must leave the place in the same condition that you found it – but allowance is made for the reasonable wear and tear that occurs with time.

Tenants must not damage the landlord's property, neither intentionally nor unintentionally. If you are a tenant, you are liable for any damage caused by your visitors.

If you wish to attach a fixture, you should obtain the landlord's consent. A fixture is an object which is attached to the property, such as a wall hanging. In order to take it with you when you leave, you must be able to remove it so that the premises are undamaged and left in their original condition.

Landlords' obligations

The landlord is obliged to maintain the premises and keep it in a reasonable state of repair. For non-urgent repairs (such as a loose tile), inform the landlord in writing. Putting it in writing could protect you from losing your bond if you leave before the repairs are carried out.

Urgent repairs include things such as gas leaks, serious electrical faults and burst water services. Contact the agent and confirm your request in writing. If the landlord does not carry them out, you might be able to arrange for the repairs yourself (although there may be some monetary limit) and then seek compensation.

ENDING A TENANCY

Fixed-term tenancies

Leaving before a fixed-term tenancy has expired can be costly. You may have to pay rent up until the expiry date unless a new tenant can be found. There is an exception where the landlord has breached the tenancy agreement – for example, by not carrying out necessary repairs. In this case, you can give notice of your intention to leave (usually 14 days) and state the reason.

Landlords also have rights to end a tenancy where the tenant has breached the agreement – for instance, by falling behind on rent or carrying out alterations without consent. If you correct the breach you may be able to stay on.

Seek advice if you are told that you have to leave because the premises are being sold. Generally you will have to go if you are given adequate notice, but the laws of some States give further protection to tenants.

If you wish to leave at the end of the term, do not simply move out on the last day. Notice should still be given, otherwise the fixed-term tenancy may turn into a periodic tenancy. In New South Wales 14 days' notice is needed.

Periodic tenancies

You do not need to have a reason to end a periodic tenancy. All you need to do is to give proper notice. As the notice period varies markedly depending on circumstances and the laws of your State, you should always check it. In New South Wales tenants need to give 21 days notice.

Eviction proceedings

Staying on after a tenancy has been lawfully terminated could result in eviction proceedings. The landlord cannot simply come and physically throw the tenant out, nor change the locks while the tenant is absent. Proceedings must be commenced before the Residential Tenancies Tribunal or before a court in jurisdictions without a tribunal.

Tenants are given notice of the hearing and an opportunity to defend their position. To succeed, a tenant would have to show that:

- they did not breach the residential tenancy agreement; or
- adequate notice to leave was not given.

It may be possible to be granted extra time to help find other accommodation.

12.2 BUYING A HOME

ARRANGING FINANCE

Before you commit yourself to buying a home, it is important to have your finances arranged. Unless the contract contains a clause which makes it subject to finance, you may be sued if you back out. Talk to a bank or building society to get an idea of how much money you can borrow – and then go house hunting armed with that knowledge.

For information on arranging a loan see 12.4 Home Loans.

Keep in mind that when you buy a home there are many ancillary expenses, such as:

- the lender's home loan fees;
- legal fees;
- stamp duty on the home loan;
- stamp duty on the purchase of the house;
- contribution to rates;
- contribution to land tax if applicable;
- home insurance;
- costs of moving.

Your bank or building society can help you plan for these costs.

FINDING THE HOME

Real estate agents

Estate agents act for the seller. It is their job to make the property sound as impressive as possible. They are not obliged to point out any faults or weaknesses in the condition of the building or land. It is therefore up to you to protect yourself – see Before You Sign below.

However, if an agent makes a false or misleading statement that induces you to buy a house you otherwise would not have bought, you may be able to take action. The statement must have been something material and objective (such as the size of the block) rather than an opinion (such as saying it is the nicest house on the street).

Auctions

Most houses bought at an auction are subject to a reserve price – auctioneers do not have authority to sell under this price. Agents cannot disclose the reserve price, so you should check what similar properties go for in that area. It is a good idea to attend a few auctions to help familiarise yourself with the procedures.

If you buy your home at an auction you are immediately committed and have to hand over the deposit on the spot (usually 10 percent of the purchase price). Cooling off periods (discussed below) do not apply, so you should make sure that you have finance approval.

Also make sure all the necessary checks have been carried out, and it is best to have the contract checked by a solicitor. Make sure that the copy of the contract you had checked is an exact copy of the auction contract, and that no last minute changes have been made. Also keep in mind that there is a possibility that you will be outbid after having incurred expenses.

Making an offer

For houses sold privately, purchasers usually make an offer lower than the asking price. When both buyer and seller agree, the purchase price is set. The estate agent will usually ask for a holding deposit as a sign of good faith. As long as you do not sign a contract, the holding deposit is not binding and is refundable if you change your mind.

The other side of the coin is that the seller (also called the vendor) is free to sell to anybody else who makes a better offer. Gazumping, as this is known, occurs most often during a booming property market.

MORE THAN ONE PURCHASER

If you are buying with another person you have to decide which system of ownership you prefer. There are two:

- joint tenants;
- tenants in common.

Joint tenants

Married couples usually buy their home as joint tenants. Under this system, when one partner dies the survivor automatically owns the entire property. A joint tenant cannot give their share to somebody else in their will unless and until they are the surviving partner, in other words, when they become the sole owner.

Tenants in common

To leave your share of the property independently in your will you have to be a tenant in common. This system of co-ownership is often preferred by friends or business partners who purchase property together.

SHOULD YOU USE A LAWYER?

Once you have arranged a loan and found a house or unit you would like to buy, it is time to decide who will do the conveyancing. Conveyancing is the term for transferring your name onto the title deeds.

Using a lawyer

A lawyer's expertise is useful, particularly in checking the contract. They recognise irregularities and can take action before they escalate into a major problem. And if something goes wrong causing you to lose money, you may be able to claim compensation from your solicitor if he or she was negligent: see 2.1 Lawyers.

Conveyancing firms

Conveyancing firms are a relatively new option in some States. They tend to be less expensive than lawyers. Residents of South Australia and Western Australia can use the long-established land brokers and land agents.

Doing it yourself

Many people choose to do their own conveyancing. If you wish to do this it is in your interests to read up as much as you can. Be prepared to do a lot of running around.

Conveyancing kits are a good idea. They include detailed instructions and forms, and also have a query service so you can ask for advice when you need it. Not all States have them, but for those that do, contact:

- Law Consumer's Association in New South Wales;
- Consumer Law Reform Association in Victoria;
- Do It Yourself Legals in Queensland.

If you want a lawyer's advice but are worried about legal costs, talk to a solicitor about sharing the work. Your solicitor can check the contract and you can do the routine leg work such as ordering searches and filing documents.

BEFORE YOU SIGN

Undoubtedly you have heard the phrase "caveat emptor" or let the buyer beware. Generally when buying a home this applies to the quality of the property – in most States the vendor has no legal obligation to warn you if the house is in poor condition. So it is up to you to check for yourself before you sign a contract.

Building and pest reports

These reports will indicate any faults in the property such as rising damp, cracks, and termite infestations. They will also provide an idea of the cost of rectification. Inspection firms can be found in the *Yellow Pages*.

What exactly are you buying?

Which household items will you retain? Curtains, light fittings and carpets usually remain with the house, but you should know exactly what is included and make sure they are listed in the contract.

Confirm your finances

The importance of arranging finance before you sign a contract cannot be overstressed.

CONVEYANCING PROCEDURES

Check the laws in your State

Laws vary markedly between States, and if you do your own conveyancing you should always check the position in your State. The following description is merely a general guide to the types of issues to look out for.

The contract

Contracts for the sale of land are in a standard form, published by the Law Society and the Real Estate Institute. Signing the contract does not make you the owner, but it does mean that you promise to buy.

The sorts of things that must be checked in a contract include:

- particulars – the particulars are the details describing the parties, the property and the purchase price. Check that they are all correct;
- the terms – the terms of the contract outline the procedures that must be followed and specify what will happen if either party defaults. Read the contract carefully, preferably with the help of a lawyer. Be particularly alert if changes have been made to the standard terms;
- insurance – this is something you should check. In some States the buyer is responsible for the property as from the date the contract is signed. If so, insurance should be taken out. In States such as New South Wales the vendor is responsible until the sale is completed, and the buyer does not need to take out insurance until that date. It may be different if you decide to move in before completion.

Disclosures by the vendor

Most States require the vendor to provide certain information. In some States vendors must warrant that their land is unaffected by certain matters unless disclosed.

In New South Wales, the following documents should be attached to the contract:

- a copy of the title;
- a copy of the plan;
- a copy of any instrument creating restrictions (eg right of way);
- sewerage and drainage certificate;
- zoning certificate;
- a copy of the strata plan (for strata units).

Vendors in New South Wales also need to disclose any government body proposals affecting the land that they are aware of (eg a proposal to widen the road).

In Victoria vendors must provide purchasers with a statement before the contract is signed. The statement will give details of matters such as planning, services and notices affecting the property. A copy of the title deed must be attached.

Cooling off period

In some States you can change your mind without giving a reason after you have signed the contract. You only have a limited number of days to do this, for example five days in New South Wales, three in Victoria. The length of time that you have is known as the cooling off period.

The cooling off period does not apply in certain situations, for instance if you bought at an auction, or in some cases if the property is under or over a certain price. Vendors sometimes refuse to sell unless a certificate waiving the cooling off period is signed.

Searches

These vary between States. Generally various searches and checks need to be done:

- title search – searches must be made at the land titles office to check that the vendor is on title and has the right to sell the property;
- government proposals – inquires should be made of various government departments to ensure there are no proposals affecting the land;
- survey – surveys identify the land, disclose overlaps of neighbouring buildings on the land (these overlaps are called encroachments) and disclose breaches of council requirements.

Exchange of contracts

Both the vendor and the purchaser sign their counterpart of the contract and then swap them. This process is known as exchange. Once contracts have been exchanged both parties are bound.

The contract's deposit is usually paid on exchange. Note that this is not the same as a holding deposit which is paid before exchange as a sign of good faith. If the buyer backs out of the contract without a legally valid reason, they may forfeit (lose) the deposit.

Settlement

Settlement (also called completion) is the last stage of the sale. The balance of the purchase price is paid in return for the title documents. Your home loan provider will get the title deeds, the transfer and the discharge of the vendor's mortgage and lodge them – making you the owner. The keys to the home are usually handed over at the settlement.

Notices of the settlement are then sent to various bodies such as the local council, the Water Board and the Valuer General, informing them that you are now the owner.

Remember to arrange connections of gas, electricity and the telephone. Home insurance should now be taken out if this is not already done. 12.5 Home Insurance provides more details.

12.3 BUILDING A HOME

Crossing your fingers and hoping is not enough when you are building a new home or renovating. You need to know how to prevent problems by making wise choices; and how to handle problems if they do arise.

CHOOSING A BLOCK OF LAND

When building a new home this first step can be the most important, so inspect the block carefully before deciding to buy. Too many people buy land expecting paradise but end up with a patch that is low in value or, worse, unhealthy and toxic.

To ensure that you make the right decision, you should:

- obtain a property report that describes the physical condition of the land;
- ask the local council what the land was used for previously;
- speak to local residents;
- compare the price to that of similar blocks in the area;

- check whether gas, electricity, water and sewage services exist;
- talk to an architect or builder about the suitability of the land for the building you had in mind.

CHOOSING BUILDERS AND ARCHITECTS

Personal recommendations are always the best. If you see a house you admire, you could ask the owners who built it. Or you could examine the work of builders that you find through advertisements in local papers and the *Yellow Pages*. Industry associations such as the Master Builders Association can give further advice.

Project home builders have standard designs that can be examined at display home villages. If you want something out of the ordinary, consult an architect.

It is a good idea to check with the builders registration authority (a government body) whether any complaints have been lodged against the builder.

Licensing and registration requirements

Different States and Territories have different laws requiring the licensing and/or registration of builders. You can check the position in your State with the builders registration authority. In areas where licences are compulsory (such as New South Wales, South Australia and Queensland) it is not enough to check that the builder has a licence. Various classes of licences exist, and you should ensure that the builder is licensed to carry out the type of work that you have in mind.

In Victoria, builders cannot enter into a contract to perform work unless a guarantee by the Housing Guarantee Fund is in force. This guarantees the performance of the builder's obligations under the contract.

Some States have compulsory insurance schemes, for instance New South Wales, South Australia and Queensland. The type of protection the house owner receives depends on the laws in their State. As an example, New South Wales owners are protected for three years for all defects except wear and tear, and for seven years against major structural defects.

COUNCIL REQUIREMENTS

Local councils regulate the construction of buildings and extensions. Various requirements must be met. For instance, the building cannot be too far forward on the block nor oversized.

It is important that you receive council approval for the building before you sign a contract with a builder. Unless there is a clause in the contract saying that it is subject to council approval, you could be bound by a contract for a house that you are not allowed to build. The builder may have the right to sue you for damages for breach of contract.

NOTIFYING THE TAX OFFICE

If the work done costs over $10,000 you need to notify the tax office of the payments you made to the builder. This is known as prescribed payments system tax.

OWNER BUILDERS

If you have experience in building you may wish to manage the project yourself, and hire sub-contractors to do the work. Being an owner builder is stressful and time consuming, and you will often be needed on site. In some States you need a permit to be an owner builder.

You are responsible for the work, so you should talk to an insurance company about taking out the following types of insurance:

- workers compensation;
- public risk;
- works in progress (in case the work is destroyed eg by fire);
- materials and loose tools – to protect against vandalism and theft;
- personal insurance;
- comprehensive insurance is compulsory in some States, and it protects not the owner builder but anyone who buys the home within a set number of years.

BUILDING CONTRACTS

As the laws vary so greatly between States, there is no national standard contract. Even within States, different contracts are in use.

Standard contracts are published by the Master Builders Association and the Housing Industry Association. Contracts are also available from some government agencies, for example New South Wales and Queensland. The "Plain English" contracts that are gaining popularity are preferable. In New South Wales the Plain English contract is expressed in simple clear terms, and is produced by the input of building industry associations, the Australian Consumers Association and Standards Australia.

Sometimes non-standard contracts are provided by the builder. This is often the case if you buy a project home.

Whichever contract you end up using, read it carefully. If you do not understand any part of it, seek advice from an independent architect or a lawyer experienced in building contracts.

As a general guide, you should pay attention to the following items:

The price

It is best to get a fixed price. Sometimes "provisional sums" are added for matters which cannot be determined by the builder until work actually begins – for instance, rocks may need to be dug up to lay down pipes. Be careful. You may be given a good initial price, but then be hit with a large bill for the provisional sum.

If you prefer to avoid provisional sums, you could obtain a geotechnical report and give it to the builder.

An allowance may have been made for items put into the home (such as ovens and toilets) known as "prime costs". Make sure the sum is reasonable by shopping around to compare prices. If you prefer, you can buy the items yourself and ask the builder to install them.

You can save some money by arranging to do some of the work yourself – such as painting or wallpapering.

Cooling off period

Plain English contracts in some States are unique in that they have a cooling off period. After signing, you have a certain number of days to change your mind and get out of the deal.

In South Australia, statute law provides owners with the right to give notice of their intention not to be bound by the contract within five business days of signing. The builder can get an order that the owner pay for any work already done or material supplied.

The deposit

Most States have legal limits on the amount of the deposit. Check with the builders registration authority, and do not pay more than the maximum legal deposit.

Progress payments

For large jobs payment is not made as one lump sum, but in stages. Payment should relate to a stage of the work being completed, not the passing of time. Generally the stages are:

- base stage;

- frame stage;
- lock-up stage;
- fixing stage.

Before making a progress payment, it is wise to get an independent inspection by an architect or building inspection firm. If there are any defects, insist that they are corrected before you pay.

Time for completion

Clauses that specify a date for completion should be included. It will protect you against builders who accept a deposit and then vanish for weeks before getting on with the job. But if the delay is not the builder's fault, for instance if it is due to bad weather or material shortages, the builder will normally be entitled to an extension of time. Ask the builder to specify the new completion time.

Liability for defects

In some States it is compulsory to have a clause making the builder liable for defects. If it is not try to have one included. Defects liability clauses specify a period after completion in which you can notify the builder of any defects. They have to be fixed without extra charge. Ring the builder, but make sure you follow it up in writing.

RESOLVING DISPUTES

If you are dissatisfied with the work, discuss it with the builder as soon as possible. There may be a valid reason that you are not aware of – if your concern is delays, then perhaps the builder is waiting for materials. If you think the work is defective, you could call the council to see if it meets legal requirements or you could call an architect or building inspection firm.

If you are unsatisfied with the reply, put your complaint in writing. Allow the builder a reasonable time to deal with it, and if you do not receive a satisfactory reply, you can talk to the builder's registration agency about lodging a complaint.

The usual procedure is that an official will meet you and the builder on site to attempt to resolve the dispute. An order can be made requiring the builder to repair or complete the work. Failure to obey could result in disciplinary action being taken.

Some States have building disputes tribunals that can hear the dispute. For general information see 4.3 Complaints and Tribunals. Or you may be able to use mediation or arbitration to resolve your dispute. These processes are described in 4.1 Out of Court Solutions.

You may be able to make a claim on the builders insurance scheme — depending on the laws of your State.

12.4   HOME LOANS

Home loans are likely to be the largest expenditure in your life. As such, it is important that you know as much as you can about them and their consequences, and that you shop around.

A home loan (also called a mortgage) is a loan where a financial institution lends money against the value of the property. If you (the mortgagor) cannot pay the money back to the lender (the mortgagee) they may have the right to sell the property to recover their loan.

WHAT COMES FIRST – THE HOUSE OR THE LOAN?

Never sign a contract to buy a house before you have written approval of finance. Unless the contract contains a subject to finance clause, you might be sued if you back out because you cannot get a loan. It is possible to find a house you like first and then approach a lender, but the delays may cause you to lose the house if the market is booming. The best method is to see a lender first and get an idea of how much you can borrow.

SOURCES OF FINANCE

Banks and building societies are the main sources. Some credit unions and cooperatives also offer home loans to members. Mortgage originators or brokers are a growing source — some offer their services through real estate agents. Some employers have special schemes for staff members, often as part of a salary package.

Private lenders are sometimes willing to make loans when conventional lenders refuse. They should be viewed with caution, however, as interest rates may be significantly higher. If you are considering such a loan, it is advisable to seek legal advice before committing yourself.

Sometimes the seller of the property is willing to allow purchasers to pay the purchase price in instalments. This is called vendor finance. Again, you need to be careful here. Do you become the owner immediately, or when all the instalments have been paid? It is important to seek independent advice if you are considering using vendor finance.

First-time home buyers may qualify for government assistance if their income is below a certain figure. The department of housing in your State can give further details.

WHAT IS EQUITY?

Your equity in the house is the amount you paid out of your own money. The amount you borrowed from the bank is known as the principal sum. Your early repayments will be paying off the interest on the loan, but as time goes by you will start to pay back the principal sum. As this happens, your equity in the property increases.

TYPES OF HOME LOANS

Spend some time shopping around to find which type of loan best suits your needs. Call on several financiers and discuss their interest rates, fees and repayment requirements.

A brief guide to understanding what is available can help you with your task:

Variable rate loans

The interest rate goes up and down in line with market forces. Most are for 25 years with monthly repayments, but many lenders allow fortnightly or even weekly repayments which lessen the term of the loan. Each instalment contains both interest and principal repayments. Early repayment of the loan is generally not penalised by the imposition of additional costs.

Fixed rate loans

The interest rate is fixed for a specified period of time, usually one to five years. Repayments generally are interest only and remain the same throughout that period. At the end you need to either repay the principal or refinance the loan.

Fixed rate loans may be to your advantage when variable interest rates are rising, but the possibility of them falling must be considered. Fixed rate loans usually have charges imposed for early repayment.

Capped loans

Several lenders offer loans at a low interest rate for a set period of time, often six months. At the end of that time it becomes an ordinary variable rate loan. The low interest period is "capped" meaning the rate cannot increase but can decrease.

Home loan application fees

While comparing different interest rates on offer, keep in mind that you will also have to pay the lender a fee for processing your application. The amount charged varies.

APPLYING FOR A LOAN

The lender's requirements

You should take as much information with you as you can to your meeting with the lender. If you go to a bank or building society, you do not usually need to have an account with them to apply for a home loan.

The lender will tell you their precise requirements, but as a general guide they will want to see:

- proof of identity – such as passport, driver's licence, birth certificate;
- income details – recent payslips and group certificates (applicants who are self-employed may need to take past tax returns);
- a list of assets and their value – include details of your car, accounts, investments, shares etc;
- details of what you owe – such as credit card accounts, personal loans, car loans;
- your budget – how much you spend per month on food, clothing, entertainment etc.

If you are buying the property with another person, the lender will also need to see their income and expenditure details.

How much can you borrow?

The exact amount cannot be determined until after you have found the house or unit you wish to buy.

This is because the lender will insist on carrying out their own valuation of the property – and they are generally unwilling to lend more than 80 percent of their valuation. If you obtain mortgage insurance they may lend up to 95 percent of the valuation (see Home Loan Insurance below).

Your income and expenditure details will also be taken into account in deciding how much you can borrow. Lenders want to be sure you can repay the loan. Generally they will not approve a home loan if you need to spend more than 25 percent to 30 percent of your earnings to make the repayments.

HOME LOAN INSURANCE

There are two types of home loan insurance serving very different purposes.

Mortgage insurance

Mortgage insurance protects the lender. It exists to help people who cannot save up for a deposit, but are able to meet repayments. The borrower pays a one-off premium to an insurance company equal to about 1 percent of the loan. This protects the lender from losses if the property ends up being sold because the borrower cannot meet repayments. As a result they are willing to lend more, often up to 95 percent of their valuation.

Mortgage providers often have a list of approved insurers. One of the largest is the currently government-owned Housing Loan Insurance Corporation.

Mortgage protection insurance

This type of insurance is different. It protects the borrower and their family. If the person responsible for making the repayments dies or becomes permanently disabled, the insurer will help pay off the home loan balance. The amount of the premium depends on various factors, including the age and state of health of the policy holder.

SECOND MORTGAGES

Where more money is required it may be possible to get a second mortgage. Second mortgages are more difficult to obtain than first mortgages. This is because if there is a forced sale by the lenders to recover their money, the second mortgagee will only be paid if there is any money left after the first mortgagee has been paid. As a result of this increased risk the interest rate charged will tend to be higher.

SELLING YOUR HOME

It is not necessary to fully pay off your home loan before selling your home. If the lender is willing, you can transfer your loan to the purchaser. This is generally not a good idea, as you will still be responsible for making repayments if the purchaser defaults. And many banks and building societies are not willing to consent to such a deal.

The most common method is to repay your loan with the proceeds of the sale. The mortgage is then discharged (released) as far as you are concerned. The purchaser can make arrangements with their own lender for their own home loan.

Bridging loans

You may find a house you wish to buy before you sell your current one. It is possible to do this by taking out a bridging loan. But a word of warning – you are paying interest on two loans. If you have trouble selling your house, repayments may become difficult. This could force you to sell your house quickly at a lower price than you anticipated.

REPAYMENT DIFFICULTIES

The extreme step of a forced sale (known as foreclosure) is rare. Lenders are reluctant to foreclose on a mortgage unless it is obvious that there is no other way that they can recover their debt.

All that concerns a lender if there is a foreclosure is that they recover their money. The result could be that the house sells for less than it otherwise would. As you only receive money if there is some left over, you could be left seriously out of pocket.

People have problems meeting repayments for various reasons – they may lose their job or fall ill. If this happens it is important to notify the lender as soon as possible. The lender may be willing to reduce the amount or the frequency of payments until you are back on your feet again.

12.5   HOME INSURANCE

Many people dutifully take out home insurance but do it blindly – only to receive a nasty shock when they lodge a claim. Failing to take out a suitable policy can cost you thousands, so it is important to shop around for the cover you need.

Insurance contracts are generally made up of three elements working together. Be sure to consider each when comparing policies. The elements are:

- the proposal – the form you fill in to apply for the policy;
- the policy – often a booklet, it sets out the general terms and conditions that apply;
- the schedule – once the policy is processed, the schedule describes what is covered and the amount of the premium.

SHOPPING FOR INSURANCE

Compare three or four different insurance companies. Premiums can vary markedly, as can the extent of the cover.

Remember that insurance companies will try to sell you their product. You can visit an insurance broker who gives independent advice if you are prepared to pay their fee.

TYPES OF HOME INSURANCE

Home buildings insurance

Check the policy to see exactly what is covered, but generally home buildings insurance covers damage to structures such as houses, garages and carports. It also covers items permanently attached to the structures whether indoors or outdoors – for instance awnings, ovens and water heaters. Some policies also cover reasonable out-of-pocket expenses incurred if you cannot live in your home, such as the costs of temporary accommodation and moving furniture.

Buildings insurance is not compulsory by law but is wise for anybody who owns a house. If you have a mortgage it is likely that the lender will insist on it.

In the case of strata units, the body corporate is responsible for taking out buildings insurance but unit owners should check the coverage. If the body corporate's insurance is too low to adequately cover a damage claim, unit owners will have to make up the shortfall (refer to 12.6 Living in a Unit).

Tenants do not need to take out buildings insurance but they may wish to check that their landlord has done so. Tenants should, however, take out home contents insurance.

Home contents insurance

Contents are items that are not permanently attached to the building. When taking out contents insurance itemise what you own, estimating the cost of each item. Particularly important or valuable items such as jewellery or collectables may need to be given specific cover. Keeping receipts or obtaining valuations will assist any claims.

Some policies provide cover for contents outside the home or in storage. Read the terms carefully if you require this – often contents such as cash or items left in a car will be excluded.

Public liability insurance

This is often a component of standard home policies, but you should always check that it is adequate. If a person injures themselves or their belongings on your land you might be liable to compensate them (see 10.2 Accidents in Public Places and Homes). Note that the person who is

217

legally responsible is the occupier – the person whose name the property is in. This means that tenants as well as home owners should take out public liability insurance.

Domestic workers compensation

If you employ cleaners or someone to mow the lawn you should consider taking out domestic workers compensation. This applies whether you are a home owner or a tenant. Contractors working on your home should have both liability insurance and workers compensation, but if they do not you might be liable if they hurt themselves.

WHAT IS COVERED?

Do you know exactly what your insurance policy covers? Storm damage? Damage by animals? Keep the following points in mind when shopping for insurance. Existing policy holders should look at their current policies to decide if they really meet their requirements.

Listed events

Some policies list the events under which you can make a claim: fire, theft, lightning etc. Damage caused by anything not listed is not covered.

Excluded events

Other policies state that you are covered for damage caused by anything except for – and then they specify what is excluded: floods, vermin, war etc.

Often a combination of both is used. You are covered for certain events unless the stated exceptions apply. Read the information carefully and make sure you understand exactly what is covered by the policy.

WHAT ARE YOU COVERED FOR?

Would you be paid the price of replacing the damaged item or would a discount be made to reflect the age of what was damaged? It depends on the terms of your policy.

Agreed value policies

If you and the insurer agree on a set value, that amount is the most that will be paid out. The market value at the time of the claim does not come into it.

Indemnity policies

The insurance company will only pay the market value of the item. This may be rather low if the damaged item is old or obsolete.

Replacement policies

You may be given the cost of purchasing a new replacement for the item claimed. As this is generally better than indemnity cover, it tends to cost more.

APPLYING FOR INSURANCE

If buying a home, you should take out home buildings insurance from the day that you become responsible for the house. This varies between States. In some States it is when the contract is signed; in others it is when the matter is finally settled.

Home contents insurance should be taken out from the day you move in, whether it be a house or unit, and whether you are an owner or tenant.

Cover notes

Cover notes provide instant temporary cover. They can often be arranged over the telephone. Cover notes usually last for 14 days while the policy is being processed. If you then decide not to take out the policy it is likely you will have to pay the insurance company for the risk they assumed during the period of the cover note.

Full disclosure

Obviously you must give honest answers to the questions on the application form, but your duty to disclose goes beyond that. Anything that would influence the insurance company's decision to insure you is termed a "material fact" and needs to be disclosed.

Is there anything that you know about, or should reasonably know, that would affect your risk? For example have you ever had insurance refused? Is there anybody in your household with a criminal conviction for theft?

Insurance companies are obliged to inform you of your duty of disclosure. If you do not volunteer the necessary information the policy can be cancelled and the claim refused.

The duty to disclose is ongoing. If circumstances change since you took out the policy that might affect your risk, inform the insurance company in writing. Often if your home is unoccupied for a certain length of time you must notify the insurance company.

If they decide to cancel your policy as a result, they generally only keep a proportion of the premium you paid to cover themselves up until the date of cancellation, and refund what is left.

MAKING A CLAIM

Notifying the insurer promptly if damage occurs is important. Make a phone call as soon as possible and follow it up in writing. The insurance company will provide you with a claim form to fill in. If you were robbed you should also call the police.

An inspector will be sent by the insurance company to look at the damage. If it is covered:

- you may be paid the agreed value;
- you may be paid the cost of repair or replacement;
- the insurance company may pay the repairer directly.

It depends on the terms of the contract and the type of policy you have.

If you insure something for its full value and it is totally destroyed you may receive the full sum due. If it is only partly damaged, you may receive a lower sum reflecting the extent of the damage.

Damage caused intentionally

It is obvious but still worth stating – insurance companies will not pay out if the damage is found to have been deliberately caused for the purpose of making a claim.

Consequences of under-insuring

Under-insuring (to keep premiums low) can backfire. Insurance companies discourage under-insurance by inserting averaging clauses into their contracts. Averaging clauses operate by proportionately decreasing the amount paid out.

Usually the averaging process cannot operate for home buildings or contents policies if you have cover for at least 80 percent of the item's value.

To avoid inadvertently under-insuring you should increase the sum insured as time passes to keep up with inflation. Insurance companies generally recommend a figure.

Consequences of over-insuring

You cannot make a profit out of insurance. If you insure something for more than it is worth and then make a claim, you will only be paid according to the appropriate value – unless you have an agreed value policy, but it is unlikely that an insurance company will agree to an excessively high value.

Duty to cooperate

You have a duty to cooperate with your insurance company. This requires providing information and documents they may require.

If somebody did something to cause your loss, and the insurance company pays your claim, they take over the right to sue the person who caused loss. This is known as subrogation. In these cases you have a duty to cooperate with your insurer. You might need to attend court to give evidence.

Your insurer may want to defend you if it is alleged that you caused loss or damage to someone else. You must cooperate by sending them any notices or court documents you receive that might relate to a claim. Do not do anything to damage the case such as admitting liability.

12.6 LIVING IN A UNIT

In the past, it was not possible to own a unit outright. You could buy shares in a company which owned a block of flats, giving you the right to live in part of the building. Or several people could purchase a block jointly and allocate the flats. Often one person owned the entire block and sold long leases on individual units.

None of these arrangements gave residents full rights of ownership over their particular flat. Permission from the other "owners" was needed to sell or lease. Raising a mortgage was often difficult due to the lack of security.

It wasn't until the 1960s that the strata title system was introduced. People could finally own a unit in the same sense that they could own a house. In addition, they own a share in the common property – areas that can be used by all residents such as driveways, corridors and gardens.

Some of the older systems of unit ownership still exist, but the advantages of strata title have made it by far the most common. This chapter will focus on living in a strata title unit.

THE BODY CORPORATE

Blocks of strata title units are managed by the body corporate. The body corporate is made up of all the unit owners. Its duties include:

- holding annual general meetings;

221

- keeping records of meetings and correspondence;
- keeping financial records and statements;
- arranging insurance;
- keeping the building in a good state of repair;
- keeping the common property in a good state of repair;
- raising levies to enable it to carry out its duties.

It is not responsible for looking after individual units – that is the unit owner's responsibility.

The council

The council is a group of unit owners or nominees elected at annual general meetings to carry out the day to day functioning of the property. Councils are commonly used in large blocks of units where the body corporate is large.

The council is responsible for performing the same duties as the body corporate, although some decisions still need to be made by the whole body corporate.

Body corporate meetings

Unit owners can attend the annual general meetings in order to vote on decisions and have their say in how the block is being run. If they wish to raise issues at other times of the year, for instance to change by-laws (see below), they can ask the secretary of the council to hold an extraordinary general meeting. The percentage of votes needed to pass a decision varies depending on the type of decision and the laws of different states.

Managing agents

Body corporates often appoint managing agents to look after the block of units. Managing agents can carry out all or any of the body corporate's functions, including keeping accounts, arranging repairs and insurance. Some decisions require full body corporate approval.

Managing agents should have proper qualifications in strata management. They can be appointed or dismissed at annual general meetings.

BY-LAWS

By-laws are rules set down by strata titles legislation in each State. Some of the rules regulate the rights and responsibilities of the body corporate (described above) and generally these cannot be changed.

The remaining rules regulate the conduct of residents. Activities that may be forbidden include:

- owning a pet without body corporate permission;
- making noise that disturbs other residents;
- obstructing common property.

Depending on particular State laws, these by-laws can be amended at general meetings if sufficient agreement is reached.

CONTRIBUTING TO COSTS

Levies

The body corporate can collect money from unit owners for the purpose of looking after the common property. Different funds exist for different purposes.

The administrative fund covers general day to day expenses including:

- administration costs – such as stationery, business calls;
- maintenance costs – such as cleaning bills;
- fees to accountants, lawyers, and the managing agent;
- insurance payments.

The sinking fund covers future needs such as buying gardening tools and painting the common property.

If unexpected expenses arise, (for instance structural repairs), the body corporate should be able to use the money from these two funds. If it is not enough, however, it has the right to charge a special levy.

How is your contribution determined?

All unit owners must contribute to the funds and levies discussed above. But how is the amount that each pays determined?

Not all units in a block of flats are of equal size and value. Usually larger flats are required to contribute more than smaller flats. The figure used to calculate the different amount paid is called the unit entitlement. The unit entitlement can also effect body corporate voting rights, although this is not always the case.

INSURANCE

The body corporate's responsibility

Requirements vary between States, but generally the body corporate must take out insurance to cover:

- the building – this includes items permanently attached to the building (fixtures) such as carpets in common areas, cupboards, sinks and light fittings;

- public liability insurance – a person injured on common property might be able to sue the body corporate for their injuries. The body corporate needs to take out public liability insurance to cover this. For information on the liability of occupiers for injuries caused to visitors, see 10.2 Accidents in Public Places and Homes;

- workers compensation insurance should be taken out if the body corporate employs gardeners, cleaners etc to work on the property;

- if voluntary workers are used in the building or on common property, voluntary workers insurance should be taken out.

If the insurance cover is inadequate to meet a claim, the unit owners would be liable to meet the amount outstanding. Unit owners concerned about the level of insurance should raise the matter with the body corporate. If this does not help, a complaint can be made to the Strata Titles Commissioner or Referee in States such as New South Wales and Queensland (see Disputes below). Or extra insurance can be taken out by the unit owner to cover their own liability.

Unit occupier's responsibilities

The body corporate's insurance does not cover non-fixed items inside individual units. Occupiers of units should take out home contents insurance to cover their personal belongings.

You may be able to receive compensation for damage to your property caused by something that the body corporate is responsible for. An example of this situation is where a water pipe that runs inside the walls and services more than one flat (and is therefore common property) leaks and causes damage inside your unit.

Public liability insurance should be taken out to cover people injured inside the unit. If people are employed to work in the unit, such as cleaners, workers compensation insurance is also advisable.

For more details on insurance to be taken out by home owners or tenants, see 12.5 Home Insurance.

BUYING A UNIT

For general information on conveyancing, see 12.2 Buying a Home.

Purchasing a strata title unit requires some additional information:

- the by-laws should be read and understood;
- inspection of the body corporate's records should be arranged;
- the amount of the levies should be checked;
- are the levies adequate to meet expenditure, or is it likely that special levies will have to be raised?
- have council orders and regulations been met (for example fire stairs)?
- is the insurance cover taken out by the body corporate adequate?
- is there a managing agent? What are their qualifications?

You could arrange for a strata inspection before you buy. It should answer many of your questions and highlight any structural defects, giving you a good idea of future expenditure.

If the block of units has not been built and you are buying off the plan you could:

- examine other blocks built by the developer;
- speak to residents of these blocks to see if they have any complaints;
- speak to local real estate agents about both the developer's reputation and their opinion as to the location of the units;
- contact the builders registration authority in your State to see if complaints have been made against the builder (see 12.3 Building a Home).

DISPUTES

When people live in close proximity it is inevitable that disputes will flare up, either between residents or between a resident and the body corporate.

The dispute may be over whether an animal should be allowed to be kept, or whether improvements should be made to the property. The body corporate cannot unreasonably withhold its consent to requests made by unit owners. If the body corporate is not performing its legal responsibilities, such as maintaining the building in a good state of repair, action may be able to be taken to compel performance.

The steps that you can take in a dispute depend on the laws in your State. In some States complaints can be made to a strata titles official – in

New South Wales you can make a complaint to the Strata Titles Commissioner, in Queensland there is a Referee. In States where there is no strata titles official, legal action is pursued through the courts. Legal advice should be obtained in this case – one of the free legal advice centres described in 1.2 Sources of Legal Advice may be able to help.

The procedure for lodging complaints with strata titles officials varies between States, but generally complaints must be made in writing. The cause of complaint and the solution desired should be specified. An officer will interview the body corporate and unit owner, and may inspect the block of units.

Orders are made having regard to the interests of all unit owners. The use and enjoyment of their units and the common property will be taken into account. If an order is made it must be followed, or else fines are payable. It may be possible to appeal against decisions made by strata title officials.

12.7   DEALING WITH TRESPASSERS

A trespasser is someone who does not have the right to be on your property. This may sound obvious, but what is not quite so obvious is who has that right. Does a salesman? A council official? What about a police officer?

WHO IS A TRESPASSER?

Trespass is committed when:

- somebody enters your house or land without either your permission or official authority; or
- you initially allowed entry, but then revoked your permission and the person refuses to leave; or
- objects are left on your property without your consent.

Any person, such as a door-to-door salesman, has the right to enter your front gate, walk directly to your door and state their purpose. If you refuse entry, or allow it but then change your mind, they must leave. If they do not, they are trespassing.

Officials such as meter readers and council inspectors have a limited right to enter your land. They must have identification, and can only enter for the purpose of carrying out their official duties. For more information on the rights of government officials to enter, see 6.1 Dealing with Government Officials.

The situation regarding the police is more complicated. Police officers have a right of entry if they hold a valid search warrant. But the mere fact that they do not have a warrant does not automatically turn them into trespassers.

Generally, police can enter to arrest a suspect, or if they have reasonable grounds to believe a serious crime has been committed. In most States, they can enter even if a crime has not been committed, but they believe it soon will be – for instance to prevent anticipated domestic violence. The police powers of arrest, entry and search are discussed in more detail in 5.1 Dealing with the Police. Their powers to enter houses in domestic violence situations are discussed in 7.2 Domestic Violence.

REMOVING TRESPASSERS

A polite but firm request to leave is the best approach. Unfortunately, this does not always work and you are entitled to forcibly remove a trespasser.

How far can you go? Force that is taken too far is assault, giving the trespasser a right to sue and the police the ability to charge you with the crime of assault. Before you try to physically remove a trespasser, it is a good idea to call the police. If the police remove the trespasser it will protect you from allegations of assault. The police presence is also advisable for your own safety. Often the mere threat of calling the police is enough to convince a trespasser to go.

Reasonable force

If you do eject the trespasser yourself, only a reasonable degree of force can be used.

What is reasonable depends upon the danger that you are faced with. You can use the amount of force necessary to protect yourself from danger and remove the intruder – but no more. It would be over reacting to use a weapon such as a gun or a knife against an unarmed trespasser. If you are small and the trespasser is large, the use of a weapon might be reasonable if the trespasser tries to attack you – it all depends on the circumstances.

INJURY TO TRESPASSERS

If you used excessive force to eject a trespasser and they were injured in the process, they may be able to sue you for assault. Trespassers sometimes injure themselves while unlawfully entering or crossing somebody's property. For instance, they may fall in a ditch and hurt their back. For details of the liability of home owners and occupiers for injury caused to entrants see 10.2 Accidents in Public Places and Homes.

LEGAL ACTION

It is possible to sue for trespass. You can sue even if no damage was caused, but it would not be worth your while as the monetary compensation (also known as damages) you receive would be very low. If the trespasser did cause damage to your property, you can sue them for compensation. This may be worth your while if the property damaged was valuable. Keep in mind that litigation is expensive and complicated, and there are never any guarantees that you will win.

Mistake on the part of the intruder is no defence in a court case. They are liable to pay damages even if they mistakenly believed that they were on their own property. It would be a defence if they entered your land by accident, for instance if they were walking past and fell.

If the trespass occurs repeatedly, you can go to court for an order that it is to stop. This order is known as an injunction, and penalties can be imposed if it is breached. Again, the legal process is lengthy. If the situation is urgent, you can seek an "interim" or temporary injunction. This order is made quickly and lasts until a more complete investigation can be made.

Anybody seeking to take legal action for trespass, either to claim compensation for damage caused or to prevent it happening again, should consult a lawyer.

FURTHER READING

Bellemore, *Your Rights as a Tenant in New South Wales*, The Tenant's Union, Sydney, 1992

Bellemore, *Tenants' Rights Manual: A Practical Guide to Renting in New South Wales*, Pluto Press, Sydney, 1991

Libesman (ed), *The Housing Handbook*, Redfern Legal Centre Publishing, Sydney, 1992

McLagan, *An Introduction to Building Contracts*, Law Book Co, Sydney, 1991

Prokhovnik, *The Strata Titles Handbook*, Redfern Legal Centre Publishing, Sydney, 1992

Smith, *Is It A Lemon?: The Complete Guide to Buying a Home, a Car, a Boat*, Allen & Unwin, Sydney, 1994

Tenants' Rights Handbook, Tenants Union of Victoria, Melbourne

See also: General references listed in Further Reading Chapter 1.

Chapter 13

YOUR NEIGHBOURHOOD

13.1 DISPUTES WITH NEIGHBOURS

Neighbours live close enough together so that the activities of one can be a source of great annoyance to those around them. Disputes arise over everyday matters such as noise, fences and overhanging trees.

Handling disputes with neighbours requires more than an understanding of your legal rights – it requires a strategy that can solve the problem without souring future relationships.

HANDLING DISPUTES

Tact is important. You will have to continue to live next to your neighbours, and continuing conflict can be a constant source of strain.

A calm discussion is the best approach. Neighbours often do not realise they are being irritating, and most are happy to discuss a solution that suits you both. Be clear about the issue. To avoid misunderstandings, state exactly what it is that is causing the upset and propose a reasonable solution.

Mediation

If the matter is important enough to you and your approaches did not work, you may consider taking it further. Rather than immediately starting legal proceedings, it is a good idea to attend a dispute resolution centre such as a Community Justice Centre. Community Justice Centres exist in many States, and they use mediation to help resolve disputes.

Mediation involves discussing the problem with the help of an uninvolved third person known as a mediator. Mediators do not impose solutions on you. Instead, the mediator's aim is to facilitate discussions to help you and your neighbour reach a solution you are both happy with. More information on mediation and dispute resolution centres can be found in 4.2 Mediation.

If a solution cannot be reached, or if your neighbour continues to breach the agreement, you may decide to consider formal legal action.

COMMON DISPUTES

Noise

Disturbing noise caused by neighbours is one of the most common sources of dispute. The law relating to noise is described in 13.2 Noise and Odours.

Dividing fences

If there is no fence dividing two properties or if the existing fence is dilapidated, the question of building or repairing the fence is likely to be raised at some stage.

The fence should be placed on the boundary between the properties. Where the position of the boundary is in dispute, a survey can be ordered.

If you wish to repair or replace a fence, discuss it with your neighbour first. Obtain two or three quotes, as prices and standards can vary markedly.

What is the situation if your neighbours do not agree with your proposal?

That depends on the quality of the existing fence. If the fence is very dilapidated or affords no privacy, they may be required to pay half the cost of a standard paling fence. If you want a more expensive fence, you will probably have to bear the extra cost yourself. If the fence was damaged by either neighbour, the other usually does not need to contribute to the cost of repairs.

The situation may be that the existing fence is adequate but you just feel you would like a new one. If this is the case, you cannot force your neighbours to contribute to the cost of a new fence against their will.

You should also keep in mind that if you want to build a fence that is over the standard height (usually 1.8 metres) you may need to obtain council approval, especially if you live in a metropolitan area.

If the fence needs replacement or repair and the neighbours refuse to comply, you can give them a written notice that the work will be carried out and advising them as to their share of the cost. Taking photographs of the dilapidated fence might be a good idea if you ever need corroboration.

Some States prescribe specific forms that must be used for the notice, other States allow you to come up with your own wording. If there is no response to your notice within the set period, you can take further action to compel compliance. To determine the situation in your State, contact your local council or one of the free advice centres listed in 1.2 Sources of Legal Advice.

What happens if your neighbour initially agrees to share the cost, but then once the fence is built, they change their mind? The person who accepts the quote and enters the fencing contract is ultimately responsible to pay the bill.

If you entered into the contract and you refuse to pay the full sum to the builders, they may have the right to sue you for the remainder. To avoid the situation of then having to try to sue your neighbours to recover that sum, it is wise to request that they enter the fencing contract with you.

Shared driveways

Next-door neighbours sometimes share a single driveway. Neither has the right to obstruct the driveway by parking their car in it, nor by dumping rubbish on it.

Theoretically you have the right to remove obstructions that unreasonably prevent you from gaining access to your property. But you have to be careful. If you damage the obstruction while attempting to remove it, you might be liable for the damage caused.

Development of your neighbour's land

People sometimes object to development being carried out on a neighbour's property. They might be stopped if they are contravening planning or building laws, or if there is a legal restriction such as heritage controls or a covenant.

Neighbours usually have the right to be given notice of proposed developments and to make objections.

Overhanging trees

Branches or roots from a neighbour's tree may overhang or overlap onto your land. You have the right to cut them off at the boundary but no further.

It would be a good idea to tell your neighbour what you are planning and check that they have no objection. It would be even better if they were able to cut the branches or roots themselves. This would prevent you getting into trouble if too much is cut off and the tree dies.

Check tree preservation orders with your local council. If the tree is over a certain height, there may be pruning restrictions. Fines exist even if you are ignorant of the law.

Tree owners also have responsibilities. They may be liable for damage caused by a falling tree or branch if they could have exercised reasonable care to prevent the fall. For example, if the tree is diseased, often the danger could have been prevented. But if an otherwise healthy tree falls over in a freak wind storm, it is unlikely that the owner could be held liable.

Overlaps onto your land

Fences or buildings on your neighbour's land that overlap onto your land are known as encroachments. They are not merely an annoyance – they reduce your available space and the value of your land. What can be done?

First make sure that you are certain where the actual boundary lies. If you recently bought your house, you should have a survey which will identify the boundaries. If not, you may have to order a new one. Surveys can be expensive, particularly in rural areas, so you need to be fairly confident of your position.

With legal assistance, you can apply to a court for a remedy. If the encroachment is very minor (say a few centimetres) the court is unlikely to take any action. But if it is substantial, you can seek a variety of orders.

An order may be made that the encroaching structure be demolished. All the surrounding circumstances will be looked at, and if this is impractical an order for compensation may be made instead. Other possible solutions are the sale, lease or granting of a right of way over the affected land to your neighbour.

People entering your land

For a description of what to do if neighbours or other people enter your land without consent, see 12.7 Dealing with Trespassers.

Animals entering your land

Owners of animals that enter your property and cause damage may be liable for that damage. For more information about the responsibilities of animal owners, see 13.3 Animals.

Water entering your property

If water flows onto your land from your neighbour's land and causes damage, it is possible that you may have some legal rights. It depends on

232

the role played by your neighbour. If the flow is due to purely natural causes you may have no legal redress.

But if it is due to your neighbour's actions, you may have some redress. This would be the situation if your neighbour caused the flow, for instance by not unblocking their drains. They may also be liable if they changed their land in some way that interfered with the natural flow of water, for instance by concreting an area that was previously grass.

If damage was caused, you might be able to seek a court order for compensation. If the problem is a continuing one, it may be possible to obtain an order to prevent its re-occurrence.

13.2 NOISE AND ODOURS

Everybody at some stage has been disturbed by loud noises or offensive odours invading their property. Some degree of discomfort is an inevitable part of modern life, but if the interference is so great as to be unreasonable, there may be something you can do about it.

You might be able to sue under the law of nuisance or take action under a pollution statute.

THE LAW OF NUISANCE

Nuisance in the legal sense means something more than merely irritating. A nuisance is a material and unreasonable interference with somebody's comfort. It is not nuisance if the person complaining is unusually vulnerable or sensitive.

If a nuisance has been committed you might be able to sue for damages to compensate you for the intrusion. Or you may be able to seek an order that the interference stop (these orders are known as injunctions). A lawyer's advice is advisable.

The law of nuisance has two branches – public nuisance and private nuisance.

Public nuisance

Widely spread nuisances affect the public as a whole or a significant proportion of the public. To be able to sue for damages you need to show that you have a special interest in the matter. In other words, you suffered harm over and above that suffered by the general public, such as personal injury, property damage, or loss to your business' earnings.

Often a public nuisance is also a crime and is more conveniently dealt with by the criminal law.

233

Private nuisance

You are entitled to use your land without unreasonable interference from noise, odours, and fumes entering from neighbouring properties.

What is unreasonable depends on the character of the area. People living on major roads can expect to live with higher noise levels than people in a quiet cul de sac. If you live near a farm you can expect to smell farmyard odours from time to time. It is only when the problem is unreasonable that you have a right to take action for nuisance.

Other solutions to the problem – pollution statutes

Specific pollution statutes exist in all States to deal with common private nuisances such as noise and odours. It is easier, faster and cheaper to take action under these statutes than to sue under the law of nuisance. A brief description follows.

NOISE RESTRICTIONS

Laws vary significantly between States but the underlying principles are the same. New South Wales law is used here as the example. To determine how the laws in your State differ, contact your local council.

Residential premises

The use of domestic appliances is restricted at night if they can be heard in a neighbour's home. Regulations set out the times that certain types of noise audible in a neighbour's house can be made. For instance lawn mowers and power tools cannot be operated before 7:00 am Monday to Saturday and 8:00 am on Sundays and public holidays. Anything that makes excessive noise can be restricted at any time of the day or night.

Local councils can issue notices to control offensive noise. Noise is offensive if it is harmful or unreasonably interferes with the comfort of a person outside the place where the noise is coming from. Interference is judged as being unreasonable by looking at the time the noise was made and its intensity. Other factors such as duration and any special characteristics such as pitch or frequency can also make a noise offensive.

Laws vary between States, but in New South Wales if a house or shop alarm rings for over 10 minutes the police can enter to turn it off. If a car alarm sounds for over 90 seconds the owner may be fined.

Inherently noisy premises

Premises that are noisy by nature, such as factories and outdoor entertainment venues, have greater controls placed on them. They need approval from the local council or in some cases from the State environment protection authority. Complaints about excessive noise can be made to the relevant authority.

OFFENSIVE ODOURS

The type of action you can take depends on where the smell is coming from. Major factories and industrial polluters need licenses, and they must prevent the emission of odours.

If the smell comes from residential premises you can contact your local council. Regulations exist prohibiting various types of activity which create offensive odours, such as non-collection of dog droppings.

DEALING WITH THE PROBLEM

Discussion

First contact the neighbour causing the problem and explain the situation calmly and rationally. This is better than immediately leaping to legal solutions. Legal action can be costly and may cause bitterness and resentment, and you will still have to live near the neighbour afterwards.

Mediation

If your attempts to talk it through are futile, in some States you can go to a dispute resolution centre such as a Community Justice Centre for help. Community Justice Centres provide a mediation service to help solve neighbourhood disputes.

Mediation involves you and your neighbour discussing the problem in the presence of a neutral third person called a mediator. The mediator will not impose a decision on you, rather he or she will facilitate discussions to help you and your neighbour reach a solution you are both happy with. Dispute resolution centres and the process of mediation is discussed more fully in 4.2 Mediation.

Making a complaint

If the above methods fail you might want to consider making a complaint to the authorities. As laws vary significantly between States it is only possible to provide a general guide.

If the noise is a one-off, such as a loud party in the middle of the night, you can call the police. You can call before midnight if the noise is particularly intense or offensive. The police can order that the noise be stopped.

If the noise or odour problem is regular, such as a dog that barks every night, you can call the council. They will monitor the problem and will most likely interview the neighbours who are causing it. The council can issue orders suitable to the situation, such as requiring a barking dog to be confined during certain hours or that a soundproofed kennel be used. If the orders are not followed, fines can be imposed. You may be required to appear in court as a witness if the council takes legal action. Or you might be able to make a complaint to the State environment protection authority, depending on the type of problem and where it is coming from.

General information on making complaints can be found in 4.3 Complaints and Tribunals.

Legal action

If the relevant authority takes no action you might be able to commence private legal action through the Local Court (called Magistrates Courts in some States). It depends on the type of complaint and the laws of your State.

In some States you could seek a noise abatement order if you can show the court that the occupation of your home is affected by noise amounting to a nuisance. The order can require the noise to be reduced within a specified time, and that action be taken to prevent its recurrence.

If the noise or odour has caused damage (for instance damage to your garden or illness in a family member) you might be able to sue for compensation. Problems that are ongoing might be solved by a court order that the action is to stop. Such orders are known as injunctions.

If you are contemplating taking legal action a lawyer's advice is recommended. Contact either a private solicitor or one of the free legal advice services discussed in 1.2 Sources of Legal Advice.

13.3 ANIMALS

Laws exist throughout Australia governing the rights and responsibilities of pet owners, and dealing with others who do not own animals but come into contact with them.

WHAT PETS CAN YOU KEEP?

Not all animals can be kept as pets. And even with those you can keep, ownership is regulated by the law.

Native animals

Few native animals can be kept as pets. To find out which can be kept and what the rules are governing ownership, check with the national parks and wildlife authority in your State.

As a general rule, you are not permitted to go out and trap native animals. If you wish to own one you will need to buy one from a licensed dealer or breeder.

While driving or bushwalking it is not uncommon to come across injured or ill wildlife. If this happens contact the wildlife authority. You will very likely be advised to give the care of the animal to the experts. If you wish to care for it yourself, ask about training courses that will give you the skills to do so.

Dogs

Dog owners have various responsibilities, including:

- registering the dog with the local council – the age at which this needs to be done varies between States, but is usually when the puppy is three to six months. You should check with the council. In New South Wales the age is six months;
- keeping the dog on a leash when it is away from home. Some councils have special areas where dogs can run free with their owners;
- cleaning up after the dog if it defecates in a public place.

Owners who fail to carry out these responsibilities can be fined. The New South Wales *Dog Act* has recently been amended to introduce larger on-the-spot fines. Council officers or the police can issue penalty notices, or take the owner to court. The court can impose a much larger fine.

Dogs that are wandering unleashed may be picked up by council officers. In New South Wales you have 14 days to claim your dog if it is registered or seven days if it is unregistered. After that time the dog might be sold or destroyed.

Dogs are not allowed in some places at all, such as in school grounds and within a certain distance of children's playground equipment.

Guide dog owners do not face the same restrictions as other dog owners. They can take their dog to any public place or on public transport. In some States it is an offence to prevent a blind person with a guide dog from entering such places.

Other animals

While some councils have adopted guidelines handling the keeping of animals, few regulations exist for animals that are not dogs, not native and not wild.

But the position regarding cats is in a state of change. Guidelines have been drawn up that may be adopted as law. It is not certain at the time of writing, but cat owners may soon be required to:

- register cats;
- desex them; and
- obey a cat curfew.

Your local council will be able to tell you whether there are any regulations in force for cats or other animals.

INJURIES CAUSED BY ANIMALS

Are owners responsible for injuries caused by their animals? If you own a domestic animal you will usually only be liable if it can be shown that you were somehow at fault. That is, if you were negligent or failed to control the animal properly.

Negligence can be established if it is shown that you knew the animal had a tendency to cause damage but still allowed it to enter such a situation.

The degree of control that can be exercised over an animal depends on the type of animal. Cat owners know that it is virtually impossible to stop cats from jumping fences into neighbouring properties. But if you know your cat is aggressive towards children you have to keep it away from children who visit you.

A much greater degree of control is expected to be exercised over dogs, because dogs can cause significantly more damage than cats, and dogs can be effectively controlled with adequate fencing.

Dogs

Dog owners may be responsible for injuries caused by their dog. Dogs should be kept on leashes in public places, and should not be able to wander off their property. If you have a guard dog it is a good idea to put up warning signs, but keep in mind that if a child too young to read strays onto your land, a sign may be of little use.

In most States farmers have the right to shoot dogs on their fenced property that worry livestock. In some States the right is automatic, in others they have to apply for a court order.

The exact responsibility of dog owners varies from State to State. The law in New South Wales can be used as a guide, but residents of other States should check the law with their local council. Vets and dog breeders may also know the legal position.

Under the New South Wales *Dog Act*, if a dog attacks outside its property:

- the owner may be liable for injury to a person, clothing, or an animal, whether or not the owner was at fault;
- the owner may be fined;
- the owner may be ordered to take steps to control the dog, such as putting up a proper fence;
- the dog might be declared "dangerous" (see below);
- the dog might be destroyed.

If the dog attacks within the boundaries of its own property the council may have the dog declared to be dangerous. Owners are notified before such a declaration is made and they have the chance to be heard.

If a dog is declared to be dangerous:

- an appropriate warning sign must be put up on the property;
- the dog must always be leashed when outside its property;
- the dog must be restrained when on its own land to prevent it from attacking people or other animals.

If a dog declared dangerous still attacks, it can result in:

- a large fine;
- an order to muzzle the dog;
- an order that the dog be destroyed.

Sometimes dogs are provoked into attacking, for instance if its owner is being attacked, it is being treated cruelly, or if it is seeing off a trespasser. In these cases the *Dog Act* measures may not apply.

NOISE AND NUISANCE

Common complaints associated with animals are concerned with noise and nuisance. Dogs barking are a common noise complaint. "Nuisance" does not mean merely irritating, it has a technical legal meaning. A nuisance is something that unreasonably interferes with the use or enjoyment of your land or home.

See 13.2 Noise and Odours for information on these two topics.

IMPORTING AND EXPORTING ANIMALS

Importing

Restrictions exist on the importation of animals. Animals can only be imported from specific countries, and even then there is a quarantine period that must be observed. Quarantine periods vary depending on the country of origin, but they typically last several months. The main disease quarantine tries to prevent from entering the country is rabies; Australia is one of the few countries in the world that is rabies-free.

Exporting

Export bans exist on most native animals.

If you are moving overseas and want to take your pets with you, you will have to obey any quarantine laws that may exist in the country you are travelling to.

CRUELTY TO ANIMALS

Cruelty to animals is a criminal offence, punishable by a fine, imprisonment or both. Laws vary between States but generally cruelty consists of:

- abandoning an animal, such as when going away on holidays or for long periods;
- not adequately feeding or sheltering an animal;
- poisoning;
- hitting an animal with a car and then not taking reasonable steps to care for it and contact the owner;
- tying an animal up for a long time or using an unreasonably short or heavy rope or chain.

If you suspect anybody of being cruel to an animal, contact the police or the Royal Society for the Prevention of Cruelty to Animals (RSPCA).

FURTHER READING

Farrier, *The Environmental Law Handbook*, Redfern Legal Centre Publishing, Sydney, 1993

Moloney, *Neighbours: A Multicultural Guide To Local Community Law*, Redfern Legal Centre Publishing, Sydney, 1994

Spender (ed), *Animal Acts: You, Your Pet And The Law*, Redfern Legal Centre Publishing, Sydney, 1989 updated 1993

See also: General references listed in Further Reading Chapter 1.

Chapter 14

YOUR CAR

14.1   Buying and selling a car
14.2   Driving offences
Further reading

14.1   BUYING AND SELLING A CAR

After a house, a car is usually the largest expenditure that people make. To avoid trouble and expense it is important to know your rights and responsibilities when owning, buying or selling a car.

OWNING A CAR

Registration

A car owner must ensure that the car is registered each year. A car is unregistered if it has no number plates, is imported from another State or country, or the registration has expired.

Driving an unregistered vehicle can lead to a heavy fine. In 1994 the New South Wales penalty was $359 and that is doubled because an unregistered vehicle is also uninsured – even if the compulsory third party "green slip" has been obtained, since cover does not start until the registration fee has been paid. Unregistered vehicle permits may be available as a temporary measure under some circumstances.

In most States cars over a certain age must have a road worthiness certificate issued by a mechanic to be registered. In New South Wales, all cars over three years of age must obtain such a certificate.

Car buyers have to change the registration into their own name. Directions on how to do this are usually printed on the back of the registration certificate. Make sure you are given one by the seller. If you buy a new car from a dealer you will need to show a receipt. If your car is from interstate you will need a certificate of clearance from that State's Vehicle Security Register.

Sellers have to notify the motor registry that they no longer own the car (see below under Selling a Car: Documents Needed). The time limit for performing these tasks is quite short, often only a few days. It is important not to delay.

Insurance

It is compulsory for car owners to take out third party insurance. Third party insurance covers injury to people other than the driver at fault. That is, it covers people such as passengers, pedestrians, and faultless drivers injured in an accident.

Whether you wish to take out any insurance beyond this (such as third party property which covers damage to another person's property) or comprehensive (which covers damage to your own car and to other people's property) or something in between, depends on your judgment and how much your car is worth.

You should at least take out third party property insurance. It does not cover your car but does protect you if you damage another vehicle – and it could be a very expensive vehicle to repair.

Safety

Vehicles must be kept safe. Police officers can stop cars to check that safety requirements are met. If there are defects a notice can be issued requiring them to be fixed.

BUYING A CAR

Everyone fears ending up with a lemon. But this need not happen if you are aware of your rights and know what to look out for.

Note that car buyers are protected by the same laws that protect buyers of other goods: see 15.1 Consumer Protection. If you buy your car on credit, you are also protected by the consumer credit laws: see 15.2 Consumer Credit.

Buyers of cars have added protection beyond these basic consumer rights. Exactly what your rights are depend on whether you are buying a new or used car and whether you buy privately or from a dealer.

Buying a new car

Generally it is wise to arrange finance before you go car shopping. Finance can often be arranged through car dealers but tends to be more expensive than that arranged through banks and other financial institutions.

If you have a good idea of what you are looking for you are less likely to be swayed by car dealers keen to sell a different type of car – usually a more expensive one.

When negotiating on the price make sure you are getting the on the road cost of the car, not merely its base price. Have you been quoted a price including any chosen options, stamp duty, dealer charges etc?

Be very sure before you sign any document. Whether it is called a contract or a purchase order it is still a contract. Among its clauses (which you should read and understand) are penalty clauses where the buyer is liable to pay a percentage of the purchase price if they decide not to go through with the purchase. This applies to both new and used car purchases.

New cars are covered by manufacturer's warranties. Most warranties last for about one year but some last three years. Under the warranty you do not have to pay for repairs that arise due to manufacturing defects. It will not cover damage caused by accidents or improper use of the car. It may be a condition of the warranty that regular services are carried out.

Some States are introducing independent Quality Assurance auditing for car dealers. The audit is carried out by a government endorsed body. Some car dealers are now gaining Quality accreditation in certain divisions of their operations.

Buying a used car from a dealer

When buying a used car you have the choice between buying privately or from a car dealer. Buying privately tends to be cheaper, but you have less safeguards than if you buy through a dealer. The most important is that you do not have a warranty from a private seller.

Legislation protects people who buy used cars from dealers. Laws vary between States, but generally used car dealers must:

- display information such as the car's make, model, year, selling price, kilometres travelled;
- provide a warranty.

Generally warranties must be provided under law for all cars except very cheap ones. And in New South Wales there is no warranty if the vehicle is priced over the luxury tax limit, has travelled over 160,000 km or is over 10 years old.

Warranties cover a fixed period or the number of kilometres travelled. Some types of repairs are often not covered. Certain defects discovered during the warranty period are covered. It is best to get the car checked by a mechanic soon after purchase. Motoring organisations such as the NRMA offer such a service.

Car dealers are required to be licensed. Dealers convicted of dishonesty may have their licenses cancelled. Fidelity funds exist in most States that protect buyers who are cheated by used car dealers. But the deception has to be something more than just the quality of the car – it may cover the situation where the dealer is not the proper owner of the car sold.

Make sure you have a cover note before you leave the dealer's premises (for new and used cars).

Avoid purchasing insurance or extended warranties through the dealer. You should check with your insurance before shopping for a car, and not have insurance added as part of your financing since you would pay interest on top of the premium. It would probably be cheaper to put the cost of an extended warranty in a bank account to cover future repairs as extended warranties are usually very limited in what they cover.

Buying a used car privately

You have less legal protection if you are buying a car privately. Basically there are three things you should check before you buy:

- the mechanical condition of the car;
- that the car is not stolen;
- that no money is owed on the car.

Often there is little you can do if you buy a car in poor mechanical condition. You might be able to take legal action if the seller made false promises, but the legal procedure is expensive and lengthy and you have no guarantee of success. Your best protection is to get an inspection performed by a mechanic. There is a risk, of course, that the seller may then decide to sell their car elsewhere – but if you are pressured into buying something prematurely it may be a warning.

If you buy a stolen car the real owner can claim the car back, even if you have already paid for it and did not know that it was stolen. You can then try to recover your money from the thief, but success is unlikely. To check whether a car has been stolen, call the encumbered vehicle register in your State.

The register will also be able to tell you if any money is owed on the car. If you buy a car that the seller has not paid off you may be liable to meet the repayments or have the car repossessed.

SELLING A CAR

People selling cars have duties. Some are required by law. Others are simply common sense steps that you should follow to protect yourself.

Advertising the car

When advertising the car, be careful not to make any statements that may be false or misleading. If you do you might be sued by the buyer.

You have a legal duty to accurately state the model and year of the car and the distance travelled. Misrepresenting these items is a criminal offence.

Documents needed

You will need the certificate of registration to prove you own the car. It is given to the buyer.

If you bought the car on credit you will need to show that it has been paid off. If you intend to pay off the loan with the proceeds of the sale you should notify the lender and ask them how to go about it.

Depending on the laws of your State, you might need to provide a road worthiness certificate.

A notice of disposal should be completed and sent as soon as you sell the car. It tells the motor registry that you are no longer the car owner. Do not wait for the buyer to transfer the ownership – or you may be liable for their parking fines and other traffic offences. Details on what you need to do are usually printed on the back of the registration slip, or you can contact your local motor registry.

You should check that the buyer, or the person who drives the car away from your premises, has a current driver's licence. It is an offence to permit an unlicensed person to drive.

Accepting payment

Only cash or bank cheques should be accepted. You are quite free to refuse to accept personal cheques from buyers.

14.2   DRIVING OFFENCES

It does not matter whether you intended to commit a driving offence – often, the mere fact that you have committed it is enough to make you liable.

TYPES OF OFFENCES

There are many different types of motoring offences, and details can vary between States. There are proposals to introduce a system of National Australian Road Rules, at present being considered by the States and their motoring organisations. For the time being, however, it is possible to make the following general remarks about some of the more common driving offences.

Parking offences

When a car is parked in a prohibited area or exceeds the time limit permitted, a parking ticket may be given by a parking inspector. It is usually left on the windscreen under the windshield wiper. It is not a valid excuse to say that you did not receive the ticket. A time limit exists in which a fine must be paid – usually 21 days.

You might wish to contest the parking ticket in court. Often this is difficult where it is your word against a parking inspector's. Keep in mind that if you lose the case you may have to pay court costs as well as the original fine: see "Penalties" below.

One defence may be that you were not in charge of the car. Usually the owner of the car is responsible, but if you can show that the car was stolen you may not be liable. You might also escape responsibility if you can show that somebody else was in charge of the car and you can supply their name and address.

Speeding

Driving at an excessive speed can attract a fine. It can also lead to penalty points being imposed (see below).

The normal speed limit for driving in a town is 60 km/h unless otherwise indicated. On country roads and freeways the upper limit may be 100 or 110 km/h depending on the State.

Police radars and speed cameras are often used to detect speeding offences. Car owners may be sent an infringement notice or drivers may be pulled over and given an on-the-spot fine. An on-the-spot fine need not be paid immediately, it just means it is issued on the spot.

If a car owner is sent an infringement notice they should notify the police if somebody else was driving their car.

Not stopping after an accident

Drivers have a duty to stop after being involved in a car accident. Failure to stop is treated very seriously by the courts. Magistrates usually consider that the reason the driver did not stop was that drinking was involved and the penalty is usually the same as a high range PCA (prescribed concentration of alcohol). The driver often has a negligent driving charge against them as well.

Where injury or death is involved it is even more serious, with gaol sentence limits being doubled from December 1994 in New South Wales and the offence of negligent driving having a gaol component added where there is death or grievous bodily harm.

Driving without a seat belt

It is an offence to drive without a seat belt. Drivers are usually responsible for unbelted passengers particularly children. People with certain medical conditions might be excused, and can check with their local motor registry. Their doctor should also know. Note that in most States pregnant women are required to wear seat belts, no matter how pregnant they are.

Driving without a licence

It is an offence for an unlicensed person to drive on a public road. The person who allows them to drive their car may also be committing an offence, but not, of course, if their car was stolen.

A person who is disqualified from holding a licence or whose licence is suspended commits an offence if they drive or attempt to obtain a licence.

Driving under the influence

It is an offence to drive while under the influence of drugs or alcohol.

Breath tests may be given to any driver randomly – the police do not need to suspect that the driver has been drinking. Drivers signalled by Random Breath Testing units must pull over, show their licence, and take a breath test. It is an offence to refuse to take the test.

To fail a breath test the driver would generally have a reading of 0.05g/100ml – lower for learners, young drivers, provisional drivers and some professional drivers. If you fail a breath test you may be arrested and taken to a police station where the test is repeated.

If the test shows an illegal blood alcohol level you may be charged with an offence. Police bail may be granted but you will not be allowed to drive again until your blood alcohol has dropped. For details on police bail and charging see 5.1 Dealing with the Police.

If the police suspect that a driver is under the influence of a drug they may have the power to require blood or urine tests in certain circumstances. The drug can be any drug that affects driving – not just illegal drugs. Drugs affecting driving can be obtained either by prescription or over the counter (for instance sedatives, cold remedies). Always check the medicine container for a warning that the drug may cause drowsiness.

Negligent driving

Negligent driving is also known as careless driving. It involves driving without reasonable care and attention. An accident need not occur for a negligent driver to be charged.

Penalties can be high, especially where somebody has been injured. For instance in New South Wales penalties increased in December 1994. Negligent driving used to carry five penalty units maximum, but was increased to 15 penalty units and/or six months imprisonment for grievous bodily harm and to 20 penalty units and/or 12 months imprisonment where death is occasioned. (A penalty unit is the basis used for calculating fines).

Dangerous driving

Dangerous driving is also known as culpable or reckless driving. It involves a person driving in a manner which can be dangerous to the public. It does not matter that in fact nobody was actually in danger. Whether the driver was driving dangerously depends on all the circumstances. It may be possible to commit this offence even when driving under the speed limit where conditions are poor (dark streets, fog, storms etc).

In New South Wales the old offence of culpable driving was changed in December 1994 to "dangerous driving occasioning death" and "dangerous driving occasioning grievous bodily harm". This was to make the offence easier to understand and to increase the penalties. The previous maximum of five years imprisonment increased to 10 years where death occurred; and from three years to seven years for grievous bodily harm. There are even higher penalties of an additional four years imprisonment where:

- the blood alcohol reading is 0.15 g/100ml or higher;
- speed is in excess of 45 km/h over the posted limit;
- death or serious injury to another person is as a result of the driver attempting to escape the police.

PENALTIES

The penalties imposed for driving offences vary between States, but similar types of penalties are imposed for similar types of offences.

Fines

Generally a fine is imposed for the less serious offences, such as parking and some speeding offences. An infringement notice may be issued either on the spot or by mail. If the fine is paid within the specified time, no further action is taken.

When a fine is not paid the motor registry may be notified. After sending reminder letters they can cancel your driver's licence or car registration or both until the fine is paid. You will need to pay both the fine and a collection fee.

If you wish to challenge a fine you can sign the election to go to court – usually found on the back of the infringement notice. A summons may be issued and the matter will go to court. (For information on the court process see 5.2 Criminal Court Procedure.) If you lose the case a larger fine may be imposed and you may have to pay court costs.

Points

Points are accumulated when driving offences are committed. Parking offences usually do not attract points. Points and other penalties can be imposed simultaneously.

When the maximum number of points has been reached, the motor registry can cancel your licence without court involvement. The maximum number of points varies between States. In New South Wales it is 12 points in three years for holders of unrestricted licences, and four points in one year for provisional licence drivers. The period of cancellation varies – it is usually three months.

Licence cancellation

Licences may be cancelled for various reasons:

- the failure to pay a fine;
- when enough points have been accumulated;
- where a serious offence has been committed cancellation might be automatic – for example dangerous driving, high blood alcohol content etc. Sometimes the period of disqualification is set by law, other times it is at the court's discretion.

Licence holders in some States might have the option to be put on a probationary licence rather than lose their licence altogether. If they are, then it only takes a small number of points to greatly increase their disqualification period.

Appealing against a disqualification might be possible, but it is best to seek legal advice. Members of motoring organisations such as the NRMA or the RACV may be able to use the organisation's legal services. If you do not belong to such an organisation, you can contact one of the free advice centres listed in 1.2 Sources of Legal Advice.

Imprisonment

Imprisonment might be imposed for the more serious driving offences – such as manslaughter or causing death or serious injury while driving. It may also be imposed for very serious drink driving offences. For information about prison sentences and alternatives see 5.3 Sentencing Options.

INTERSTATE DRIVING

Motor registries in some States and Territories are able to exchange details about points with other jurisdictions. This is expected to be extended to the whole of Australia. In other words if you break the law in another State you may still have the points recorded on your licence at home.

FURTHER READING

Canning and Graham, *Cashed Up For A Car: Your Guide To Buying A Used Car*, Department of Consumer Affairs, Sydney, 1993

Motor Accidents: Drink Driving And Beyond, Legal And Accounting Management Seminars, Sydney, 1994

Smith, *Is It A Lemon? The Complete Guide to Buying a Home, a Car, a Boat*, Allen & Unwin, Sydney, 1994

See also: General references listed in Further Reading Chapter 1.

Chapter 15

PURCHASER'S PROBLEMS

15.1   Consumer protection

15.2   Consumer credit

Further reading

15.1   CONSUMER PROTECTION

What would you do if your new leather shoes split the first time you wore them? Or if that expensive cologne smelt like vinegar? What if you were cajoled into buying something you didn't really want?

Knowing your rights when something goes wrong and recognising unfair sales tactics can save you time and money.

CONTRACTS

All sales are contracts, whether they are written or not. In contracts for the sale of goods, some terms and conditions are expressly stated, while others are implied by law.

Express terms can be in the form of a contract or warranty. Make sure you understand all the implications before you sign anything. Express terms need not be written, and they can include promises made in advertisements.

Implied conditions protect consumers when they buy unsatisfactory goods. They are imposed by the Commonwealth *Trade Practices Act*, which applies throughout Australia, and by State legislation.

Sellers cannot override the statute's implied conditions. Your rights will still exist even if you have signed a contract that tries to remove them.

UNSATISFACTORY GOODS

The implied conditions set out by legislation are:

The product's purpose

Goods must be fit for the purpose for which goods of that type are commonly bought. A heater must heat and a sewing machine must sew. This is known as the merchantable quality condition.

Merchantable quality conditions do not apply when:

- the defect was specifically drawn to your attention before the sale. Tags marked "factory seconds" and "as is" may be a warning that the protection does not apply;

- you had an opportunity to examine the product, and could have discovered the problem had you looked carefully enough.

Buying by description

Buying goods "by description" would refer, for example, to mail order or self-service products. There is an implied condition that goods will match their description.

Unless the deviation is trivial you can reject the goods. You can do this even if they are still of merchantable quality.

Specific purpose

At times you may ask a seller what product would best suit a specific purpose you had in mind, especially where there is need for expertise in making the decision. For example, you might ask a gardening shop which tool would be best for lopping branches.

If you relied on their skill and judgment in making your purchase, there is another condition implied by law: the product must be fit for the purpose you indicated.

An exception – auctions

A word of warning – the implied conditions do not apply to goods bought at auctions. You will only have redress if the seller or auctioneer made false statements about the product, enticing you to buy.

Safety

Unsafe goods can be returned to the store and you can ask for a refund or replacement.

Under Trade Practices legislation, if somebody is injured and suffers loss as the result of a defective product, they can claim compensation. If the product was supplied by the manufacturer from 9 July 1992, it does not matter whether the injured person was the purchaser or the consumer. Neither is it necessary for the loss to have been foreseeable.

If the injury resulted from misuse of the product, then compensation may be reduced. Manufacturers are obliged to warn consumers of the anticipated potential consequences of misuse.

For goods supplied before 9 July 1992, it may be harder to sue, particularly if the person injured was not the purchaser or consumer, and if the loss was not reasonably foreseeable.

UNSATISFACTORY SERVICES

Even when you buy a service rather than a product (for instance hiring a plumber) you still have rights conferred by consumer protection legislation.

Implied conditions apply in the same way:

Care and skill

The person carrying out the work for you must apply due care and skill. The standard that must be met is the standard of care and skill that a competent tradesman in that field would reasonably meet.

Service fit for purpose

If you specify a particular purpose for the work, it must be met. For instance if you ask for handrails to be installed and you specify that they are to help a disabled person, the handrails must be at the right level to be of use.

Appropriate materials used

Materials used to carry out the service must be suitable for the purpose intended and must be of reasonable quality. As an example, if a new doorway is put in using cheap and inappropriate materials causing the ceiling above to collapse, an implied condition has been breached.

UNFAIR PRACTICES BY TRADERS

Even if there is nothing wrong with the product, you may feel that unfair tactics were used to entice or trick you into buying something against your better judgment.

The use of false or misleading statements is prohibited by the *Trade Practices Act*. Unfortunately it is often quite difficult to prove that this has taken place. Your best protection is to be aware of the type of tactics used and simply take your business elsewhere.

Common tactics to be aware of include:

Free gift

A free gift may be offered to encourage you to buy something. But is the "gift" really free? Or are you actually paying the full price of both the product and the gift? Look for proof, such as receipts and advertisements for the pure product, that convince you that the gift is legitimate.

Bait advertising

A product is advertised very cheaply to attract customers. On entering the store, you are told they "just ran out" and "happen to have a better model". This better model is, of course, the expensive item that the retailer really wanted to sell.

Legislation prohibits retailers from failing to have reasonable quantities of the cheap product advertised. But how do you prove it? What is a reasonable quantity? And what if they did legitimately run out of stock? Just be aware of this technique, particularly if you were not warned that the offer only existed while stocks last.

Pyramid selling

What is being sold is not so much the product, but the right to recruit others to sell that product. Each seller gains a commission from introducing new recruits.

Endless chains are formed. More sellers exist than the demand for the product justifies. Saturation point is reached, and those lower down on the chain cannot recoup their investment. The people who initiated it, however, make a fortune.

Certain types of conduct involving pyramid selling are prohibited by law.

Unsolicited goods

Products sent to you without your permission are unsolicited goods. You do not have to pay for them.

For most goods you have two options. You can hold onto the goods for three months, and if the sender hasn't collected them in that time, you can keep them.

Or you can give notice to the sender that you did not order the goods, and that they can be collected. If they have not been collected within a month, you can keep them.

Door-to-door sales

Pressure to purchase from a door-to-door salesman can be very high, and you cannot just walk away.

If you buy something from a door-to-door salesman but then change your mind, you may be protected by a cooling off period. The length varies between States. You should be given a statement regarding the cooling off period at the time of the sale, but if you are not, check it with Consumer Affairs.

The most important thing to remember is that you may lose your rights to a cooling off period:

- if you invited the salesman to call – and this includes them phoning you and asking if you want them to visit; or
- if you paid cash up front. It is wisest to pay a small deposit by cheque. Do not pay cash until the goods have been delivered and you have inspected them.

GETTING YOUR MONEY BACK

If your problem is that you have changed your mind and no longer want the product, all you can do is rely on your ability to persuade the store to give you a refund for the sake of customer goodwill. Many of the large department stores have unconditional warranties, allowing exchange or refund without difficulty.

If the product does not measure up to either the conditions implied by law or expressed in the contract, you have legal rights which can be enforced against either the retailer or the manufacturer.

Signs that declare "we exchange but do not refund" are pure bluff. They may not have to return your money just because you do not like the goods, but if an implied condition was breached, repair is impossible and no suitable exchange exists, the store is obliged to refund your money.

Your first step in getting a refund is to return the product to the store. Most of the time you will have no trouble. But if they refuse, try a letter to the manager. Keep a copy, and make sure you include:

- a description of the product;
- the date and place of purchase;
- specific details about the problem;
- what action you expect.

If you have not received a reply within one to two weeks, send another letter repeating the above, and give them a time limit. Choose a reasonable date, say a fortnight, and warn them that if you have not received a satisfactory reply by that date, you may take further action to secure your legal rights.

Consumer Affairs

What happens if you still get no response? You can report the store to the Department of Consumer Affairs. They can give you advice over the telephone.

Consumer Affairs offers a mediation service. Mediation differs from court proceedings in that the parties are encouraged to reach a solution themselves. This may be better than a decision that has been imposed on you by a court. Mediation also tends to be faster and cheaper than court. For details on mediation generally, see 4.2 Mediation.

Small Claims Tribunal

Do not forget that if you see a lawyer, you have to pay their fees whether you win your case or not. If the product is under a certain monetary limit (which varies between States) you could make a claim yourself in the Small Claims Tribunal.

The Small Claims Tribunal is called the Small Claims Court in some States, and the Consumer Claims Tribunal in New South Wales. Ring the tribunal to find out what their monetary limit is, and ask them to send you an information leaflet which describes how to make a claim.

The hearings are informal, and generally you cannot be represented by a lawyer (unless you are making a claim against a lawyer). It is basically up to you to prove your case. But do not worry, you do not need to be an expert on the law. Cases are decided on their facts.

Preparing for the hearing involves collecting documents such as:

* contracts;
* warranties;
* advertisements and promotional leaflets;
* quotes, invoices and receipts;
* letters;
* photographs.

You can have witnesses, including expert witnesses. Expert witnesses have qualifications in the relevant area, and are able to give their opinion. Witnesses can either appear in person or submit written evidence on sworn or solemnly declared documents known as statutory declarations or affidavits.

Both sides present their case. Again, you are encouraged to reach an agreement, but if you cannot, the tribunal will make an order. This must be followed. It can require the seller to exchange, repair or refund. If the order is not followed, contact the tribunal or the Department of Consumer Affairs.

Small Claims Division – NSW Local Courts

Local Courts in New South Wales have a Small Claims Division. It hears actions where the amount claimed is under $3000 (although this figure may rise in the future).

Cases are heard by assessors or magistrates. Compared to normal court cases, proceedings in the Small Claims Division are relatively informal, and the technical rules of evidence do not need to apply.

Parties are encouraged to reach a mutually acceptable settlement. The assessor or magistrate can then make a judgment to give legal effect to the terms of the settlement.

Further loss

Loss or damage that goes beyond the faulty product purchased can sometimes occur. For instance, a defective video cassette may ruin your VCR. If the defect amounted to a breach of the consumer protection laws, you could sue for the cost of the VCR.

Loss that goes beyond monetary terms can also be sued for in certain circumstances. In one famous case, an unfortunate woman drank a bottle of ginger beer, and then found the remains of a snail in the bottle. She became ill, and was able to sue for negligence.

For either of these types of action, seeing a lawyer is advisable.

15.2 CONSUMER CREDIT

Paying cash is the cheapest way to buy something. If you use credit you have to pay for it. You pay, not only for the product, but for use of the money. Of course, it is not always possible or practical to rely solely on cash, but it is possible to minimise the risks associated with debts.

Credit can be provided by the seller – stores often allow purchasers to buy a product and pay it off over a set period of time. Or the credit can be provided by an outsider, such as banks and credit unions. In this case the purchaser enters into an agreement with the lender to repay the money plus interest over a fixed term.

A debt arises when someone (the debtor) borrows money from a lender (the creditor).

CONSUMER CREDIT LAWS

At the time of writing, different laws apply in different States. The protection provided to consumers is somewhat patchy, and so a new uniform Credit Code has been agreed to. Basically, the same laws will apply throughout Australia. The law has passed parliament in virtually all States, but will not come into operation until March 1996 at the earliest.

One major difference between the old and new laws is that the new laws apply to nearly all credit contracts and providers. The old laws only apply to certain types of contracts made by certain types of lenders, and monetary limits exist.

This discussion will focus primarily on the new law. Details regarding the old law can be checked in individual States.

BEFORE YOU SIGN

Avoiding debt problems

Problems with debt can arise in several ways. The most common is over-commitment. Always be aware of how much the product you are buying will actually cost, and whether you can afford it.

Another way that problems can arise is if you have a change in circumstances. Losing a job or falling ill can reduce your ability to repay debts.

Purchasing defective goods on credit can also lead to problems. If this happens, do not simply refuse to pay. Write to the seller, explaining the problem, and try to return the product: see 15.1 Consumer Protection.

Always keep all documentation relating to credit purchases – such as quotes, invoices and receipts.

If you have problems with debt it is advisable to contact a financial counselling service.

Right to information

Under the new protection laws, credit contracts must be in writing. You have a right to be given sufficient information with which to make an informed choice as to whether to sign the contract. The right to information means that:

- the contract should be understandable;
- the contract should warn you not to sign unless you understand it;
- it must describe what is being purchased;

259

- the full cost must be specified in the contract – including the cash price, repayments, details of credit charges, interest, credit fees, enforcement expenses, commissions and insurance.

CHANGES TO CREDIT CONTRACTS

Under the Credit Code, creditors must provide debtors with notice of any changes to interest rates, credit fees or charges.

IF YOU RECEIVE A DEMAND FOR PAYMENT
Check the debt

If you receive a letter demanding that you pay a debt, first check that you really are obliged to pay it. Look through your records – it is not unheard of for a payment to have been made but not recorded. If this is the case, write to the creditor explaining the situation and enclose a copy of the receipt.

If you have not paid, check the amount the creditors are claiming. Ask for an itemised list of money owed to be sent to you if necessary.

Who pays?

Debts can be owed by more than one person – the debtors are then known as joint debtors. Creditors can seek to recover the whole sum from any one of the joint debtors. If one debtor does end up paying the entire amount, they can claim contribution from the others.

A joint debt arises where two or more people buy something on credit together or borrow money together. Spouses are not automatically joint debtors, and property belonging to a debtor's spouse cannot be seized to pay off the debt.

Guarantors are liable to pay a debt if the debtor does not make the repayments. As the responsibility of a guarantor is as great as that of the borrower, guarantors should carefully consider entering such a commitment, preferably with the help of an independent advisor.

INABILITY TO MAKE REPAYMENTS

If you are having difficulties meeting repayments make sure you notify the lender as to your circumstances as soon as possible.

Renegotiating the contract

Try to renegotiate the terms of the credit contract. Under the protection laws, you have the right to ask for the contract to be varied if you are suffering hardship because of illness, unemployment or some other reasonable cause.

Parties can agree to whatever arrangement suits them, but if you go by the law it provides that any such variations should either:

- postpone the date on which payments are due during a specified period; or
- extend the contract and postpone the repayment dates; or
- extend the contract and reduce the amount of each instalment.

If the creditor refuses you can ask Consumer Affairs for advice or you could apply to the credit tribunal (called the Commercial Tribunal in New South Wales) for an order varying the contract.

Unjust contracts

Contracts that are unjust because unfair tactics were used to entice you to sign, or because the terms are harsh, might not be binding. If you think this is the case you should seek legal help – it may be worth disputing the contract in court or the credit tribunal.

A tribunal could consider:

- whether you obtained independent legal or other expert advice before signing the contract;
- how easy the contract is to understand;
- whether all the terms and conditions were finalised or still subject to negotiation at the time you signed;
- whether unfair pressure or undue influence was used;
- whether the credit provider knew or could have known that you were over-committing yourself.

If the tribunal believes the contract is unjust it can make a range of orders, including:

- setting the contract aside either wholly or in part; or
- ordering that any mortgages be discharged; or
- ordering an appropriate sum to be paid.

STEPS CREDITORS TAKE

Legal action is rarely the first step that a creditor will take if you owe them money. Usually the first thing that will be done is that they will contact you, reminding you that payment is due. Always respond to any steps taken – they may be willing to negotiate.

If you do not respond to their preliminary steps, or if the creditor is not satisfied with your response, they may hire a debt collector to chase the debt up for them. Debt collectors are not allowed to harass buyers. Harassment includes badgering and threatening violence or publicity. Report any such action to the creditor.

Repossession

Very often, if goods are bought on credit the lender takes a mortgage over the goods. In other words they can be repossessed if payments are not made.

Consumer credit laws offer some protection – you must be given at least 30 days' notice in writing of the creditor's intention to repossess the goods. You can use this time to attempt to renegotiate and vary the contract.

After repossession a notice must be sent outlining how you can regain the goods. Paying for the goods means that they will be returned to you.

If you cannot recover the goods they will be sold to pay off the debt. Any sum still outstanding after this will have to be paid. Sellers are obliged to try to get the best price they can, and you may wish to get the items valued before they are repossessed.

Legal proceedings

Most proceedings begin in the Local Court (called Magistrates Courts in some States) unless the monetary value in dispute is too high.

The first you will know of it is when you receive a letter of demand sent by the creditor or its solicitor. It threatens that unless payment is received by a certain date, legal proceedings may be taken without further notice.

The document that formally commences court action is the summons or Statement of Claim. For information on court procedures see 3.4 Suing or Being Sued.

If you lose, you may have to pay:

- the debt;
- any interest that arose before the court case; and
- the legal fees which often include court costs.

ENFORCING A JUDGMENT

If the creditor goes to court and obtains a judgment in their favour they are then known as judgment creditors. They have several ways to ensure that the debt is paid:

Instalment orders

Paying off a debt by instalments tends to be the most favourable for the debtor. It involves the least financial hardship. If an instalment order is made the creditor cannot take further action unless repayments are missed. If you forget or are unable to meet an instalment you should make another application to pay by instalments. The creditor cannot take action while that application is pending.

Examination of debtor

Creditors often want to learn more about your financial position. If you receive an examination summons you must go to the court and give evidence under oath as to your income and assets. Take all relevant documents with you such as bank accounts, tax returns, title deeds etc.

If the court finds that you have sufficient means to pay, it will make an order accordingly. An order can be made to pay by instalments.

Seizure of property

Judgment creditors can get a writ of execution. This authorises a sheriff or bailiff to seize the debtor's assets and then sell them to pay off the debt. Bailiffs cannot force entry into your home, but it is an offence to obstruct them in the exercise of their duties.

Not all assets can be taken. Rented products, spouse's property and household goods to a certain value cannot be seized.

Garnishee order

When you are owed money by someone else, such as wages from an employer or rent from a tenant, the judgment creditor can apply for a garnishee order. That is, a proportion of the money that you are owed would go directly to the creditor. There are limits on the amount that can be removed each week and for the duration of the order.

Bankruptcy

Bankruptcy is the last resort. The judgment creditor begins proceedings by applying to the Federal Court for a Bankruptcy Notice. If you do not pay the debt within the stated time (usually 14 days) you have committed an act of bankruptcy. The creditor can then apply to have you declared bankrupt.

People with severe debt problems can consider voluntary bankruptcy, but should consult with debt counsellors and legal practitioners first.

FURTHER READING

Bingham, *Credit Handbook*, Consumer Credit Legal Service, Melbourne, 1991

Bowen, *The Complete Consumer*, ABC Books, Sydney, 1993

Campbelltown Legal Centre, *Debtors Guide To Local Courts*, Redfern Legal Centre Publishing, Sydney, 1991 plus 1993 supplement

Department of Consumer Affairs, *The Consumer Handbook: A Practical Guide For Consumers in New South Wales*, Sydney, 1994

White, *Debt Recovery In Victoria: A Guide To The Law*, Longman Professional, Melbourne, 1993

See also: General references listed in Further Reading Chapter 1.

Chapter 16

WILLS

16.1 MAKING A WILL

Did you know that if you do not make a will, parliament will make one for you? A set of rules, known as the intestacy laws, will automatically apply.

Intestacy laws are impersonal and inflexible, and no one's pretending they'll coincide with your wishes. Your family cannot simply sit down and share your property as they think best.

IF YOU DO NOT MAKE A WILL

Once debts and taxes have been repaid, there are various categories of people who are entitled to a share of the property. Each is ranked in order of priority.

If one person is alive from any category, everybody below that is automatically excluded. They are left with no gift at all. There is an exception if you leave both a husband or wife and children. Your spouse will take nearly everything. Your children may get something, but that depends on the value of your property and the particular laws of the State you live in.

The intestacy formula has some variations between States, but generally the order is:

- husband/wife;
- children (or grandchildren in their place);
- parents;
- brothers and sisters;
- grandparents;

- uncles and aunts; and finally
- the government.

Of course, you may be happy to leave everything to your partner. But that does not mean you do not need to write a will. The process tends to be quicker and cheaper where there is a will.

Appointing a guardian

Anybody with children should give thought to appointing a guardian. This can be done in a will, and is preferable to leaving this decision to a court. It is best to discuss the matter first with the person you have in mind to make sure they are willing to undertake the responsibility. Guardians have the same rights and duties as parents – discussed in 8.1 Parents' Rights and Duties.

Partners that live together

People that live together as husband and wife but are not legally married are known as de facto partners. De facto relationships are gaining recognition in the eyes of the law: see 7.1 Living Together. De facto partners now have rights on an intestacy in some States.

In States such as New South Wales, if there is a de facto partner but no legal spouse, the de facto is in the same position under the intestacy formula that a legal spouse would have been in.

Complications arise where there is both. The result varies between States, and depends on factors such as how long the partners were living together. It requires evidence that is messy to prove and emotionally draining. The best way to avoid these problems is with a will.

Administrators

If there is no will, or the will does not appoint an executor, the court will appoint somebody to distribute the deceased's estate. This person is known as an administrator. They have the same duties as executors. See 16.2 Executors and Administrators.

MAKING A WILL

How should you go about getting a will made?

Obviously you can see a solicitor. A typical charge for drawing up a will is around $100. You may have to pay again if you want to make changes.

Or you can go to a trustee company. Often they do not charge for wills, but they insist on being appointed as executor. They then charge a fee for distributing your assets, which will be taken from your property after your death.

It is also worth considering the government trustee offices. Called the Public Trustee in most States (or State Trust in Victoria), these government bodies have some advantages over the privately run companies. Rates charged tend to be lower. The Public Trustee is not answerable to shareholders, and it cannot go bankrupt nor leave the State.

WRITING YOUR OWN WILL

Complex wills

If you want to create a trust, a life interest or conditional gift, it is best to see a professional rather than attempting to write the will yourself.

A trust involves holding and investing property for a child for their benefit until they reach a certain age. A trustee needs to be appointed, and the wording and limitations of the trust need to be clearly expressed.

A life interest involves leaving property for someone to use but not dispose of during their lifetime – the typical scenario being a life interest in a house to a wife. She can live there, but cannot sell it. On her death, the house passes to the children.

A conditional gift means that a gift will only be given if a certain condition is met, for example "I leave my house to my wife on condition that she does not remarry". This area of law is very complicated, and a lawyer's advice is essential.

Conditional gifts may fail for a number of reasons, and what happens then? Will the person receive the gift without fulfilling the condition, or will they lose the gift whatever they do? As you won't be there to say what you intended, it is essential that the correct wording is used in the first place.

Writing your own simple will

If you only have something simple in mind you may prefer to write your will yourself.

A will must be written. It cannot be taped, as tapes are easily tampered with. You can use a Will Form but it is not necessary. Will forms are inexpensive and are available from stationers.

The person making the will is called a testator if male or a testatrix if female. For a will to be valid, the testator/testatrix must have "mental capacity". That is, they must be able to understand:

- the general nature of a will;

- the extent of their property; and
- the nature of their relationships with family members.

Being intoxicated while making a will could result in the will being invalid for lack of mental capacity.

When writing a will, you must follow the basic structure:

Opening

The document must state expressly that it is a will. The name, address and occupation of the testator must be stated in the opening along with the date.

An example of a correct opening is "This is the last will and testament of [name] of [address], [occupation], dated [date]."

Revoking earlier wills

If you have written a previous will, the earlier will must be revoked in order to avoid the confusion of having more than one will in operation. Even if this is your first will, using a revocation clause is wise.

After the opening clause, you should state "I revoke all former wills and codicils made by me". (A codicil is an addition to a will.)

Executors

The next step is to appoint an executor. An executor deals with your property after your death. They have to list and control assets, pay off debts, deal with land tax and capital gains tax problems. 16.2 Executors and Administrators provides more information.

You can appoint whoever you like, but keep in mind that the duties are onerous, and often distressing for family members. Appointees can refuse to act, and the chance of their death or illness should be considered. Appointing a trustee company or a solicitor avoids these problems.

Gifts

The next step is to describe the actual gifts. The person who a gift is left to is called a beneficiary. If you wish to leave everything to one person, you could write "I leave to [name] of [address] all my property both real and personal absolutely". Real property refers to land, houses, units, etc while personal property includes cars, jewellery etc.

If you wish to make specific gifts to a number of people, you must make sure that all your property is covered. Anything omitted would pass according to the laws of intestacy. This does not mean that you should list everything you own item by item. You are likely to acquire new things in the future, and they won't be covered.

The best approach is to make specific gifts of particular items that you feel strongly about, and then leave all of the remainder to a named beneficiary.

Be careful how you describe the gifts. It is better to leave "the cars I own at the date of my death", than to describe the car you currently own. If you make a gift of something, but then dispose of it while you are alive, the gift in the will fails.

If you and your partner own a house as joint tenants, the survivor automatically owns the entire property when the other dies. To leave your share independently in your will, you have to be tenants in common. Most married couples own their house as joint tenants, but check with your solicitor.

Funeral directions

You can state your preference in your will – you may prefer burial to cremation, or you may wish to donate your body to science. If you have strong feelings about this matter, discuss it with your family. Often a will is not looked at for several days after the death, and by then it might be too late.

Signature

The will should be signed and witnessed at the end. You need to have two witnesses, both over the age of 18. Everybody should sign the will in each other's presence using the same black pen. The witnesses do not need to see the contents of your will.

A good signature clause to use is "Signed by [the testator/testatrix] as his/her last will and testament before us both simultaneously and signed by us as witnesses in his/her presence and in each other's presence".

Most States allow some departure from strict compliance with these rules, but they should still be followed to avoid trouble and expense later on.

Witnesses are not allowed to benefit under the will, nor be married to a beneficiary. In most States, a gift to a witness would fail.

Your will should always be kept in a safe place, such as a bank or with a solicitor. Make sure there is only one signed original of your will in existence.

ALTERING AND REVOKING A WILL

Wills can be altered or revoked at any time. Alterations are best made by writing a whole new will or, if the change is small, a codicil. Do not make any changes on the original will or they may be invalid.

To revoke a will you should destroy it completely by burning or tearing – do not simply crumple it up. Old wills are revoked by new ones if a revocation clause is used.

The effect of marriage and divorce

Marriage revokes a will, unless it was written in contemplation of marriage. This should be stated expressly.

Divorce has no effect on a will in some States, but in others it can revoke either the gift to the former spouse or the whole will. To be on the safe side it is best to write a new will if you marry or divorce.

CHALLENGING A WILL

Even if a will is correctly drafted and signed it might still be challenged. Testators are required to make adequate provision for their dependants' welfare under Family Provision legislation. If they are not adequately provided for, they may be able to challenge the will.

The range of people who are entitled to be adequately provided for varies between States. Generally it includes a spouse, and, in some States, de facto spouses. Dependent children are entitled to adequate provision, and in some States, dependant parents are too.

Testators sometimes have strong reasons for wanting to disinherit someone. They should make a statement of their reasons in the form of a statutory declaration and keep it in a sealed envelope separate to the will. This might be used as evidence in court.

It will then be up to the court to decide if the reasons justify depriving that person of a share of the estate. Adultery used to deprive partners of their share, but it wouldn't now. Physical abuse might, depending on the circumstances.

UPDATING YOUR WILL

Wills should not be left to gather dust and grow more and more out of date as the years go by. Time changes the effect of your will.

For instance, if a beneficiary dies before you, their estate does not inherit the gift. A specific gift would go to the person you left the remainder to. If that person is also dead, the gift would pass as if there was no will – that is, according to the laws of intestacy.

As a general rule, you should update your will when any of the following occur:

- you get married or divorced;
- you have a child or adopt one;
- an executor, guardian or trustee dies;
- a beneficiary dies.

It is also a good idea to review your will every 5-10 years as taxation laws and economic conditions change.

16.2 EXECUTORS AND ADMINISTRATORS

TERMINOLOGY

When somebody dies, their debts have to be paid off and their assets distributed. A deceased person's assets and liabilities are known as his or her estate. The distribution is carried out by either an executor or administrator. They have similar duties, but are appointed in different ways. Both executors and administrators are known as a deceased's "personal representative".

Executors

An executor is appointed in a will. The executor distributes the assets according to the terms of the will. More than one executor can be appointed.

The executor can be a solicitor, a trustee company, or a friend or relative (even if they receive a gift in the will). Professionals charge a fee for doing the work, and there may be a clause in the will stating this.

Executors obtain their authority to deal with the estate by a grant of probate (described below). Until then, they cannot deal with the property. Probate is not necessary in all cases, such as where the estate is very small or where all assets are jointly owned.

Administrators

An administrator is appointed where:

- there is no will; or
- there is a will but an executor has not been appointed; or
- there is a will but the named executor is dead or does not wish to do the task.

Often a relative applies to the court and asks to be appointed as the administrator. If not, the court can make an appropriate appointment. Administrators get their authority from a grant of administration by a court.

Where there is no valid will, the administrator distributes the estate according to the laws of intestacy, described in 16.1 Making a Will.

AFTER A DEATH

Various steps must be carried out when a person dies. The first thing that must be done is to find the will if it exists.

Finding the will

The will is likely to be kept with a solicitor, a trustee company, a bank safe custody box, or in the deceased's home with their other important papers. There is no government body that registers wills, so it is wise for anybody making a will to tell someone (preferably the executor) where it is kept.

If a will cannot be found, and nobody recalls a will having been made, the property might be distributed according to the laws of intestacy.

Locating the will early is important. The person who made the will (the "testator" if male or "testatrix" if female) may have specified the type of funeral they preferred. While these directions are not legally binding in most States, it can be distressing if a cremation was performed and then it is discovered that burial was requested.

Finding people named in the will

If a will is found, it is then necessary to find the people named in it and to check that they are still alive. This would include the executor(s), plus those who have been promised gifts. People receiving gifts under a will are known as beneficiaries.

Registering the death

Deaths must be registered with the Registrar of Births, Deaths and Marriages, who will issue a death certificate. Death certificates are needed to deal with matters such as allocating property, and claiming life insurance and superannuation.

The Registrar will not issue a death certificate unless there is a medical certificate prepared by a doctor stating the cause of death. Sometimes a doctor cannot write a medical certificate, and must report the death to a coroner. This is the case if the death:

- was violent;
- was unnatural or suspicious;
- was sudden and inexplicable;
- occurred within 24 hours of a general anaesthetic;
- occurred in a prison or institution;
- occurred without a doctor attending for a certain time before death and the cause of death is unknown.

The coroner may order a post mortem. If the death is found to be due to natural causes, a death certificate will be issued. If not, an inquiry may be held.

Arranging the funeral

Relatives usually make the funeral arrangements. The costs of the funeral are covered by the property left by the deceased at their death, but the person who orders the funeral is ultimately responsible to ensure that costs are paid.

Banks may be willing to release funds from the deceased's account to pay for the funeral if necessary. It may also be possible for people receiving social security to obtain financial assistance to help cover funeral expenses. The Department of Social Security should be contacted for details.

Looking after dependants

Often the deceased will have left behind people reliant on them for their day to day survival. Unfortunately, it takes time before they receive the money and property promised in the will, so what can they do in the meantime?

Various steps can be taken:

- bank accounts held jointly with the deceased can still be operated by the surviving partner;
- there may be an entitlement to social security – dependants should contact the Department of Social Security;
- part of a superannuation fund may be released early;
- a bank may agree to make a loan, using the interest in the estate as security – but this has the drawback that fees and interest will have to be paid.

DUTIES OF EXECUTORS AND ADMINISTRATORS

Basically, executors and administrators deal with the deceased's estate. This involves:

- listing all property and debts – this can be done by carefully going through the deceased's papers and belongings;
- collecting money owed to the estate;
- paying debts, which may require selling some property;
- distributing what is left in accordance with the terms of the will, or, if there is no will, in accordance with intestacy laws.

The responsibilities are onerous, and often distressing for family members. If you have been appointed as an executor, there is no compulsion for you to take on the task. The court may appoint someone else, or you may prefer to employ a solicitor or trustee company to handle it for you. You can choose to be co-executors, in which case you have an ongoing role.

Legal assistance

As the duties of an executor are complex, if you decide to take on the responsibility it is advisable to consult a lawyer.

Time will be saved if you know what documents to take to the first meeting with your lawyer. Try to have ready:

- a list of all property owned by the deceased at the date of death;
- a list of money owed by the deceased;
- a list of money owed to the deceased;
- taxation records;
- life insurance and superannuation policies;
- bank accounts and statements;
- bonds and share certificates;
- property title deeds;
- the will, a copy of the will, or details of where it is kept.

Also take details of:

- the deceased's date of birth and date of death;
- the deceased's address;
- the place where death occurred;
- marital status;

- details of family members;
- details of the beneficiaries – where they can be found, whether they are still alive, and their ages – especially if they are children.

All of this information can be obtained by talking with family members, friends, work mates, banks, and by searching through the deceased's papers.

The lawyer will check the will to ensure there are no irregularities. Some irregularities, such as problems with signatures and witnesses, can be overcome. But the added expense and delay illustrates the need to ensure wills are properly drawn up in the first place.

Matters are complicated if the deceased owned property in another country or died overseas. If this is the case, try to collect as much information as you can, and inform your lawyer. Generally, wills written overseas by people that subsequently migrate to Australia are valid. It is a good idea, however, for migrants to draw up a new will to avoid confusion and complexities.

APPLYING FOR AUTHORITY TO DEAL WITH THE ESTATE

If there is an executor, he or she must apply to court for a grant of probate. A person wishing to be an administrator must apply for letters of administration.

Requirements vary between States, but generally courts wish to see:

- evidence of the death;
- evidence that the fact of the death has been published (eg in a newspaper), giving anybody holding a later will the chance to come forward;
- details as to the assets and liabilities of the estate;
- evidence of a valid will (if there is one);
- an oath by the executor or administrator.

DISTRIBUTING THE ESTATE

Collecting money owed

After the grant of authority, the executor or administrator can collect money owed to the deceased. This includes money in bank accounts, shares, and rent if the deceased was a landlord. Money received may be kept in a solicitor's trust account, or in a separate estate account opened by the personal representative. Detailed records of all transactions should be kept.

Paying off debts

Debts owed by the estate must be paid off first. If not, the personal representative may have to personally pay the debts. This problem is avoided by publishing a special notice in certain newspapers (usually a major paper and a local one). The notice tells creditors to make their claim by a set date. If they do not, they can lose their right to claim. The notice must be done properly, so legal advice is advisable.

Most estates have several different types of debts. How do you know which should be paid first? Generally the order is:

- funeral expenses;
- costs of administering the estate (such as legal fees, costs of tracking down the beneficiaries);
- taxation;
- money owed to secured creditors (a secured debt is a debt where property is used to cover repayment failures – mortgages are an example);
- money owed to unsecured creditors.

Some assets may need to be sold to enable debts to be paid. But what happens if there is not enough money to pay off all the debts? Such an estate is known as an insolvent estate. It would be made bankrupt, and is usually handled by a trustee in bankruptcy. As an executor, you are not under an obligation to administer an insolvent estate.

The terms of the will

Once debts have been paid, the estate is distributed among the beneficiaries according to the terms of the will. Personal goods not covered by the will, such as clothing, can be divided up as the family desires.

Sometimes, after the debts have been paid, there is not enough money left to pay all the beneficiaries the amounts promised in the will. In these situations, there is a proportionate reduction in the share that each receives.

If there is no will, the administrator must follow a formula set by the laws of intestacy.

Account statements

Account statements should be prepared, showing what money was paid into the estate account and what money was paid out. Debt repayments and payments to beneficiaries should be shown. The statement should be given to the beneficiaries and may need to be filed with the court.

FURTHER READING

Renton, *The Australian Wills And Record Keeping Book: Everything You Need To Know About Wills*, Family Assets And Record Keeping, Investment Library, Melbourne, 1990

Spender (ed), *Rest Assured: A Legal Guide To Wills, Estates And Funerals*, Redfern Legal Centre Publishing, 1994

See also: General references listed in Further Reading Chapter 1.

GLOSSARY

A

acquit Find an accused not guilty at a criminal trial.

Act Law made by parliament.

adjourn Postpone a court hearing either temporarily or indefinetly.

administrator Person responsible for dealing with the assets of a deceased person where there is either no will or no executor appointed in the will.

admissible Permitted to be used as evidence in a court hearing.

advocate Person who argues your case, such as a lawyer.

affidavit Written statement made under an oath or affirmation and witnessed by an authorised person.

affirmation If a person has no religious beliefs or if their beliefs prevent them swearing on oath, they can affirm that something is true.

annul Declare something to be legally void.

appeal Ask a higher court to correct a decision made by a lower court.

arbitration Alternative to court where a binding decision can be made.

assets Property of a person that can be used to pay outstanding debts.

attest Affirm that something is true, such as a signature.

award Decision made by an arbitrator.

B

bail When an accused person is allowed to go free while waiting for the court hearing.

bankruptcy Proceedings to distribute a debtor's property to his or her creditors and to relieve the debtor of the unpaid balance.

barrister Lawyer who does court work and must be approached through a solicitor in some States.

beneficiary Person left something in a will.

bond Written promise to do something, refrain from doing something, or pay money at a future date.

breach Failure to carry out a legal promise or duty.

burden of proof The person who bears the burden of proof in a court case is the one who must prove that their story is true. In criminal cases the burden is held by the prosecution. In civil cases it is usually held by the plaintiff.

C

charge Allegation that a person has committed a criminal offence.

civil law Law involving individuals or companies taking action against each other, for instance over contract or personal injury disputes.

codicil Document that adds to or amends a will and satisfies the same formal requirements as a will.

cohabitation agreement Document dealing with the property rights of people who are living together.

committal proceedings When a Local Court decides whether a person charged with an indictable offence should be sent to a trial in a higher court.

common law Law based on traditions and customs such as judges' decisions, as distinct from statutes.

conciliation Resolution of a dispute through the process of discussions aided by an independent third party.

contract Legally binding agreement entered into where there is a promise to do or not do something.

contributory negligence Where a person's own negligence contributed to the injuries they suffered, and their ability to receive compensation is either reduced or removed.

cooling off period Time to change your mind.

creditor Someone money is owed to.

cross claim Claim made by a defendant aginst a plaintiff and heard at the same time as the plaintiff's claim.

cross-examination Questions that an opposing lawyer asks a witness.

custody Daily care and control of a child. In criminal cases it refers to imprisonment and confinement.

D

damages Court order that a sum of money be paid to compensate a party for loss the other party caused.

debtor Somebody who owes money.

decree absolute A final court order in divorce proceedings.

decree nisi Provisional court order in divorce proceedings, but neither person can re-marry until the decree absolute is made.

deed Legal document that has been signed, sealed and delivered.

de facto In fact, not law.

default Failing in a duty.

default judgment Judgment entered by a court against a defendant who did not defend the case.

defendant Person who is being prosecuted or sued.

disbursement Out-of-pocket expenditure paid by one person on behalf of another.

discharge Release from an obligation.

dissolution Divorce.

E

easement Right to use another person's property for a specified purpose, for example a right of way.

estate Assets and liabilities of a deceased person.

eviction Forcing a tenant to move out by the use of legal proceedings.

executor Person appointed in a will to distribute the estate according to the terms of the will.

ex nuptial Child born to unmarried parents.

ex parte order Court order made when one party to the proceedings is not present.

F

fixture Item permamnently attached to a building or land.

foreclosure Forced sale to pay off a debt.

forfeit Give up or lose something.

G

garnishee order Court order allowing a creditor to recover their money from somebody who owes money to the debtor — for instance where an employer owes the debtor wages, part of those wages can be paid directly to the creditor.

guarantee Undertaking that an agreement, duty or liability will be carried out.

guardian Person responsible for the long-term welfare of a child.

H

hearsay Evidence of a fact not personally experienced by a witness.

I

indictable offence Serious criminal offence such as murder, tried by a judge and jury.

injunction Court order to do something or refrain from doing something.

inquest Investigation into the cause of death.

insolvent Inability to pay debts.

intestate Dying without leaving a will.

J

joint tenants Ownership of property by more than one person, where when one person dies the other automatically owns their share.

judgment Court decision.

jurisdiction Area in which particular laws have authority.

L

lease Contract between a landlord and tenant related to the renting of the landlord's property. Also called a resdiential tenancy agreement.

legislation Laws made by parliament.

liability Legal duty or responsibility.

litigate Taking court action.

M

magistrate Similar to judge but sits in a Local Court (also called Magistrates Court)

mediation Resolution of a dispute involving face-to-face discussions in the presence of a neutral person who facilitates the discussions.

minor Somebody under 18.

mitigation Lessening responsibility or loss.

mortgage Loan where property is used as security for the repayment of money.

mortgagee Lender in a mortgage agreement, often a bank.

mortgagor Person who borrows money in a mortgage agreement.

N

negligence Failure to use the standard of care required.

negotiation Bargaining the terms of an agreement.

nominal damages Very small sum of damages awarded where the plaintiff's

rights were breached but no loss was suffered.

nominal defendant Victims of motor accidents can sue the nominal defendant if the driver at fault cannot be found.

nuisance Unreasonable interference with somebody's comfort, convenience or enjoyment of their property.

O

oath Solemn appeal to God to witness the truth of a statement.

ombudsman Independent official who investigates complaints made against the government.

P

parole Release of a prisoner from part of their prison sentence if they meet certain conditions.

party Participants to a court case or to a contract.

perjury Lying under oath in court.

plaintiff Person who commences court proceedings.

precedent Court decision used to guide a later decision.

pre-nuptial agreement Document made before marriage purporting to deal with property rights on separation and divorce.

probate Court proceedings proving the validity of a will.

probation When a person convicted of an offence can stay out of prison if they meet certain conditions.

prosecution The initiating and carrying on of criminal proceedings, usually by the police.

R

real property Property in land and buildings.

recognisance Promise to a court to do something.

remedy Legal solution.

residential tenancy agreement See lease.

S

standard of proof Level of proof that a court requires. In criminal cases the standard is "beyond reasonable doubt", which is higher than the civil standard "on the balance of probabilities".

statute Law made by parliament.

subpoena Order to appear in court as a witness or to produce certain documents.

sue Take legal proceedings in a civil case.

solicitor Lawyer who performs a wide range of legal tasks, such as seeing clients, preparing documents, running cases and appearing in court.

specific performance Court order requiring that existing obligations be carried out in the terms of the agreement.

summons Order to appear at court.

summary offence A relatively minor criminal offence decided in a Local Court before a magistrate.

surety Person who promises to be responsible for another.

T

taxing Having a lawyer's bill checked by a court.

tenants in common Ownership of land by two or more people, where each owner can dispose of their share independently in their will.

testator/testatrix Person making a will. Testatrix is the term used for women.

title Ownership of property.

tort Wrong giving rise to a civil case that is not based on breach of contract, for example trespass.

trespasser Person present on land without official authority or the occupier's permission.

tribunal Body outside the court system that hears and resolves diputes in a specific area.

V

verdict Final decision made by a jury.

vicarious liability Responsibilty of an employer for the acts of its employees.

void No legal effect.

warranty Promise made that an item being purchased meets certain characteristics.

W

will Document stating how a person wants their property to be dealt with after their death.

INDEX

(For definitions, refer also to the Glossary)

Body corporate
 complaints, 225
 duties, 221
 insurance, 224
 levies, 223
 managing agents, 222
 meetings, 222
Bonds
 good behaviour, 69
 rental, 198
Boundaries
 overlaps, 232
Breath tests, 248
Bridging loans, 216
Builders
 choosing, 208
 complaints against, 211
 licensing and registration, 208
 owner-builders, 209
Building
 choosing builder, 208
 choosing land, 207
 contracts
  cooling off period, 210
  general, 209
  payments, 210
 council approval, 208
 disputes, 211
 reports when buying house, 204
Car accidents
 admission of liability, 177
 duty to report, 176
 duty to stop, 175, 248
 exchange of particulars, 176
 personal injury, 179
 property damage, 178
Car insurance
 claims, 178
 loss of cover, 177
 personal injury, 179
 property damage, 178
 types, 177
Care proceedings
 court orders, 133
 court procedures, 132
 meaning, 131
 need of care, 131
Cars
 buying

 dealers, 244
 new, 243
 privately, 245
 used, 244
 insurance *see* Car insurance
 registration, 242
 selling, 246
Child support
 child support scheme, 114
 general, 112
 post October 1989, 114
 pre October 1989, 113
Child Support Agency
 calculation of child support, 114
 collection of child support, 114
Children
 alcohol, 129
 contracts with, 129
 crimes by, 133ff
 damage by, 126
 discipline by parents, 124
 discipline by schools, 127
 divorce and, 116
 employment, 129
 injured while trespassing, 168
 leaving home, 128
 marriage, 130
 police and, 133
 school attendance, 124, 126
 sexual relationships, 130
 witnesses, 33
 see also Students' rights
Children's Courts
 care proceedings *see* Care proceedings
 criminal law, 133ff
Civil law
 court procedures, 38ff
 meaning, 6
Codicils, 270
Cohabitation agreements, 96
Committal proceedings, 61
Common law
 meaning, 5
Community Justice Centres
 role of, 47
Community Legal Centres
 advice by, 11
Community service orders, 70